DATE DUE

WITHDRAWN

Asset Allocation
Techniques and Financial
Market Timing

ASSET ALLOCATION TECHNIQUES AND FINANCIAL MARKET TIMING

Carroll D. Aby, Jr.
Donald E. Vaughn

QUORUM BOOKS
Westport, Connecticut • London

Library of Congress Cataloging-in-Publication Data

Aby, Carroll D., Jr.
   Asset allocation techniques and financial market timing / Carroll D. Aby, Jr. and
Donald E. Vaughn.
      p.   cm.
   Includes bibliographical references and index.
   ISBN 0–89930–761–2 (alk. paper)
   1. Investment analysis.   2. Speculation.   3. Asset allocation.
I. Vaughn, Donald E.   II. Title.
HG4529.A29   1995
332.6—dc20   94–45275

British Library Cataloguing in Publication Data is available.

Library of Congress Catalog Card Number: 94–45275
ISBN: 0–89930–761–2

First published in 1995

Quorum Books, 88 Post Road West, Westport, CT 06881
An imprint of Greenwood Publishing Group, Inc.

Printed in the United States of America

The paper used in this book complies with the
Permanent Paper Standard issued by the National
Information Standards Organization (Z39.48–1984).

10 9 8 7 6 5 4 3 2 1

CONTENTS

ILLUSTRATIONS

TABLES

FIGURES

CHARTS

EXHIBITS

PREFACE

As we enter the last decade of the 20th century, indecision and turbulence prevail in the financial markets. Investors appear preoccupied with escalating political and economic instabilities. Meanwhile, attempts to identify major price swings dominate investment strategies. Perhaps more than ever before, individuals seem unable or unwilling to venture into investment decision making. Growing numbers of individuals depend on portfolio managers to obtain acceptable investment returns. If asset managers are to accommodate increasing client expectations for better performance, asset allocation, and timing, strategies in financial markets must play a larger role.

This book represents a collection of investment analyses and asset allocations for portfolio managers. The book provides a unique blend of pragmatic investment management concepts and real-world applications geared for financial managers and portfolio specialists. However, the approaches that will be discussed should also appeal to individual investors with diversified portfolios, because they are presented in a way that is both readable and easily understood. For the most part, academic jargon and mathematical emphasis have been minimized to both facilitate the readers' understanding and to avoid either mathematical or theoretical "overkill."

Chapters 1 and 2 provide an overview of financial assets, guidelines for evaluating the allocation of assets within the overall economic framework, and the impacts on financial decisions from cyclical swings in the economy. Chapter 3 focuses on the fundamental analysis of individual stocks, and Chapter 4 introduces technical analysis of equity issues through the medium of vertical bar charts.

Chapter 5 offers some seldom understood strategies involving the use of vertical bar charts. Chart configurations are presented to aid portfolio managers in making swift, accurate portfolio decisions. Forecasting the extent of price movements and determining price objectives make the treatment distinctively unique. Chapters 6 and 7 introduce readers to point and figure charting. We stress clarity of presentation to ensure readers that chart patterns are not shrouded in mystique. They are not smoke screens cast by veteran analysts to divert the attention of budding technicians from techniques mistakenly thought to be more relevant to actual security analysis. Presentation of advanced analytical charting techniques follows in easily understood terms.

The book includes an integrative approach toward investment decisions in different financial markets and climates. Chapter 8 examines many tools of technical analysis used in forecasting general stock market trends. Whereas Chapter 9 exposes portfolio managers to group stock movement patterns, Chapter 10 enables serious investors to understand the impacts that market anomalies have on security prices. Portfolio managers learn that markets contain many inefficiencies that lead to superior returns for managers who employ this information.

In Chapter 11, we address tenets associated with fixed-income portfolio management. Interest rate risk, duration, convexity, immunization, and similar concepts are dealt with in a concise, fundamental manner. Mortgage-backed securities, taxable and tax-exempt bonds, and money market instruments are also discussed. Chapter 12 introduces the idea of managing portfolio risk. Derivative securities such as options and futures contracts occupy a key role in risk management practices for both equity-oriented and fixed-income portfolios.

An interesting aspect of the book relates to selecting obscure or out-of-favor stocks. Logically, buying low and selling high makes it virtually impossible to focus all efforts on glamour issues experiencing large price advances. We discuss innovative ways of profiting from lesser known firms. Chart configurations, relative strength, and other frequently misunderstood techniques help identify supply and demand imbalances and pinpoint issues poised for price moves in either direction.

Although it would be more conventional to present a sequential approach, the book's innovative structure allows readers to single out specific areas of interest for immediate study. Despite the continuity and flow of the book, readers will find that individual sections can stand alone.

There are a number of things that make this book different from others in the field. We draw on more than fifty years of practical experience in asset evaluation, selection, and allocation techniques. Our emphasis centers on making complex subjects matter and reducing them into a workable presentation. Concepts previously regarded as esoteric by some are made lucid by supporting illustrations.

In summary, this book offers a total perspective on portfolio management. We continually espouse the view that undervalued and overvalued assets offer uncommon profit opportunities. Our coverage is in sharp contrast to the arcane view that all markets are efficient and that returns may be increased merely by assuming additional risk. Here, risk consists of stating that all known information about a security is embodied in its current market price. Securities will adjust instantaneously to new information disseminated about different firms. In other words, academicians propose that undervalued and overvalued assets either do not exist or do not exist in sufficient magnitudes to permit profiting from them. Therefore, it is virtually impossible to earn superior returns or outperform the market for any given level of risk. Although we concede that the market for certain stocks, such as IBM, Exxon, and General Motors, may indeed be efficient, such established, well-known issues do not offer the most profit potential. We introduce readers to potential profits from less obvious investment opportunities.

Carroll D. Aby, Jr.
Donald E. Vaughn

ACKNOWLEDGMENTS

Any large undertaking requires the devotion and commitment of special people. We are most fortunate to have received support from such individuals who helped bring this project to fruition. Our support staff "went the extra mile" to facilitate the completion of this manuscript.

Our friendship with Michael Burke, John Gray, and the entire staff at Chartcraft/ Investors Intelligence, Inc., spans quite a few years. Supportive contributions from this staff are endless. All reproduced point and figure charts scattered throughout the book are provided by Mike and John. Mike also took time away from his busy schedule to make editorial contributions and suggestions. Comments from one of Wall Street's finest minds and strategists were certainly welcome and invaluable. Chartcraft deserves its reputation as one of the finest investment advisory firms in the United States.

All vertical bar charts were furnished by Ken Lutz, President of Trendline, Inc., a division of Standard and Poor. Like Mike, Ken is a long-time friend and enjoys an impeccable reputation in the investment community. Trendline prepares vertical bar chart services that are next to none in the investment business. Thanks are also expressed to Earl Zeligman and Pauletta Avery at SIUC (Southern Illinois University at Carbondale) for final manuscript preparation.

We are indebted to Mernita Branch, Willie Mae Carter, and Romayne Olivier for placing the book in its final form. Without their computer assistance and construction of many charts and graphs, the preparation of the text would have been impossible. Others at Northwestern State University of Louisiana also provided key support. Among them are President Robert Alost, Dr. Ed Graham, Dr. Randy Webb, and Dr. Barry Smiley.

Finally, any project of this magnitude requires the understanding and patience of families. We are blessed to have the finest spouses and children in the world. Thanks for everything.

Chapter 1

INTRODUCTION

THE INVESTMENT CLIMATE

As we push onward toward the end of the 20th century, indecision and turbulence prevail in the financial markets. This provides opportunities to asset managers in the asset allocation process to earn above average returns when they are able to gauge expectations correctly but to penalize those that fail to plan for these changes.

Each decade of the post–World War II era seems to have differed from the others in many ways. Many different challenges have confronted the United States, and the climate for financial securities has been quick to respond to anticipated impacts on the sales and earnings levels of affected corporations. Years of the hot and cold wars with Communist nations witnessed the national interest, and governmental spending, being directed toward greater defense efforts. Years of peace generally encouraged greater world travel and purchase of larger amounts of consumer goods. Years of rising interest rate levels, due to the acceleration in price inflation (from about 1966–1980, generally, with brief years of some retracements), resulted in a shift in values of fixed and variable return securities. These shifts in values are implied from the swings in (1) long-term market yields on selected types of fixed return financial securities, as shown in Figure 1.1, and (2) the average earnings yield at which corporate issues traded in the post–World War II era, as reflected in Figure 1.2.

After the Soviet Union's collapse in late 1991, the prospect of a post–cold war world opened opportunities for increasing the exports of goods and services to free Europe, several of the former Soviet republics, and particularly China. Al-

Figure 1.1
Long-Term Market Yields on Bonds

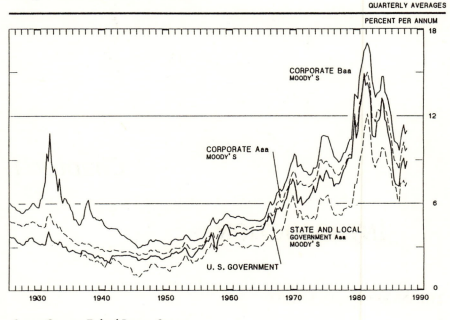

Source: Courtesy Federal Reserve System.

though the United States and other free-world nations have been welcomed as trade partners, their assistance has also been sought in educational, economic, and technical areas.

Portfolio managers must be aware of important worldwide events and gauge the impacts of these events on the expected risks and potential returns for the assets they manage. Fiscal and monetary policies are also important, because they impact on the earning ability of certain groups of firms, the general inflation rate, and the level of yields in the market places. These forces in turn have a significant impact on fluctuations in the market prices of corporate shares, as do the underlying forces of growth in overall population, population demographics, innovations, and demands exerted due to major law and environmental regulation changes. Several of these major market influences are explored in Chapter 2, which deals with general economic indicators and the theory of business cycles.

The financial sector was beset by many problems during the late 1980s and early 1990s, including magnitudes of business failures unseen since the early 1930s. Inability to forecast impacts of shifts in interest rate levels on values of real and financial assets was one underlying cause of such problems to many financially distressed institutions. Other factors that have contributed to weaknesses in the financial sector include increased mobility of investment funds, greater institutionalization of securities markets, the criticism and speedup in

Figure 1.2
Long-Term Bond and Stock Yields Compared

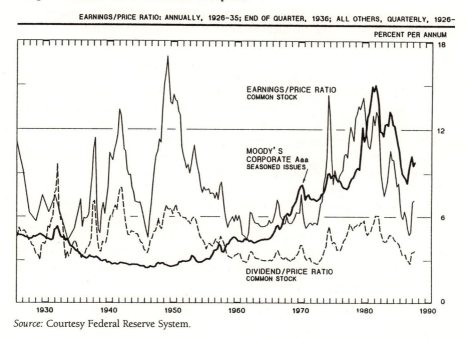

EARNINGS/PRICE RATIO: ANNUALLY, 1926-35; END OF QUARTER, 1936; ALL OTHERS, QUARTERLY, 1926-

Source: Courtesy Federal Reserve System.

Federal Deposit Insurance Corporation (FDIC) regulation in the liquidation of failed savings and loan associations and insured banks, and scandals in the underwriting of government and other primary securities.

The collapse of the junk bond market, combined with overbuilding of commercial real estate (office space, recreational facilities, shopping centers, etc.), led to financial weakness for many institutional investors that committed large sums of funds to speculative real estate ventures (i.e., savings associations, banks, life insurance companies, pension accounts, and real estate investment trusts). Some large insurance firms, which previously were immune to financial troubles, are now coming under closer scrutiny by regulators; meanwhile others are losing assets through the withdrawal of deferred annuity funds by frightened holders. Some firms have even had their quality ratings downgraded by Moodys and Standard and Poor (S & P) Corporation. Such weaknesses, if widespread, may lead to national laws that regulate some aspects of the life insurance industry (currently done at the state level).

The aging population and its need for growing amounts of medical care is on the front burner for national attention and legislation. The aging of the U.S. population will have a significant impact on the demand for certain types of consumer products and health care over the next thirty years. How to afford the level of health care needed by our segment of low-income working population and the growing retirement ranks is and will continue to be one of the major issues facing the United States in the decade of the 1990s. In addition, spending billions of dollars to combat drug traffic and to house the 4.5 million incarcerated persons in the United States will leave less money for other social programs.

Interest rates trended lower in the 1980s, as inflation forces were waning, promising a climate potentially conducive to economic growth in 1993 and beyond. U.S. firms are faced with stiff competition from other industrial countries on imports of goods, while opportunities abound for expanding into eastern European countries regaining their independence after fifty years of military control (by Germany and then Russia); other changes will occur as the result of the downshifting of military spending to other federal programs (or just a contraction in the red ink) in the U.S. pension accounts and certain mutual funds have become significant holders of the security issues of international and/or foreign firms and governments. These changes, when recognized early, offered unusual profit-making opportunities to asset managers astute enough to take advantage of them.

The investment arena visited by the major financial institutions in the nations has increasingly become a worldwide one; and some of the events outlined briefly here will be traced in later chapters as the dominant factors in the shifts in investor sentiment for certain types of securities, depending on their assessed strengths and weaknesses impacts on financial assets.

The Array of Financial Assets

We define financial assets as those that are traded freely in the auction markets for securities, and those that represent claims against other assets, either real or financial in nature. This will include marketable U.S. government securities, marketable federal agency issues, marketable municiples, real estate mortgages, corporate bonds, corporate preferred issues, corporate warrants and options, corporate common shares, and derivative issues (such as puts and calls, financial futures, commodity futures, etc.) that are bought and sold by individual and institutional portfolio managers. Pension account managers or mutual fund managers concentrating on foreign issues would, of course, extend this universe to foreign issues. The scope of this book, however, is intended to primarily deal with domestic issues, other than derivative issues, rather than foreign ones.

A quick look at the financial pages of any leading business or financial newspaper makes clear the wide array of marketable issues in which we may choose to place savings. Our investment options include the approximate 1,600 common issues on the New York Stock Exchange (NYSE), the 400 or so preferred issues on the NYSE, the approximately 1,200 issues on the American Stock Exchange (AMEX), the few hundred companies that trade their issues on regional exchanges, and the thousands of stock issues that trade in the over-the-counter markets. Add to this list the 3,500 or so mutual funds whose shares are actively quoted, those of several hundred each of money market funds, closed-end investment company shares, and real estate investment trust shares from the finance sector.

Fixed return issues include direct marketable issues of the U.S. Treasury, short- and longer-term municipal issues, government agency securities, short and long-term corporate issues, corporate bonds (straight debt and convertible), fractional shares in mortgage market pools, and preferred stocks (straight and convertible) issued by corporations.

The term "residual equity issues of corporations" refers to the common shares. As sweeteners to aid in the sale of other issues, firms sometimes issue stock purchase warrants or rights.

In 1960, financial intermediaries, such as life insurance companies, trust departments at commercial banks, and investment companies, were not dominant factors in the secondary markets for stocks. Instead, they were substantial buyers of high and intermediate grades of bonds. By the 1980s, however, the picture was reversed, as institutions (pension funds, life insurance companies, and mutual funds, especially) generated an estimated 55% of the trading stock volume on major exchanges and perhaps half this level in over-the-counter stock trading. Trading at retail amounted to about 18%, whereas member firms accounted for the balance of trading on the NYSE. The stock markets, then, have increasingly become institutionalized.

Growing dominance of stock markets by financial institutions in the United States is described by Gary L. Gastineau in the book, *Investment Management*.[1] For example, NYSE reported annual trading volume of about 2 billion shares in 1965 but 36 billion volume by 1986. The average issue on that exchange was trading 5,000 shares daily in 1965 compared to 90,000 by 1986. By the mid–1990s, daily trading volume was about 50% above the mid–1980 level. Moreover, many large block trades (10,000 shares or more) are made in the fourth market directly between institutional buyers and sellers.

Many small and large individual securities investors have withdrawn from the battle of wits and nerves with the stock markets. They have, instead, placed increasing amounts of their savings in pension funds, insurance companies or mutual funds through income deferral arrangements, or in trust with commercial bank trust departments to manage the accounts. Some managers of large portfolios prefer to limit their stock investments to the top 500 or 700 largest U.S. firms. Still others select some large worldwide and international firms. Many have begun to seek out emerging firms in the American Stock Exchange and over-the-counter (OTC) markets. Standard and Poor's Corporation, Value Line, Mansfield, and other publishers of financial data track institutional holdings of issues being reviewed. It is not unusual to discover that 70 or 80% of some well-known issues are institutionally held. From zero to upward of a quarter of the shares of many OTC issues are now held by institutional investors, especially in emerging industries such as health care. Discoveries of such companies are often made by security analysts or other trackers from their computer data banks of accounting and financial information. Large volumes of purchases, of course, cause the equity prices to rise. Conversely, broad dumping of disappointing issues depress their prices.

Some individual investors limit their own commitment of financial assets to insured accounts at commercial banks, savings associations, or credit unions. Still others with significant amounts of funds buy U.S. government, high-grade municipal bonds, and some corporate bond issues. Increasingly, individual investors are buying shares in no-load or low-load mutual funds, or placing deferred income accounts with life insurance companies or other professionally managed groups.

Before deciding to invest, the prospective security buyer should assess the return and apparent level of risk associated with each type of investment being considered. Comparative yields on savings accounts at major types of financial institutions are published annually by the U.S. League of Savings Associations. Relative market yields may also be found in publications of the Federal Reserve System (*Federal Reserve Bulletin* and individual Federal Reserve Banks' monthly reviews), *Survey of Current Business,* Moody's *Bond Survey,* and numerous other sources. Market yields on many types of issues are shown daily or weekly in the *Wall Street Journal* and *Barron's,* respectively, and are published weekly or monthly by many of the twelve Federal Reserve Banks. Expected returns on common stock issues are reviewed by some investment advisory services (especially S & P and Value Line), and financial analysts and other investors spend many long, tedious hours daily or weekly in pouring over historical financial statements, national economic series, worldwide events, and the like, in attempts to forecast likely futures of companies under review. This type of analysis, fundamental analysis, is described in greater detail in the following.

FACTORS INFLUENCING SECURITY PRICES

Several types of risks are associated with claims for payment against a borrower (or even a user of equity funds provided by sale of stock). These risks are broken down into the following categories:

1. The business or credit risk is the ability or willingness of the borrower to adequately service the debt.

2. The interest rate risk is the risk from fluctuating levels of returns brought about by the shift upward or downward in interest rate levels (influenced substantially by estimates of price changes in consumer price levels), and their impacts on market values of fixed return issues.

3. The liquidity risk is the inability to convert an issue to cash with little loss in value.

4. The market risk is associated with swings in the general level of stock prices. Market risk is often defined as the beta, or relative price volatility, of an issue, referenced around some market average, such as the S & P 500 or the NYSE Index.

5. Monetary value risks and political, social, and economic instabilities exist in some foreign countries and financial markets.

The impacts of these risks on the collective desires of financial portfolio managers to hold certain types of financial assets rather than others provides never-ending challenges to portfolio managers in their concerns with asset allocation.

The United States is said to have a dynamic, ever-shifting economy. The strength in (1) the overall economy, (2) certain major sectors, and (3) specific industries may be greatly affected by such changes as the passage of an important tax law, a shift in monetary policy, or rumors of war or peace; the anticipated responses to these events may ultimately affect the earnings of many firms. Ultimately, the level of return on a fixed rate security (such as a T-bill) is influenced highly by the rate of anticipated inflation. Supply, relative to demand due to limited funds for such investment, might also cause the market yield to be swollen. In 1991, for example, the U.S. Treasury issued about $100 billion more in Treasury bills than it rolled over, as a portion of its deficit spending, including funds used in the thrift bailouts, were financed with T-bills. Yields on Treasury notes, Treasury bonds, high grade corporate bonds, and across the extended risk spectrum for fixed rate instruments, ran even higher, in most years, than on those for T-bills. Similar magnitudes of deficits in Federal spending over taxation (about $250 billion annually) occurred in the early 1990s. A combined tax increase in 1993 and some spending reduction by the U.S. Congress appeared to be bringing the U.S. deficit below $170 billion annually by mid–1994.

A common stock trades on the basis of its dividend yield and anticipated long-term growth prospects. That is, a stock with an infinite growth assessment of 12% and with a market capitalization rate of 14% should trade at a 2% dividend yield. Such a stock that is paying 0.15 dividends quarterly (or $0.60 yearly) should justify a price of 0.60/0.02 = $30. Growth should be in terms of expected growth in earnings per share (or perhaps in terms of growth in book value per share—or in the net asset backing per share) if one assumes that the firm will maintain about the same debt/equity mix and has potential investment opportunities to earn a rate of return at least equal to current returns on assets.

An upward surge in inflation, if expected to continue, is highly unhealthy for stocks in the electric and gas utility industries, for telecommunication stocks, and for those in most areas of retail trade. This is due to their failures or limited successes at passing along the inflationary impact to their users of goods or services. Financial institution shares might also be squeezed, as disintermediation (withdrawal of deposits seeking higher market yields elsewhere) might reduce the spread between what they are earning on their portfolio of invested assets and what they pay to credit providers, or depositors.

Booking (or cancellation) of a major government contract for big ticket items (such as military planes) or the stretching out or acceleration of an option by an airline firm to accept several commercial jets will have a very rapid impact on the market price of the impacted manufacturers—Boeing, GD, Lockheed, McDonnell-Douglas, and the like.

Rising interest rates have an adverse affect on the construction industry, as higher mortgage rates price many would-be home buyers out of the market for new homes. For example, an average Veterans Administration (VA) mortgage of $84,500 with thirty years for repayment requires a monthly payment of $741 at 9.0% (summer 1991 rate) but fell to about $650 when the VA mortgage rate dropped to 8.5% effective September 20, 1991. Mortgage rates continued to drop to about 6.75% by fall 1993 before moving upward. During periods of high interest rates, say 10% or above, many families continue to rent or add rooms to their inadequate owner-occupied homes. Higher rates also spell trouble for sellers of large ticket items such as autos, home furnishings, and major appliances and to providers of discretionary services such as recreational facilities (i.e., hotels, motels, restaurants, tourist firms, casinos, airlines, etc.). More money being spent for interest on loans leaves less for other discretionary spending. As rates fall, autos and homes become affordable by a larger number of persons. This was evident in 1993 when auto and housing sales rebounded vigorously.

The discovery, patent, and licensing of certain products thought to provide big bucks to its patent-holding firm meets with almost instantaneous positive market response. Introduction of a competing, or perhaps a better alternative, product marketed by a competitor, sends the shares for the impacted issue into a tail spin. The list goes on and on, but factors that are assessed as producing a higher level of profits for a given firm will ordinarily send it upward in price. Those thought to be derogatory will cause it to fall in value.

Some undervalued or super growth companies become targets for takeovers by wealthy individuals or groups of wealth holders. Partial or total buyouts are almost always at premium prices, and sometimes at ridiculously high price-earnings levels. In 1990 and 1991, if financing could be arranged, many leveraged buyouts were done with intermediate- or low-quality bonds. More shares in U.S. markets in those two years were retired than issued in the primary markets, according to some sources. The sellers of common shares might enjoy their unexpected wealth, but the buyers, in attempts to shore up the high prices of their acquisitions, might begin to fire personnel in the acquired firm(s) to trim corporate overhead. Thus professional corporate managers (owning little equity) in poorly or inadequately managed firms often find themselves in the job market. The market shares of the buying and selling firms often run up in price in anticipation of a combination or buyout and then spend several years in drifting downward. Charts of price action are shown later in the book to illustrate several of these examples.

Historical Returns

Historical returns on investments are provided in a number of sources. Some of the Federal Reserve banks publish charts monthly. Several rate-of-return series were provided in Figures 1.1 and 1.2. Annual editions of *Fact Book,* published annually by the U.S. League of Savings, compares annual average returns on several types of savings media, such as rates of interest being paid by commercial banks, savings associations, savings banks, and yields on Treasury bills. Published studies were made by Lawrence Fisher and James H. Lorie, *A Half Century of*

Figure 1.3
Annual Returns and Variations of Major Financial Assets, 1926–1991

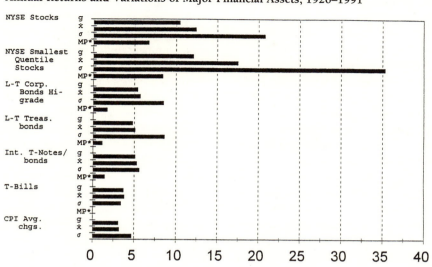

*Based on R$_g$ returns of T-bills and other issues.
Source: Developed from Charles P. Jones, *Investments,* New York, John Wiley & Sons, Inc., 1994, p. 126, from the Ibbotson/Singuefeld study.

Returns on Stocks & Bonds, and periodic updates are made to *Rates of Returns on Bills, Bonds and Stocks,* by R. G. Ibbotson and R. A. Singuefeld.[2] Rates of return and standard deviations of returns for major types of financial assets, 1926–1991, are shown by the Ibbotson study, and are summarized in Figure 1.3.

A review of the previously cited sources shows that the rate of interest earned on Treasury bills, considered by financial analysts to be a (virtually) risk free investment, is about 0.5 to 1% above the expected inflation rate, in most years. Due to their greater value fluctuation with each shift of a percentage point (or 100 basic points) in the market interest rates, Treasury notes and bonds carry premium rates above those of Treasury bills. Thus an upsloping yield curve prevails during most points in time, or the investor is compensated for the additional interest rate risk of holding intermediate or long-term issues. A risk premium of an additional 0.5% on Treasury notes and perhaps still another 1% on twenty- or thirty-year Treasury bonds appears warranted due to their higher interest rate risk.

The capital asset pricing model (CAPM) theory assumes that an investor expects a yield on a certain security equivalent to the risk free rate (say that rate achievable on six-month Treasury bills) plus a premium based on market variability of return × a market risk premium. Over the past decade, the market risk premium on listed U.S. common stocks appears to have been about 6.5%, according to statistics published in the *Quarterly Review,* Winter 1991, by the Federal Reserve Bank of New York[3] (though the Ibbotson study found it to exceed 8% from the mid–1920s through 1987). Thus in a period of 4% inflation, the T-bill rate might be appropriately 4.5 to 5%; a four- or five-year Treasury note should have a yield of 5.5 to 6%; Treasury bonds should yield a percent higher than this; and corporate bond yields should have even higher returns to compensate for their additional credit or business risk.

The capital asset pricing model for this scenario suggests that annual returns on low-beta electric utility might be .05 + .50 beta (.065) = 8.25%. About 75% of this might come from dividends and the balance from expected growth in dividends over an extended time period. By contrast, an average stock with a beta of 1.00 should provide a rate of return of 4.5 to 5.0% plus the market premium of 6.5% or between 11 and 12%.

A high-beta stock (one operating in a cyclical industry, for example) with a beta, or relative market volatility in price, of 1.50 should provide a market return of 5.0% + 1.50 (0.065) or about 15%. We could convert these from earnings-price ratios to price-earnings (P-E) ratios and determine that the electric utilities, in this scenario, should trade at about a 12 × P-E ratio and the high-beta stock should trade at a P-E ratio of about 6 to 7 ×. Three-year average (smoothed) earnings for these type firms have, in fact, provided about these P-E levels for highly cyclical stocks during recent years. The problem is in how to evaluate above average or super growth rate for non- or low-dividend-paying stocks, a topic of major concern to investment fundamentalists and considered in Chapter 3.

Since stocks are bought on the basis of expected returns for the next year (or for several years into the future), a perceived shift in the rate of inflation (or of the interest rate level), will send most common stocks to higher or lower levels. Strength of the overall economy, the sector in which the firm operates, its own industry's strengths and weaknesses, and individual firm's characteristics likewise have a bearing on the assessed market value of equity issues. In fact, this hypothesis is agreed on by most fundamentalists and technicians.

The approach recommended by most investment fundamentalists moves from the macro to the micro analysis. First of all, we should determine if the overall stock market is the place to be. Next, we should zero in on the industries that are showing above-average strength. Next, we should select individual firms that are likely to lead others in their respective industries.

In general, the security market line, at a given point in time, appears to do a reasonably efficient job of explaining differences in expected yields on alternative types of financial issues. The capital asset pricing model is merely a graph showing the anticipated yields on securities traded in money and capital markets with varying degrees of financial risk. The trend line that joins the points on the graph is referred to as the security market line. Market yields are shown on the y (vertical) axis and the variability of return on the x (horizontal) axis. Alternatively, the average yields reported in current financial literature might be charted on the line and the approximate risk of variability read on the base. Let us illustrate the

Figure 1.4
Security Market Line Illustrated

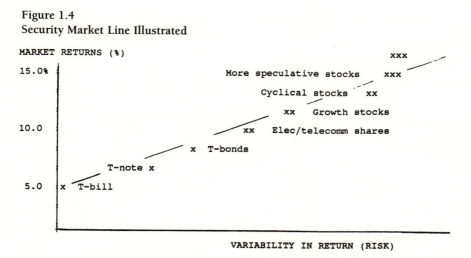

concept graphically with the following assumed yields: three-month T-bill yield of 5%, four-year T-note yield of 6%, twenty-year T-bond yield of 7.5%, AAA corporate long-term bond yield of 8%, fixed-rate mortgage yield of 8.5%, and stock returns running from a low on electric utilities to a high on cyclical and speculative issues (see Figure 1.4).

As yields shift upward on short-, intermediate-, and long-term government issues, bond yields will generally rise, meaning that bond prices decline, whereas stock prices will begin to fall (or price-earnings ratios decline). When yields on fixed-return government issues decline, conversely, stock prices usually move upward, although some at faster rates than others. Factors that tend to influence upward and downward shifts in common stock prices for selected groups of stocks are described in later chapters.

FUNDAMENTAL INVESTMENT CONSIDERATIONS

The financial analysts that hold to the fundamental view base their analysis of the strength of corporate issues on such factors as forecasts for sales, assets, earnings, cash flows, products and services provided, markets for products, quality of management of the firm, and other factors. The overall economic analysis considers U.S. gross domestic product, the level and direction of movement in industrial production, employment strength, interest levels currently and expected, present and anticipated fiscal policy, and other factors. Strength in individual business sectors and industries are evaluated on the basis of competition, impact of shifts in supply and demand due to interest rate movements or fiscal spending, the degree of merger activity for selected groups of stocks, and so forth.

Evaluation of individual issues often takes one or more of the following approaches:

1. The constant or multi-stage dividend discount model;
2. The P-E model based on recent past P-Es and near-term estimate of E/S;
3. Value Line's cash flow per share model;
4. The intrinsic value model developed by Benjamin Graham and refined by others, that incorporates growth, dividends, earnings, and book value per share into the equation.

With the constant growth model, a justified market rate of return is determined by applying the capital asset pricing model, as explained and illustrated in Figure 1.4. The growth rate for the stock is then estimated, and the value of the infinite stream of dividends is computed in the following manner.

In the CAPM, we define Value = annual dividends $(1 + g)/(R - g)$, where R is the required rate of return and g is the constant growth rate in cash dividends. Thus a stock paying $1.00 in annual dividends, having a 10% growth rate, and having a market capitalization rate of 12% should have a theoretical (or underlying fundamental) price of $1.00/(0.12 - .10) = $50. The idea is to buy the stock if its actual price is substantially below this level and to sell it if it exceeds this level by more than 10 or 20%. Fundamentalists believe that stocks are somewhat mispriced in the market in the short run and attempt, through analyzing estimated quantitative values, to uncover underpriced issues. Important fundamental measurements for individual stock issues are explored in Chapter 3, whereas later chapters analyze overall market forces and industry responses to different market stimuli. We believe that this knowledge is vital in the asset allocation process followed by portfolio managers.

The dividend growth model variation might assume that the 10% growth would prevail for a few years, and then trend downward for a few years to about average in the nation, where this rate of growth would continue forever. A realistic infinite growth rate might be the rate of inflation (e.g., unit price increases to offset consumer price index [CPI] changes), plus 1% for population growth and another one or two percentage points for productivity gains. Growth in book value per share, due to the retention of E/S, might be another contributing factor, where a firm has reinvestment opportunities.

Some stock portfolio managers attempt to gauge price-earnings levels for the overall market, groups of stocks, and individual issues on the basis of their averages for the past several years, say five to ten, and assume that this average is a fair assessment of what it should return to in a year or two. Earnings per share are then estimated for the anticipated holding period, such as one or two years, the product is determined, and the actual price is compared to the estimated underlying value. The most (apparently) underpriced stocks are bought, whereas apparently overpriced ones are avoided or liquidated from the portfolio.

Value Line Investment Survey maintains that a closer five-year moving average correlation exists between most stocks' prices and their cash flows per share than between earnings per share and price. Where little non-cash expense (depreciation, depletion, amortization) exists, they use the P-E multiple, since it is approximately identical to the cash flow multiple. For stocks bought for their dividend yields, such as real estate investment trust (REIT) shares, closed-end investment shares, and electric utility shares, for example, they work out the usual relation between similar grades of long-term corporate bonds and the stocks. Some investors follow their advice, adding to their portfolio of holdings those stocks whose prices lie below the *value line* and avoid (or liquidate) those issues that rise substantially above the five-year moving average cash flow per share line.

Professor Benjamin Graham, the founding father of security analysis, and some associate writers (Dodd and Cottle) developed what has become known as the *intrinsic value* model. This model assumes for the long term that a non-growth stock should probably have a multiplier of about 8 to 8.5. Add to this a premium of about two times the seven- or ten-year anticipated growth rate (measured in terms of earnings per share, dividends per share, book value growth, etc.). We have what Graham, Dodd, and Cottle (GDC) refer to as the multiplier. The next step in the formula is to multiply this value by the actual dividends per share being paid plus one third of the earnings per share. This is the preliminary intrinsic value, but if the actual price is less than one half or more than two times this "value," then book value per share is weighted in as one fourth of the total and growth, dividends, and earnings carry the balance of the weights. Many security analysts continue to use the GDC model or some version of it in attempting to locate underpriced and overpriced issues.

Still other fundamentalists attempt to uncover stocks that appear to possess market anomaly characteristics. That is, small firms' shares, if bought and held for a substantial time period, usually provide better risk-adjusted returns than do those in larger firms, but at the sacrifice of wider price movements for the smaller stocks. Stocks often move upward or downward during certain months, weeks, or days of the year. Some portfolio managers play these odds in adding to or reducing portfolio stock holdings. Identifying stocks that are candidates for mergers or leveraged buyouts are attempted by still others, whereas the contrarians attempt to buy stocks that are (only, they hope) temporarily out of favor. That is, they buy stocks that trade at very low price-earnings multiples on a historical basis. Still others attempt to locate groups of stocks that are about to move into the information dissemination limelight. This might be due to going public, listing the stocks on the AMEX or NYSE, or becoming favorites for mutual funds emphasizing emerging companies. Each of these topics are explored in greater depth in Chapters 10–12.

TECHNICAL APPROACHES TO INVESTING

Pure stock technicians often disregard the fundamental strengths and weaknesses of an individual stock (or the market as a whole), while attempting to gauge the demand and supply for the issue(s). The technicians study price movements, relative strength, volume of trading, price trends, and certain key patterns that often indicate strength or weakness, support and resistance level, and estimated moves. Technicians attempt to interpret chart action, usually in the form of vertical bar or point and figure charts, although a few chart services are constructed with simple or weighted average line charts for price and/or volume of trading.

Technicians hold the view that the popular stock averages is one of the early leading indicators, and that certain groups of stock lead these averages. Their efforts, then, are attempts to gauge these early movers (upside or downside) long before the market average or economy (viewed by the economists and fundamentalists) makes it turn. Thus the technicians attempt to take early positions in equities before fundamentalists suggest such justification and to exit them before they take a nose dive. Usual tools and rules followed by technicians in recommending stocks, options, commodity futures, and the like, are provided in several following chapters. Chapters 3–5 address vertical bar charts, whereas later chapters describe and illustrate the usage of point and figure charts.

Allocating Financial Assets to Investment Types

An individual investor (and an institution) develops an overall investment plan or long-term goals and develops investment strategies designed to accomplish these goals. A prudent investor desires to have near cash reserves to be used to meet near-term planned expenditures, to respond to emergencies that might occur, and to build up safe liquid investments to be used as partial payment for large ticket items. More remote goals might call for building an equity in a home, building a fund for paying for college education for dependents, acquiring insurance to cover various categories of risk contingencies (income continuation, loss of assets due to fire or other destructive elements, personal liability risks, health care risks, etc.), to build one or several pension accounts, and to create an estate.

Insured savings might be suitable for some of these needs, whereas positions in well-managed security portfolios are of growing importance to the average or above average income earning family.

The development of professionally managed portfolios of financial assets has accelerated since the early 1980s when national legislation encouraged people to make provisions for their retirements. Greater emphasis, through tax incentive programs, was placed on the deferring of income until withdrawal during retirement years (generally from aged sixty or seventy and beyond). Thus life insurance companies, mutual fund managers, and trust departments at full service commercial banks began to more vigorously compete for tax deferred pension accounts. These income deferral plans generally fall into about five categories, although we could subdivide some of these.

Important tax-deferred pension accounts might result from deferred income of employees in one or several vehicles, including the following:

1. Deferred income savings plans for federal and state workers;
2. Corporate plans (401-k), both defined benefit and defined contribution plans;

3. Section 403-b income deferral plans intended for supplemental income retirement for municipal employees, employees of not-for-profit institutions, and the like;
4. Keogh plans intended for self-employed persons (i.e., business persons such as proprietors, partners, and shareholders in an S Corporation);
5. Individual retirement accounts, generally for income earners or spouses of income earners not eligible for one of the preceding deferral accounts.

The federal income tax laws that limit the amounts of such contributions and withdrawals from these plans change from time to time, so a participant and fund manager should stay attuned to such changes and operate within the federal statutes.

Most large life insurance companies and mutual fund management groups compete vigorously for deferred income deposits. Trust departments at commercial banks are expected to become major competitors in this arena during the 1990s and later years. It is not unusual for a "family of funds" to provide portfolios that include (1) money market instruments, (2) intermediate- and long-term government securities, (3) federal agency securities, (4) high-grade corporate bonds and preferred stocks, (5) blue-chip common stock funds, (6) income-oriented stock funds, (7) growth-oriented large company stock funds, and (8) emerging growth company funds. Some design sector, industry, or geographical area specialty funds. Merrill Lynch, Fidelity, and other large fund managers, for example, offer more than forty different choices. Life insurance companies often develop pools of assets meeting many of the preceding areas and attempt to attract pension funds into these pools.

The professional managers offer several benefits not generally achievable by a small, independent investor. Large pools diversify into the financial assets of many different issuers, thus reducing the risk from possible failure of one or a few issues that might be bought by an individual. Transaction costs are less on large trades than on small trades, so this is a usual savings. The managers offer a degree of professional management that (should, at least) monitor the issues held in the portfolio. Last of all, records for tax and other purposes are maintained, and security holdings are safeguarded. For these services, a management fee (usually running about 0.5% of assets annually) and operating expenses (usually ranging from 0.25 to 1.25% of managed assets yearly) are charged on fixed return and actively traded equity funds.

Mutual fund and other professional managers of financial assets are often criticized for earning less than what is achieved on the popular averages. Changes in the S & P averages, however, are value weighted, and change over time with primary issues, as does the NYSE index. Results of the funds are net of operating expenses. Since the institutions are making up such a large share of the market holdings and trading, it is not reasonable to expect half or more of them to perform "above average." A fund that performs about 90% of market average return, allowing for the management and operating expenses, is a more reasonable expectation.

Some portfolio managers attempt to shift their holdings from certain classes of issues to other groups in attempts to benefit from expected market price changes over the business cycle. Still others use a mathematical equation such as the Markowitz efficient portfolio or the single index model developed by Sharpe. These models attempt to derive the portfolio that (1) maximizes the anticipated level of return for a given level of risk (uncertainty of return) or (2) minimizes the level of risk for a stated target goal of anticipated return. These models, although slow and tedious to apply with hand calculations, have been computerized so that the portfolio manager only has to plug in some established values for anticipated returns and risk to receive a percentage breakdown of classes of financial securities, such as T-bills, T-bonds, high-grade corporate bonds or preferred stocks, and high-grade common shares. The personal computer investment module that accompanies *Investments,* by C. P. Jones, is recommended.[4]

The mix of financial securities that should be included in a financial portfolio generally depends on three factors. These are the expected return on each investment class (or security), the beta, the residual standard deviation (defined as the beta × the standard deviation of returns computed in the usual way), and the level(s) of return desired. The computer printout provides several choices of portfolio weights. This is illustrated in Table 1.1 using the "Single Index Inputs" and approximate market returns and residual standard deviations for four groups of financial securities.

Assume the following scenario of values in the market at a given point in time. Six-month Treasury bills with a yield of 4%; a beta of .10, and a return standard deviation (RSD) of 3.0%; from three- to five-year Treasury notes with a yield of 5.4%, a beta of .15, and an RSD of 5.0%; a diversified portfolio of investment grade utility bonds with a market yield of 8%, a beta of .30, an RSD of 8.0%, a diversified growth stock portfolio of financially strong common shares with expected return of 11%, beta of 1.00, and an RSD of 20%; and a market standard deviation on returns on financial assets of 15%. The efficient mix of these elements, for a return ranging from 7 to 10%, runs from a balance of T-notes, utility bonds, and high-quality growth stocks of 45%, 49%, and 6%, respectively, with an expected portfolio return of 7% and a standard deviation in expected returns of 5.2% on the low-risk, low-return side to a portfolio of 33.3% high-grade utility bonds and 66.7% growth stocks with a high expected return of 10% and a standard deviation of 17.8% for the high-return, high-risk portfolio. Other mixes are found in Table 1.1.

Still other large portfolio managers of financial assets attempt to weight their portfolio with some market index. The CREF (College Retirement Equities Fund) variable annuity fund managed by TIAA (Teachers Insurance and Annuity Association) is constructed along these lines.

Sales people vying for funds to be professionally managed usually attempt to match available choices with perceived needs of the buyers. That is, a young family seeking a high level of safety in its investments should consider only those alternatives meeting this preset goal or objective. A middle-aged physician, dentist, or

Table 1.1
Balancing a Portfolio for Risk and Return

```
                        EFFICIENT PORTFOLIOS
                      THE INVESTMENT CALCULATOR
                INVESTMENTS: ANALYSIS AND MANAGEMENT   3/E
                          By Charles P. Jones
```

```
     Input Variables                                      Current Value
MMMMMMMMMMMMMMMMMMMMMMMMMMMMMMMMMMMMMMMMMMMMMMMMMMMMMMMMMMMMMMMMMMMMMMMMMMMM

     Number of Securities                                       4
     (W)ith or With(O)ut Short Sales                            O
     Range of Returns to Calculate Efficient Portfolios
          Upper Bound                                        10.00 %
          Lower Bound                                         7.00 %
     Number of Efficient Portfolios to Calculate                4
     (M)arkowitz Model or (S)ingle Index Model                  S
```

```
                          SINGLE INDEX INPUTS

                 Expected Return       Beta      Res Standard Deviation

MMMMMMMMMMMMMMMMMMMMMMMMMMMMMMMMMMMMMMMMMMMMMMMMMMMMMMMMMMMMMMMMMMMMMMMMMMMMMM.
     Security  1        4.00 %         0.10             3.00 %
     Security  2        5.40 %         0.15             5.00 %
     Security  3        8.00 %         0.30             8.00 %
     Security  4       11.00 %         1.00            20.00 %

     Market
     Standard Deviation     15.00 %
```

```
MMMMMMMMMMMMMMMMMMMMMMMMMMMMEFFICIENT PORTFOLIOS RESULTSMMMMMMMMMMMMMMMMMMMMMMMMMMMM

     Portfolio #            1            2            3            4

     Return              7.000        8.000        9.000       10.000
     Standard Deviation  6.212        8.429       11.700       17.808

     Weight   1          0.000        0.000        0.000        0.000
     Weight   2         45.013       14.888        0.000        0.000
     Weight   3         49.309       72.208       66.667       33.333
     Weight   4          5.678       12.903       33.333       66.667
```

Source: PC data input and run from C. P. Jones, "The Investment Calculator," provided with
   Investments: Analysis and Management, 4th ed., New York, John Wiley & Sons, Inc., 1994.

corporate manager might want to defer income until retirement, and thus prefer
shares (or interest in) long-term growth accounts. Persons nearing retirement
desire less risk in their portfolio, because they have fewer years to recoup possible
losses, and should select high-grade fixed-return funds, utility stock funds, or
perhaps industry specialized funds composed of relatively low-beta, high-quality
stocks.

OVERVIEW OF THE BOOK

This book contains twelve chapters. This chapter provides an overview of financial assets, considers important factors that influence security prices and their
historical returns, defines the usual scope of activity of the fundamental security
analyst and the stock technician, and provides a brief description of how profes-

sional managers determine an appropriate mix among financial assets to be held in a balanced portfolio. Chapter 2 considers strengths and weaknesses in the overall economy in an attempt to determine whether a portfolio manager would be better advised to concentrate funds in low-risk short-term marketable issues; long-term bonds; common shares; or other types of financial assets. Keys to fundamental evaluation of common stocks are provided in Chapter 3, including fundamental measurements provided by Trendline Corporation on its chart services, and ways for detecting out-of-favor stocks and those with rapid profit potential.

Five chapters are devoted almost exclusively to the technical approach and its application and illustration. Chapter 4 provides the basic theory of vertical bar charting. Here, we consider the construction of charts. In addition, we focus on constructing trendlines, recognizing strong and weak patterns, estimating stock price moves, recognizing relative strength, assessing the importance of moving averages, and detecting usual points of support and resistance on the charts. Chapter 5 develops some trading strategies when using vertical bar charts. We attempt to develop a theory of when to buy and sell an individual stock, targeting the probable near- and longer-term moves for an issue. Chapter 6 provides coverage for point and figure charts, including how they are constructed, how different bullish and bearish patterns appear, how a trend line is estimated, when a breakout occurs, estimating a probable move, determining support and resistance levels for the stocks, and miscellaneous topics useful to a technician. Point and figure chart theory is then extended in Chapter 7 to trading strategies, including the development of short-, intermediate-, and long-term strategies; fine-tuning of price objectives; and understanding relative strength, buying and selling climaxes, and bull and bear traps. Chapter 8 provides technical indicator review for the overall U.S. stock market. We review sentiment indicators, breadth of the market indicators, market momentum measurements, monetary pressures, and other forecasting tools. Both vertical bar and point and figure chart theory are applied to overall stock market evaluation.

Chapters 9 and 10 are more fundamental in nature than technical, because they review, largely with computer data banks of information, stock attributes in the past that positively or negatively impacted on their market returns. Chapter 9 addresses the importance of being in the right group of stocks, sequencing the stock holdings for different stages of the stock cycle, and ways to identify laggards and leaders from an industry or broader sector. Industry group charts are then contrasted to the fundamental analysis. Market anomalies, as described here, and ways to profit from recognizing them, are identified and incorporated into suggested trading strategies in Chapter 10.

The two concluding chapters address portfolio management. Chapter 11 provides important intermarket analysis and fixed-income allocation strategies. Chapter 12 shows how asset allocation management and risk reduction may be achieved by using leading mutual funds and their trading strategies as gauges of the markets.

SUMMARY

We do not hold to the efficient market view, but instead believe that most securities are somewhat mispriced in the short run. We feel that this mispricing is more easily recognized by a portfolio manager who has a good understanding of the technical strength the issue appears to be displaying; however, unless technical strength (or weakness) is reinforced with fundamentals in a few months, there is likely to be little follow-through in price movement for the issue (or price objective might be short of its target). Consequently, we consider both technical and fundamental analysis to be important. Funds placed in financial institutions are continuously shifting into issues with perceived advantages from the expected risk-return trade-off. The factors that influence and are expected to influence the market spread among various types of financial assets are assessed in designing an appropriate portfolio of financial assets to meet certain predetermined objectives or goals. The sequencing of the chapters in this book has been designed to facilitate a greater understanding of these views, and hopefully, as an aid to the serious investor in the financial asset allocation process.

NOTES

1. F. J. Fabozzi, ed., *Investment Management* (Cambridge, Mass.: Ballinger Publishing Company, 1989), 101–113.

2. R. G. Ibbotson and R. A. Sinquefeld, *Stocks, Bills, and Inflation* (Chicago, Ill.: Dow Jones-Irwin, 1989), 14 and L. Fisher and J. H. Lorie, *A Half Century of Returns on Stocks and Bonds* (Chicago, Ill.: The University of Chicago Graduate School of Business, 1977).

3. Federal Reserve Bank of New York, *Winter Review 1991* (New York: Federal Reserve Bank of New York, 1991), 24.

4. C. P. Jones, *Investments: Analysis and Management,* 4th ed. (New York: John Wiley & Sons, Inc., 1994).

Chapter 2

EVALUATING THE ECONOMY

AGGREGATE MEASUREMENTS

Before determining which financial assets are appropriate for a portfolio, it is important to evaluate the overall economy. In the United States, the entire national economy is often measured in terms of gross domestic product (GDP), the final round of sales of goods and services, adjusted for imports and exports. GDP is generally measured either in current dollars or with a deflator index that converts it to some recent base year, such as 1987. Another aggregate measurement is the index of industrial production, which includes contract construction as well as the manufacturing and utility sectors. Data for the GDP are collected by the U.S. Department of Commerce, whereas the Federal Reserve System collects data and publishes the index of industrial production on a quarterly basis.

The ten business sectors in the U.S. economy include agriculture-related firms, extracting firms, construction firms, manufacturers, transportation and utility firms, wholesale trade companies, retail trade concerns, financial service companies, general service firms, and government service concerns. Since agriculture, retail trade, and service sectors are included in the GDP but not in the index of industrial production, the GDP is the less volatile measurement.

The GDP deflated figure is expected to normally rise by about 3% yearly due to a 1.1% expected annual increase in population and a 2.0% approximate increase in productivity of workers (due partially to improved mechanization, increased computerization, and greater application of quantitative analysis). The monetary authorities usually accommodate the nation's fiscal needs by expanding the monetary base by 3 to 5% yearly. Excess credit is thought to be inflationary,

Chart 2.1
Gross Domestic Product

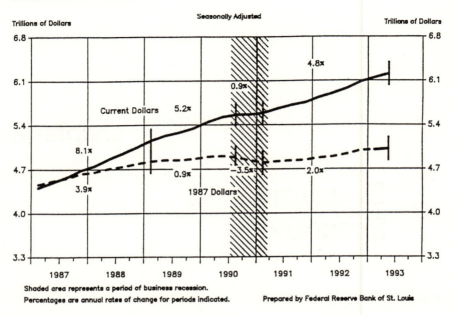

Source: Federal Reserve Bank of St. Louis, July 29, 1993.

leading to above average positive changes in wholesale and consumer prices. A deficiency of credit (or money) could stifle the ability of the economy to meet its growth potential.

Gross domestic product figures are gathered and reported by the Federal Reserve System and several of its Federal Reserve Banks. The figures are reported in current dollars and constant dollars, such as 1987 dollars. Chart 2.1 reflects GDP in current and constant 1987 dollars for 1987 to mid-1993. In boom years, GDP usually grows from about 1 to 4% yearly. Meanwhile, during recession periods, the real contraction may range from 0.5 to 1% annually.

Another measurement of the overall well-being of the nation's economy is the nearness to full employment at a given moment in time. If, for example, the nation contains 120 million adults aged fourteen and above who are willing to work, and some 6 million of them do not have jobs, then the unemployment rate is said to be 6/120 or 5.0%. This 5.0% appears to be about as low, when using total population figures, as the country is able to go without seeing a heating up of wage rates and prices of consumer goods. At this level, some jobs are available, but those desiring them are either not trained for them or not living in the proximity where the jobs are available.

The total U.S. population is growing by about 1.1% annually. Adult population beyond the age of forty-five is growing somewhat faster than this rate. As a result,

Chart 2.2
Civilian Employment and Unemployment Rates

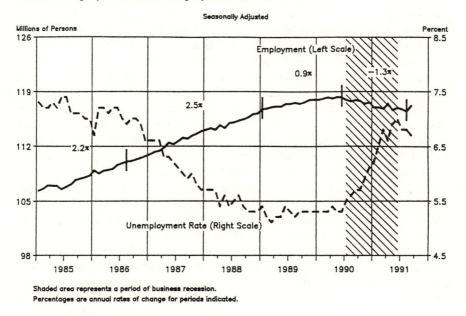

Seasonally Adjusted

Source: Federal Reserve Bank of St. Louis, October 4, 1991.

jobs should be created by about 1.2 to 1.5% yearly to maintain unemployment figures at about 5 to 6%. As employment growth exceeds this 1.2%, the unemployment rate falls, but as the rate slows to about 1% or even falls in total numbers, as reflected in Chart 2.2, the unemployment rate turns up. This occurred in late 1990 and continued into 1991 and early 1992. The low interest rates that prevailed in late 1991 through late 1993 were expected to exert economic expansion pressure, especially in the housing and other durables goods sectors, and thus lead the U.S. economy out of its recession.

Not all components of the labor force have equal opportunity for gainful employment. Teenagers, for example, have little job experience. Many are seeking part-time or seasonal employment, whereas others live at home and cannot travel to the locations where suitable jobs might be available. To a lesser degree, some of these same circumstances apply to persons falling into the prime college age (nineteen–twenty-five) group. Consequently, teenaged unemployment might run 15 to 25% of the total of that group, whereas only 3% of the married males and perhaps 3.5% of married females (seeking employment) are out of work at any point in time. Senior adults, those above fifty-five years of age who become unemployed, often find that retooling for another job is slow and difficult; however, many business firms have recently begun to woo older workers on a part-time basis to gain their high level of work ethics and to obtain years of experience at very little incremental wage cost. Moreover, the part-time workers, including many adults aged fifty-five or above who may be retired and have their own health care benefits, are usually paid fewer fringe benefits (vacation days, health care insurance, sick days, and deferred income packages) than are younger, full-time workers. Many firms use a blend of full-time workers, with fringe benefits, and part-time persons with fewer fringes as their work force.

Some occupations have greater job security than others. When, for example, a military defense contractor completes a major contract, or one is canceled or stretched out, some of the workers are terminated. Likewise, when motor vehicle sales are slow during a recession period, some assembly plants are closed. Some might be reduced to three or four days of work per week. The same might be true of major appliance manufacturers, manufacturers of other durable goods, and firms, such as those involved in publishing or trucking, whose sales are highly cyclical. Sales are more stable in the nondurable goods sector, wholesale trade, retail trade, and many types of services, including government service. Firms with stable or increasing sales are usually not discharging workers, on balance, but are usually hiring new workers to replace those terminating or retiring.

One could regress the sales within a given industry or for a company on the level of gross domestic product to determine its susceptibility to business downturns and upturns. When this is done, we would discover that residential housing construction, commercial construction, auto assembly, and the manufacturing of durable goods, along with the production of their raw materials and component parts, are very sensitive to strength in the overall economy. As sales in an industry or firm lag, certain costs are fixed in nature and profits either shrink or vanish entirely. The market prices of these issues, in the anticipation of lower future earnings, usually fall from six to twelve months before declines in reported earnings occur. Other, more stable industries include consumer nondurable goods (those that are bought for near-term consumption or usage), such as heating fuels, motor fuels, foodstuffs, beverages, and a wide array of health and personal care items, as well as those involved in the wholesale and retail trade of these items; public utilities (water, gas, electric, and telecommunications); and many types of services. Studies into the usual impact from overall cyclical swings in the U.S. economy on selected industries are provided in the last section of this chapter.

INTEREST RATES AND THE ECONOMY

The Federal Reserve System (FRS) was created in 1913 to provide central banks (twelve Federal Reserve and twenty-four branch banks), in addition to a central monetary authority located in Washington, D.C. The FRS, usually referred to as the FED, was designed to promote a healthy monetary economy, to work toward a level of full employment, and to promote international trade. These broad objectives are sometimes at odds with one another, meaning that the FED must let one suffer to some extent while promoting the other(s).

The monetary authorities have several tools useful in promoting a healthy economy (i.e., one that provides credit expansion to meet business and consumer needs, but yet is designed to minimize the likely rate of overall price changes, the inflation level). These monetary tools include the reserve requirements placed on member commercial banks, the rate of interest charged at the rediscount window from member and other commercial bank borrowers; in addition, they involve the open market action of buying or selling government securities from the FED's own substantial portfolio of U.S. Treasury issues so as to exert upward or downward pressures on interest rates. As the rates of interest on government issues move upward or downward, other money market and capital market rates usually move in tandem with them.

As the economy overheats during a long business boom, interest rates tend to rise, making credit more expensive. The tight money action followed by the FED (higher rediscount rates, selling Treasury securities in the secondary markets, and possibly raising the banks' reserve requirements) squeezes billions of dollars of credit out of the total U.S. monetary systems; and this leads to a slowing of business activity and (ideally) a decline in the rate of price inflation in wholesale and consumer goods. The reverse action is taken to make new housing and autos more affordable to potential buyers. When pent up demand is met with purchases of these big ticket items, inventories of these items and their component parts are expanded, credit is expanded, more jobs are created, the unemployment level generally declines, and the uptrend in growth in the overall nation is resumed. Adjustments made by the FED are usually gradual so as not to create more imbalances than necessary. Fighting inflation with its monetary tools creates some swings in employment. As interest moves to above-average levels, international investment dollars may flow to this nation and create some swings in monetary exchange units (relative value of the dollar and other measurements of international trade) of our trading partners (free European countries, Canada, Japan, etc.). When interest rates fall too far too quickly, dollars may flow out of this nation and toward other investment opportunities abroad that promise higher levels of returns.

Selected interest rates are reflected in Chart 2.3. The discount rate charged by the FED for member banks' short-term borrowing are reflected from late 1990 to December 1991 and are shown to fall from 7.0 to 3.5%, a very dramatic decline. The Federal funds rate, or the rate that one bank pays another for buying excess reserve deposits with the FED, moved from about 8 to 4%. Market yield on five-year treasuries declined from about 8 to 6% over the period.

The prime rate charged by large banks for loans acquired by high credit rated customers is shown in Chart 2.4 to have declined over the late 1990 to the end of 1991 from 10 to 6.5%. The market yields on Aaa corporate bonds and municipal bonds fell also, although not so dramatically. The yields on high-grade commercial paper fell from about 9 to 5% over the time period.

During a period of easy money policy pursued by the FED, most types of money and capital market rates tend to move downward. When the FED is deliberately

Chart 2.3
Selected Interest Rates

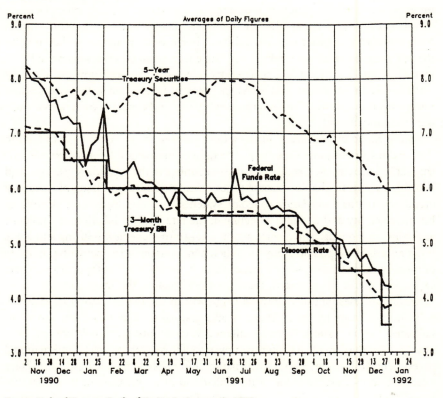

Source: Federal Reserve Bank of St. Louis, January 3, 1992.

pursuing a tight money policy, rates are being pushed up and most tend to move in the same direction.

BUSINESS CYCLE COMPONENTS

The theory of business cycles was studied by Mitchell and Burns almost 100 years ago. Census and other series of data have been collected in the United States since about 1790, and an analysis of some of these series appears to support the theory of a long-term trend, a cyclical swing that lasts from just over one year to perhaps as long as ten years, and a seasonal swing in some series of monthly or quarterly data. Other movements are considered to be random in nature. The long-term secular trend (in housing, for example) may last for several cycles. Some writers have determined that the long-term trend in housing is from forty-eight to sixty years. It would seem reasonable to assume that it would move parallel to the growth, stability, or shrinkage of adult population, and the life expectancy of

Chart 2.4
Yields on Selected Securities

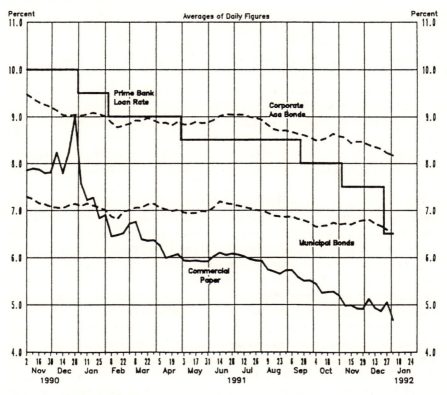

Source: Federal Reserve Bank of St. Louis, January 3, 1992.

an adult, say twenty years of age, to about seventy-five (or an additional fifty-five years). Given that credit is available on favorable terms, most adults prefer to own their own residences than to depend on relatives or landlords for living quarters.

Seasonal variations, swings that occur with a high degree of regularity from year to year, may be caused or influenced by several factors. Some raw materials are available only on a short production cycle. Prices may be much lower during the months of substantial harvests. The temperatures (seasons) may have some adverse effect on the ability to do certain things. Housing starts, for example, are low from about December to March, especially in frigid northern climates due to inability and general expense of laying cement during freezing weather. Boating and vacation activities tend to be concentrated more heavily in the warmer months. Hunting is concentrated in the fall and early winter months and so on. Sale of textiles tend to be highest prior to Easter, the back-to-school period, and just prior to Christmas. Perhaps consumers are more oriented to shopping during these periods, or perhaps retailers use heavier promotion, but there are definite retail trade bulges during these periods for many types of consumer products.

An irregular movement in business activity might be caused by a strike, a temporary plant closure due to utility outage or inclement weather, delays in making a large shipment, shortages of raw materials or key component parts, discharge of workers due to falling product demand or reorganization, and the like.

A statistician often massages a series of business data to remove components other than the cycle, before attempting to estimate its four phases. These four phases are prosperity, crisis, depression, and revival (or perhaps recession, contraction, revival, and expansion phases). We might also refer to a business cycle as having a peak, downturn, trough, and upturn. The duration of a business cycle is usually measured from the bottom of one trough to the bottom of the ensuing one.

The massaging of monthly business data so as to eliminate irregular, seasonal, and trend influences is often done in that order. Irregular movements usually occur for only a short duration. Either three- or five-month averaging is sometimes used. The impact of the seasons are determined by evaluating them for several years and then the index figures are divided into the raw data values so as to deseasonalize them. The index to the upward (or downward) secular trend is divided into the data so as to eliminate the impact of the trend forces. The residue is assumed to be the result of the impact from the business cycle.

Economic indicator data are gathered and reported by the Bureau of Economic Analysis of the Department of Commerce. Although several hundred series have been gathered and analyzed over the years, the twelve leading indicators, four coincidental indicators and seven lagging indicators, have become the ones most viewed by economists and statisticians. Chart 2.5 reflects movements over the seven business cycles from about 1965 to 1993 for the eleven business cycle components that make up the overall leading indicator. The reader should now study these and attempt to gauge how they lead the shaded area, or that of recession periods.

We may wonder why statisticians, economists, and politicians even bother with the study of business cycles. The answer is that they must forecast business activity of various sorts. They must estimate these impacts on earned income and the tax burden of individual, business, and government consumers and project needs for funds to support certain welfare programs (unemployment compensation, for example) due to layoffs and inadequacy of jobs in the labor markets. The working, consuming public also forecast their likelihood of continued employment, pay cuts, pay raises, and the like, and factor these estimates into their plans for buying a larger home, along with some new appliances and furniture; replacing the family auto or repairing and maintaining the older one; replenishing the wardrobe; buying hobby items (i.e., golfing gear, fishing equipment, guns, boats, etc.); retiring; taking a part-time job; and so forth. During a business contraction, consumers on balance begin to retire debt even though interest rates may be declining.

Reversing a downtrend in the overall economy can sometimes be spurred by making credit cheaper and more available to borrowers. The theory is that they may borrow more heavily to finance the purchase of the large ticket items mentioned above. When the U.S. Congress operates near a balanced budget, deficit spending (through tax cuts, road-building programs, or other capital outlays or increase in government labor force) is a stimulant to the economy. When the government programs are already in the red by 10 to 15% of its tax collections, national leaders have less flexibility in fiscal stimulation of the economy. Reinstatement of the investment tax credit on equipment for businesses and shortening of the depreciation tax guidelines on equipment and structures for businesses are also sometimes done to stimulate the business sector of the economy. Tax credits up to some limit to first-time home buyers have been used to encourage an increase in residential home sales. In late 1991, the upturn in the U.S. economy appeared to stall even though interest rates were at levels similar to those existing in 1978 (i.e., prior to the double-digit inflation and interest rates of the 1979–1981 years). Low interest rates had been promoted by the auto manufacturers, from time to time, for many months. The upturn in construction was delayed several months due to the inclement weather (December through February). Some congressional movement appeared to be toward some tax relief for the middle-income earners, who are said by some politicians and economists to shoulder more than their fair share of the federal tax burden. In time, lower interest rates are likely to make an impact, but as mentioned earlier, buying of new housing is much stronger in the second and third quarters of a year than in the other two quarters. It is likely that the U.S. Congress will take some fiscal action for political and other motivations. Hopefully, it will not be so substantial as to require heavy-handed monetary action that pushes interest rates back into their widely swinging patterns so as to curb rising inflationary trends from a future overheated economy.

FORECASTING STOCK PRICES WITH THE BUSINESS CYCLE

The national Bureau of Economic Analysis (BEA), a part of the Department of Commerce, began studying hundreds of economic series in the 1930s in an attempt to determine leading indicators. Some were identified in the late 1930s, and the best twelve leading indicators were combined into a composite index in 1968. Today, the list includes eleven leading indicators (plus the composite), four roughly coincidental indexes, and seven lagging index series. These, along with their average leads/lags from shifts in the overall economy as measured by the GDP deflated is as follows:

	Average Lead Time (months)	
Leading Indicators	Peaks	Troughs
Average weekly hours, manufacturing	−2	−3
Average weekly initial claims for unempl. insurance	−5	−1

Chart 2.5
Composite Indexes: Leading Index Components

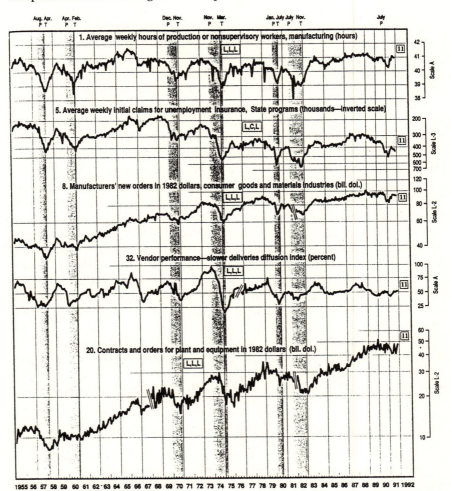

Chart 2.5 Continued

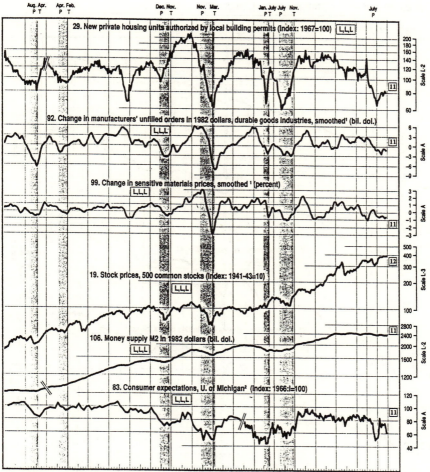

29. New private housing units authorized by local building permits (Index: 1967=100) [L,L,L]

92. Change in manufacturers' unfilled orders in 1982 dollars, durable goods industries, smoothed[1] (bil. dol.)

99. Change in sensitive materials prices, smoothed [1] (percent)

19. Stock prices, 500 common stocks (Index: 1941-43=10)

106. Money supply M2 in 1982 dollars (bil. dol.)

83. Consumer expectations, U. of Michigan[2] (Index: 1966:I=100)

1955 56 57 58 59 60 61 62 63 64 65 66 67 68 69 70 71 72 73 74 75 76 77 78 79 80 81 82 83 84 85 86 87 88 89 90 91 1992

1. This series is smoothed by an autoregressive-moving-average filter developed by Statistics Canada.
2. This is a copyrighted series used by permission; it may not be reproduced without written permission from the University of Michigan, Survey Research Center.
NOTE.—Current data for these series are shown on pages C-2, C-3, and C-4.

Chart 2.5 Continued

Composite Indexes: Coincident Index Components

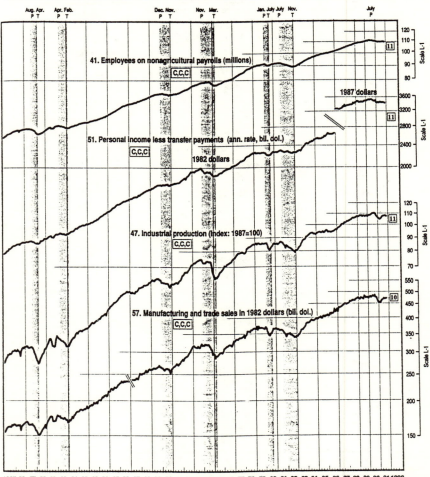

1955 56 57 58 59 60 61 62 63 64 65 66 67 68 69 70 71 72 73 74 75 76 77 78 79 80 81 82 83 84 85 86 87 88 89 90 91 1992
NOTE.—Current data for these series are shown on page C-2.

Chart 2.5 Continued

Composite Indexes: Lagging Index Components

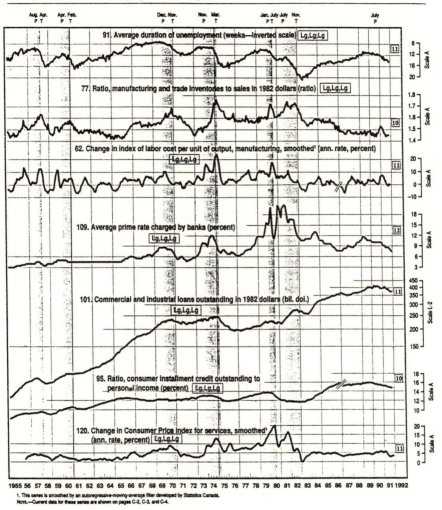

Source: Bureau of Economic Analysis, *Survey of Current Business,* June 1991.

New orders in 1982 dollars, consumer goods and materials	−2	−2
Vendor performance, slower deliveries diffusion index	−3	−4
Contracts and orders for plant and equipment in 1982 dollars	−5	+1
Building permits, new private housing units	−9	−6
Change in unfilled orders in 1982 dollars, for durable goods, smoothed		
Change in sensitive materials prices, smoothed	−4	−8
Stock price, 500 common stocks	−4	−4
Money supply M2 in 1982 dollars	−5	−4
Index of consumer expectations	Too few cycles	

Coincident Indicators

Employees on nonagricultural payroll	−2	0
Personal income less transfer payments in 1982 dollars	0	−1
Industrial production	−3	0
Manufacturing and trade sales in 1982 dollars	−3	0

Lagging Indicators

Average duration of unemployment (inverted)	+1	+8
Ratio, mfg. and trade inventories to sales in 1982 dollars	+2	+3
Change in labor cost per unit of output, mfg., smoothed	+8	+11
Average prime rate	+4	+14
Commercial and industrial loans in 1982 dollars	+2	+5
Ratio, consumer installment credit to personal income	+6	+7
Change in CPI for services, smoothed	Too few cycles	

ADJUSTING A BALANCED PORTFOLIO FOR BUSINESS CYCLE PHASES

The idea of reallocating a financial portfolio from the standpoint of risk-return measurements was introduced in the last section of Chapter 1. We now extend this four-security portfolio for different phases of the business cycle, expansion periods and contraction periods. Recent work published by Peter I. Berman[1] are highly useful in this endeavor. According to the Berman study, with summary statistics reported in Figure 2.1, the mean duration of expansion periods was forty-six months from October 1949 to July 1981. An eighth double-cycle then occurred from November 1982 to December 1990. The average duration of the

Figure 2.1
Average Returns and Risks of S & P 500, Twenty-Year T-Bonds, Ten-Year T-Notes, and Twenty-Day T-Bills for Seven Business Cycles, 1949–1982

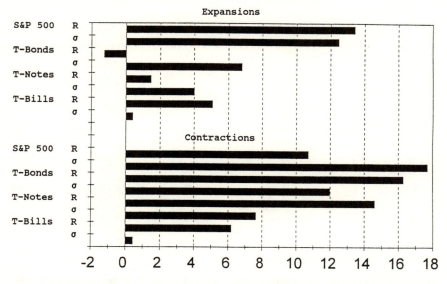

Source: Developed from Peter I. Berman, "An Asset Allocation Primer for Post-War Business Cycles," *American Business Review* 10 (January 1992), pp 88–92.

seven contraction periods was eleven months from July 1953 to November 1982. Holding stocks during an expected expansion in the economy is usually rewarding to astute asset allocation strategists.

The mean returns for the holding periods, along with standard deviations of returns, were reported for the S & P 500 stocks, for long-term Treasury bonds, for intermediate-term Treasury notes, and for Treasury bills. These returns and standard deviations (risk measurements) were factored into the Investmaster module (see Chapter 1 for description) so as to determine an appropriate mix of stocks, T-bonds, T-notes, and T-bills to hold in an efficiently balanced portfolio. Summary results are printed in Table 2.1, and suggests the following efficient portfolios:

Expansion periods	40.7% bills, 59.3% stocks
Contraction periods	57% bills, 30.0% notes, 13.0% bonds

if one desired an average return of 10% during each of these periods. In the expansion period, the standard deviation of return ran 12.0%, whereas it was only 3.4% during the contraction period (due mainly to the large holding of relatively risk-free T-bills during contraction periods) on the constructed efficient portfolio. Other values for assumed levels of returns and computed standard deviations are shown in Table 2.1.

Table 2.1

Examples of Efficient Portfolios during Expansion and Contraction Periods, Based on Historical Returns and Risk Measurements

Expansions

		Expected Return	Beta	Res Standard Deviation
		MMMMMMMMMMMMMMMMMMMMMMMMMMMMMMMMMMMMMMMMMMMMMMMMMMMMMMMMMMMMMMMMMMMMMMMMMM		
Security	1	13.40 %	1.00	12.46 %
Security	2	-1.27 %	0.22	6.77 %
Security	3	1.46 %	0.15	4.00 %
Security	4	5.05 %	0.10	0.40 %

Market
Standard Deviation   15.00 %

Portfolio #		3	4	5	6
Return		9.000	10.000	11.000	12.000
Standard Deviation		9.848	12.037	14.230	16.425
Weight	1	47.305	59.281	71.257	83.234
Weight	2	0.000	0.000	0.000	0.000
Weight	3	0.000	0.000	0.000	0.000
Weight	4	52.695	40.719	28.743	16.766

Contractions

		Expected Return	Beta	Res Standard Deviation
		MMMMMMMMMMMMMMMMMMMMMMMMMMMMMMMMMMMMMMMMMMMMMMMMMMMMMMMMMMMMMMMMMMMMMMMMMM		
Security	1	10.70 %	1.00	17.69 %
Security	2	16.28 %	0.22	11.97 %
Security	3	14.60 %	0.15	7.62 %
Security	4	6.17 %	0.10	0.43 %

Market
Standard Deviation   15.00 %

Portfolio #		3	4	5	6
Return		9.000	10.000	11.000	12.000
Standard Deviation		2.759	3.389	4.053	4.736
Weight	1	0.000	0.000	0.000	0.000
Weight	2	9.567	13.163	16.759	20.354
Weight	3	22.097	29.647	37.197	44.747
Weight	4	68.336	57.190	46.044	34.899

Source: Developed by PC using "The Investment Calculator," provided with *Investments: Analysis and Management,* 4th ed., by Charles P. Jones, New York, John Wiley & Sons, Inc., 1994.

In actual practice, many portfolio managers have a relatively fixed core of commitment of funds to stocks or fixed-return issues and shift only a portion of the total portfolio into more stocks, heavier holdings of treasury issues, or commitment in corporate bonds or other types of issues.

Although these mathematical models provide an appropriate mix of security types from a reward-risk standpoint, it is necessary to determine exact securities needed to make up these components. For the selection of stocks, the following chapters emphasize the importance of considering fundamental and technical

Chart 2.6
Dow Jones Industrial Average and S & P 500 Index, 1982 to Early 1993

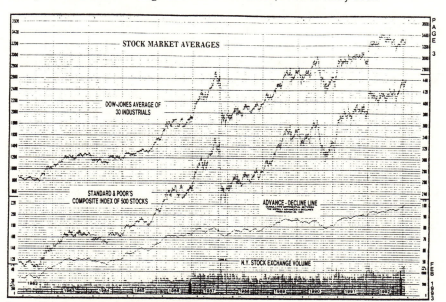

Source: Courtesy Standard & Poor's/Trendline.

strengths of individual issues. Further insight is also provided into estimating the overall strength of the economy and for industry groups of stocks.

TIME-SERIES MOVES IN STOCK AVERAGES

Long-term upward (or downward) trends occur in stock price indicators, often lasting at least three cycles or longer. The rise in stock prices that began in about 1933 (after the stock market crash of 1929–1932), faltered in 1937 but resumed its upward trend until about 1966. The market then moved in a sidewise consolidation pattern until about 1982, when an upward phase was again begun. A portion of these long bull markets can be seen from a review of Chart 2.6.

Rising markets are called bull markets, whereas falling markets are referred to as bear markets. From the bottom of one bear market to the bottom of the next has been highly regular in the United States since the end of World War II, lasting about four years on average. With some consolidations, bull markets usually last about three years followed by a bear market of one year or less. These apparent four-year movements may be fueled to some degree by legislative action taken to spur or to slow down the economy. Bull market moves usually begin from about four to eight months before it becomes apparent that other leading indicators are pointing toward a boom period. Stock price averages usually turn down several months prior to the completion of a boom period and the beginning of a contraction in the economy.

Stock price movements are somewhat seasonal in nature. January, for example, is usually a very good upside moving month, whereas February and March are lackluster. April usually advances. May and June see little upward pressure. July is usually higher, as is December. The other months may witness runs on the upside or downside. The reporting of corporate profits or year-end stock trading for tax reasons may account for some of the apparent seasonal movements.

Stock prices are usually stronger certain days of the week than on others. Friday is usually a strong, upside day. Monday is usually weak, at least until the last hour of trading on the major exchanges. Tuesdays, Wednesdays, and Thursdays are about average.

On a daily basis, the market frequently moves early in the United States in the same direction as set in the Tokyo or London stock markets. There is some tendency for a weak market on one close to carry over the early trading on the following day (unless reversing news becomes apparent overnight). Some investors attempt to fill large buy orders on weakness, or roughly the mid-trading hours of Mondays. Smart traders often sell into strength so as to get higher execution prices. More often than not, this is the late mornings of Fridays.

These topics are pursued and illustrated more completely in Chapters 9 and 10.

SUMMARY

The strength in the overall economy may be measured in a number of ways. The growth rate in the gross domestic product or in the index of industrial production are sometimes used. Both of these measures should rise, over time, due to growing population in the nation and increasing productivity.

The economy, and most economic series of data, tend to have four recognizable components: (1) the long-term secular trend, (2) the business cycle, (3) seasonal variations, and (4) random movements. The stock market averages, and long-term charts on individual stocks, tend to follow similar patterns as the general business climate, as shown by GDP, but stock market prices tend to lead the economy by about one half year.

The Bureau of Economic Analysis tracks and publishes about a dozen leading indicators that are followed closely by some economists and stock market analysts. Other indicators tend to move concurrently with or tend to lag the economy. These twenty-two business indicators are described in this chapter.

Last, the stance of the Federal Reserve System and the U.S. Treasury Department in monetary and fiscal matters, as they influence stock prices, are reviewed. Stock and bond prices are very sensitive to increases and decreases in interest rates of U.S. Treasury issues.

NOTES

1. Peter I. Berman, "An Asset Allocation Primer for Post-War Business Cycles," *American Business Review* 10 (January 1992): 88–92.

2. Refer also to Charles P. Jones, *Investments: Analysis and Management,* 4th ed. (New York: John Wiley & Sons, Inc., 1994).

Chapter 3

KEYS TO FUNDAMENTAL EVALUATION OF COMMON STOCKS

STOCK EVALUATION APPROACHES

Most holders of financial assets do not concentrate all of their resources into one type; rather they practice an asset allocation process. That is, a portion of the financial portfolio is made up of safe, liquid assets such as insured bank deposits, short-term Treasury securities, or money market funds. Another part may include bonds; but the largest portion may be allocated into a higher expected returning portfolio of common stocks or of mutual fund shares. This chapter is concerned with fundamental evaluation of individual issues that make up a common stock portfolio, inasmuch as returns on stocks vary widely over the stock cycle, and certain groups of stocks perform much better than do others during intermediate-term time horizons.

The successful evaluation of common stocks requires the use of more than one tool or philosophy. It is our belief that neither technical or fundamental factors nor modern portfolio management theories should be used exclusively when making a decision on individual common stock investments. The best method for obtaining thorough knowledge of a stock appears to be with a combination of fundamental and technical considerations.

Some stock fundamentalists place importance on reviewing a series of balance sheets and income statements for a given company (trend analysis) to detect changing trends in sales, profit margins, financial safety, or an appropriate mix of debt and equity. Meanwhile, some analysts go so far as to compare percentage (common-sized) financial statements for several firms in the same industry or to use published benchmark ratios. Some important sources of these statements are explained in the following section before extracts of important financial information are shown.

Trendline's charts are thought to be among the most useful and comprehensive sources of information available for studying common stocks. Trendline publishes four different sets of charts, including *Current Market Perspectives, Trendline's Daily Basis Charts, Trendline's Chart Guide,* and the *OTC Chart Manual.* All of these services are used in this chapter and/or the ones that follow with major emphasis placed on *Current Market Perspectives* and the *OTC Chart Manual.* All of these Trendline publications use weekly basis stock charts with the exception of the *Daily Basis Charts.* In Chapters 4 and 5, we explain that the weekly basis stock charts are for longer time periods and usually lead to fewer interpretational errors than daily basis charts. However, where short-term trading vehicles, such as puts and calls, are being used, the daily basis charts are indispensible.

FINANCIAL STATEMENT ANALYSIS

Companies that list their securities for trading on major exchanges, or those with 500 or more shareholders that trade in the over-the-counter (OTC) markets, are required to file annual reports (10-k) with the Securities and Exchange Commission. Most firms publish a colorful edition of annual reports for their shareholders. Enterprising publishing firms, such as Moody's Investors Service, gather financial statements and other important financial information on outstanding debt and equity issues and their characteristics, operating divisions, territories or routes of many firms, and other data and assemble it into bound volumes for usage by subscribers. Many public and private university libraries obtain *Moody's Investors Service,* which has been published for more than ninety years.

Industry-wide balance sheets and financial statements are published in the federal document, *Quarterly Financial Reports (for Manufacturing, Mining and Trade Corporations), Value Line Investment Survey,* Morris Associates' *Statement Studies,* Dun & Bradstreet's *Key Business Ratios in 800 Lines,* and other sources. Key financial ratios are provided along with these composite statements in many of these sources. Although the compilation of this data is a tedious task, review of key trend ratios may be useful in discovering apparently over- or underpriced shares in the market.

The U.S. Department of Commerce publishes quarterly updates in their study, *Quarterly Financial Report,* which contains balance sheet and income statement data on about twenty-five major manufacturing groups and for all mining corporations, selected retail trade firms, and a sampling of wholesale trade corporations. Five quarters of data showing industry-wide balance sheets for food and kindred products firms are reflected in Table 3.1. The statement is developed along a standard format that shows a breakdown of current assets, other longer-term assets, debts, and stockholders' equity accounts. Key balance sheet ratios are reflected at the bottom of the statement.

Some investors are more interested in income statement data than in balance

Table 3.1
Balance Sheet for Corporations Included in SIC Major Groups 20 and 21

Item	Food and Kindred Products[1]				
	2Q 1990	3Q 1990	4Q 1990	1Q 1991[3]	2Q 1991
ASSETS	(million dollars)				
Cash and demand deposits in the United States	3,207	3,151	3,631	3,152	3,412
Time deposits in the United States, including negotiable certificates of deposit	1,399	1,371	1,337	1,879	1,450
Total cash on hand and in U.S. banks	4,606	4,522	4,968	5,030	4,862
Other short-term financial investments, including marketable and government securities, commercial paper, etc.	5,813	5,960	5,335	6,462	7,569
Total cash, U.S. Government and other securities	10,419	10,482	10,303	11,492	12,431
Trade accounts and trade notes receivable (less allowances for doubtful receivables)	28,313	29,371	28,561	29,136	28,377
Inventories	37,944	40,583	41,338	41,532	39,013
All other current assets	6,307	6,453	7,286	7,538	7,324
Total current assets	82,983	86,890	87,487	89,699	87,145
Depreciable and amortizable fixed assets, including construction in progress	142,939	144,566	146,660	150,013	151,850
Land and mineral rights	5,636	5,702	5,681	5,985	5,950
Less: Accumulated depreciation, depletion, and amortization	55,746	56,389	57,993	60,196	61,388
Net property, plant, and equipment	92,829	93,879	94,348	95,802	96,413
All other noncurrent assets, including investment in nonconsolidated entities, long-term investments, intangibles, etc.	123,943	131,271	133,139	132,100	132,455
Total Assets	299,754	312,040	314,974	317,602	316,013
LIABILITIES AND STOCKHOLDERS' EQUITY					
Short-term debt, original maturity of 1 year or less:					
a. Loans from banks	5,143	6,810	7,508	6,817	6,042
b. Other short-term debt, including commercial paper	7,568	7,687	8,140	7,616	6,811
Trade accounts and trade notes payable	20,698	21,040	21,877	19,984	20,199
Income taxes accrued, prior and current years, net of payments	4,180	4,499	4,395	4,189	3,684
Installments, due in 1 year or less, on long-term debt:					
a. Loans from banks	1,913	1,771	2,157	2,743	2,432
b. Other long-term debt	4,046	3,816	4,714	5,887	6,024
All other current liabilities, including excise and sales taxes, and accrued expenses	21,876	23,312	25,691	24,952	23,948
Total current liabilities	65,423	68,935	74,481	72,188	69,140
Long-term debt (due in more than 1 year):					
a. Loans from banks	30,175	30,960	30,395	27,208	27,728
b. Other long-term debt	74,671	74,678	76,025	78,435	76,517
All other noncurrent liabilities, including deferred income taxes, capitalized leases, and minority stockholders' interest in consolidated domestic corporations	31,905	33,312	32,104	33,762	33,962
Total liabilities	202,174	207,885	213,005	211,594	207,366
Capital stock and other capital (less treasury stock)	19,260	22,966	23,723	27,064	28,974
Retained earnings	78,321	81,189	78,246	78,944	79,673
Stockholders' equity	97,581	104,156	101,969	106,008	108,647
Total Liabilities and Stockholders' Equity	299,754	312,040	314,974	317,602	316,013
NET WORKING CAPITAL					
Excess of total current assets over total current liabilities	17,560	17,955	13,006	17,511	18,006
SELECTED BALANCE SHEET RATIOS	(percent of total assets)				
Total cash, U.S. Government and other securities	3.5	3.4	3.3	3.6	3.9
Trade accounts and trade notes receivable	9.4	9.4	9.1	9.2	9.0
Inventories	12.7	13.0	13.1	13.1	12.3
Total current assets	27.7	27.8	27.8	28.2	27.6
Net property, plant, and equipment	31.0	30.1	30.0	30.2	30.5
Short-term debt including installments on long-term debt	6.1	6.5	7.2	7.3	6.8
Total current liabilities	21.8	22.1	23.6	22.7	21.9
Long-term debt	35.0	33.8	33.8	33.3	33.0
Total liabilities	67.4	66.6	67.6	66.6	65.6
Stockholders' equity	32.6	33.4	32.4	33.4	34.4

[1] Data for quarters in 1990 were restated to reflect principally industry reclassifications, as well as respondents' corrections of submitted data subsequent to original publication.
[2] Tobacco industry data have been collapsed into food industry data. Major merger and acquisition activity in recent years resulted in the reclassification of a significant portion of gross receipts and assets from tobacco to food. The remainder, composed of data from highly specialized tobacco manufacturers, is too small to be considered publishable as a separate industry.
[3] Revised principally to reflect respondents' corrections of submitted data subsequent to original publication.

Source: U.S. Department of Commerce, *Quarterly Financial Report,* Second Quarter 1991.

sheet data for a group of firms. This governmental publication of composite income statements from *Quarterly Financial Report* (*QFR*) for major SIC groups of 20 and 21 (or for food and kindred products) is shown in Table 3.2, presenting income statement items in millions of dollars as well as in a percentage format. The government document was published in hard copy through mid–1993 but is currently being distributed on microfiche. Recently, composite financial statements and key ratios are provided for several size classes for numerous standard classification code groups (SICs). An example of key operating ratios and balance sheet ratios for one industry, as shown in a recent issue of *Quarterly Financial Report,* is reflected at the bottom of Table 3.2.

A complete listing of the major industry groups covered in the *QFR* statement comparison is provided in Table 3.3, along with percentages of income before and after income taxes for each of the business lines, for the five quarters beginning with quarter two of 1990 and extending through quarter two of 1991. A financial analyst may very easily join together quarterly data for several years so as to determine the usual impact on reported pretax and after-tax profits during the latter stages of a boom period and early stages of a recession. Note that profits for all manufacturing firms fell by about half from the last boom quarter in 1990 to the lowest quarter of the recession in 1991. Actual losses occurred in the poorest quarter(s) for textiles; rubber and miscellaneous plastic products; stone, clay, and glass products; primary metal industries, especially iron and steel; and motor vehicles and equipment. After-tax profits, on balance, declined by about 25–30% in the nondurable manufacturing corporate sector but fell by roughly 90% in the durable goods sector during recession quarters. The mining sector is somewhat countercyclical so far as profit reporting is concerned. Profits in the retail trade sector are highly seasonal, with substantial rates of profits reported in the fourth quarter. Profits as a percentage of stockholder's equity are below average in wholesale trade, but tend to shrink about one half during recessions.

In comparative analysis, some financial analysts work out common-sized (ratio) financial statements for a company under review and match them up with the industry total. The previously stated references provide estimated industry-wide income statements and certain key balance sheet ratios. The user can thus compare trends for the firm in relation to the larger industry group from which it is drawn. Multiline firms are classified into the SIC code group that accounts for the largest share of its revenues.

Outlook within a given industry for a year or longer is facilitated by a review of information published and updated periodically in such widely read publications as the Department of Commerce's *U.S. Industrial Outlook,* Standard & Poor's *Industry Survey,* and *Value Line Industry Survey.* Some public libraries and most college or university libraries subscribe to one or more of these investment aids.

Rather than review complete financial statements for business firms, however, some fundamentalists merely refer to key financial data such as those provided on Trendline's *Current Market Perspectives* charts.

Table 3.2

Income Statement for Corporations Included in SIC Major Groups 20 and 21

Item	Food and Kindred Products[1]				
	2Q 1990	3Q 1990	4Q 1990	1Q 1991[3]	2Q 1991
	(million dollars)				
Net sales, receipts, and operating revenues..........................	99,059	99,474	103,828	96,807	101,609
Less: Depreciation, depletion and amortization of property, plant, and equipment..........	2,467	2,500	2,573	2,539	2,599
Less: All other operating costs and expenses, including cost of goods sold and selling, general, and administrative expenses..	87,991	88,473	91,665	86,530	89,957
Income (or loss) from operations.............................	8,601	8,501	9,590	7,739	9,053
Net nonoperating income (expense)................................	(1,004)	(838)	(4,955)	(735)	(1,172)
Income (or loss) before income taxes	7,597	7,663	4,635	7,004	7,882
Less: Provision for current and deferred domestic income taxes	2,428	2,546	2,340	2,012	2,721
Income (or loss) after income taxes	5,169	5,117	2,295	4,992	5,160
Cash dividends charged to retained earnings in current quarter	1,434	1,654	1,642	1,858	2,107
Net income retained in business.....................	3,735	3,463	653	3,134	3,054
Retained earnings at beginning of quarter	75,348	78,723	80,160	79,753	77,908
Other direct credits (or charges) to retained earnings (net), including stock and other noncash dividends, etc................................	(762)	(997)	(2,568)	(3,944)	(1,288)
Retained earnings at end of quarter	78,321	81,189	78,246	78,944	79,673
INCOME STATEMENT IN RATIO FORMAT	(percent of net sales)				
Net sales, receipts, and operating revenues...........................	100.0	100.0	100.0	100.0	100.0
Less: Depreciation, depletion, and amortization of property, plant, and equipment	2.5	2.5	2.5	2.6	2.6
Less: All other operating costs and expenses	88.8	88.9	88.3	89.4	88.5
Income (or loss) from operations.............................	8.7	8.5	9.2	8.0	8.9
Net nonoperating income (expense)................................	(1.0)	(0.8)	(4.8)	(0.8)	(1.2)
Income (or loss) before income taxes	7.7	7.7	4.5	7.2	7.8
Less: Provision for current and deferred domestic income taxes	2.5	2.6	2.3	2.1	2.7
Income (or loss) after income taxes	5.2	5.1	2.2	5.2	5.1
OPERATING RATIOS (see explanatory notes)	(percent)				
Annual rate of profit on stockholders' equity at end of period:					
Before income taxes	31.14	29.43	18.18	26.43	29.02
After income taxes................................	21.19	19.65	9.00	18.84	19.00
Annual rate of profit on total assets:					
Before income taxes	10.14	9.82	5.89	8.82	9.98
After income taxes................................	6.90	6.56	2.91	6.29	6.53
BALANCE SHEET RATIOS (based on succeeding table)					
Total current assets to total current liabilities	1.27	1.26	1.17	1.24	1.26
Total cash, U.S. Government and other securities to total current liabilities	0.16	0.15	0.14	0.16	0.18
Total stockholders' equity to total debt........................	0.79	0.83	0.79	0.82	0.87

[1] Data for quarters in 1990 were restated to reflect principally industry reclassifications, as well as respondents' corrections of submitted data subsequent to original publication.
[2] Tobacco industry data have been collapsed into food industry data. Major merger and acquisition activity in recent years resulted in the reclassification of a significant portion of gross receipts and assets from tobacco to food. The remainder, composed of data from highly specialized tobacco manufacturers, is too small to be considered publishable as a separate industry.
[3] Revised principally to reflect respondents' corrections of submitted data subsequent to original publication.

Source: U.S. Department of Commerce, *Quarterly Financial Report,* Second Quarter 1991.

Table 3.3
Annual Rates of Profit on Stockholder Equity by Division and Major Group

(Percent)

Industry	Income before income taxes[1][2]					Income after income taxes[2]				
	2Q 1990	3Q 1990	4Q 1990	1Q 1991	2Q 1991	2Q 1990	3Q 1990	4Q 1990	1Q 1991	2Q 1991
All manufacturing corporations	19.2	16.0	10.4	10.2	12.3	13.5	11.2	7.1	6.9	8.7
Nondurable manufacturing corporations	21.4	21.8	15.6	17.2	16.1	14.9	15.1	10.9	12.4	11.3
Food and kindred products	31.1	29.4	18.2	26.4	29.0	21.2	19.7	9.0	18.8	19.0
Tobacco manufactures[3]	NA	NA	NA	NA	NA	NA	NA	NA	NA	NA
Textile mill products	12.9	8.5	2.2	1.1	10.4	8.1	4.2	(0.6)	(0.3)	6.3
Paper and allied products	20.6	16.5	7.3	10.9	10.3	14.2	10.7	5.4	7.4	6.8
Printing and publishing	13.5	15.8	13.7	7.7	9.4	7.9	9.8	8.7	4.5	4.6
Chemicals and allied products	27.4	26.2	20.1	20.9	20.1	19.0	18.5	15.4	14.9	15.3
Industrial chemicals and synthetics[4]	27.9	18.4	15.4	18.7	10.5	19.0	13.2	11.1	12.6	8.9
Drugs[4]	34.0	37.8	36.1	32.2	31.0	23.5	28.3	30.9	23.7	22.7
Petroleum and coal products	15.0	19.3	16.3	17.0	8.9	11.5	14.3	13.6	13.7	7.2
Rubber and miscellaneous plastics products	16.3	9.8	3.7	1.7	10.1	11.6	6.5	0.6	(0.7)	6.2
Other nondurable manufacturing corporations	12.1	23.5	12.6	13.4	14.9	8.9	17.4	6.6	8.7	10.2
Durable manufacturing corporations	17.0	9.9	5.0	2.8	8.2	12.1	7.2	3.2	1.1	5.8
Stone, clay, and glass products	27.6	14.4	(10.3)	(13.6)	4.2	20.4	11.0	(9.8)	(11.5)	2.1
Primary metal industries	23.6	16.8	(4.0)	4.4	5.9	16.5	11.8	(4.1)	2.5	3.6
Iron and steel[4]	32.5	21.0	(21.7)	(11.7)	0.5	21.3	14.3	(25.5)	(12.8)	(2.7)
Nonferrous metals[4]	20.5	15.4	1.6	9.5	7.6	14.9	10.9	2.6	7.4	5.6
Fabricated metal products	22.0	18.8	8.8	7.8	20.2	15.2	13.1	5.1	5.4	15.7
Machinery, except electrical	11.3	9.9	12.7	(2.7)	1.3	8.5	7.5	9.6	(3.7)	0.3
Electrical and electronic equipment	15.1	14.9	6.1	12.5	14.7	9.6	9.4	1.4	8.4	9.8
Transportation equipment	15.1	(3.1)	(7.3)	(4.8)	0.2	11.3	(1.2)	(4.3)	(3.7)	0.7
Motor vehicles and equipment[4]	14.3	(16.7)	(17.5)	(17.0)	(11.6)	10.7	(10.0)	(11.7)	(11.6)	(7.8)
Aircraft, guided missiles, and parts[4]	16.5	22.7	5.6	15.2	17.3	12.1	16.2	4.5	9.3	13.4
Instruments and related products	23.8	12.2	16.4	15.2	20.0	17.2	9.6	12.8	11.4	15.7
Other durable manufacturing corporations	23.8	20.6	7.8	6.4	17.5	16.6	13.6	4.4	1.2	11.9
All mining corporations[5]	6.4	14.0	12.2	6.7	5.9	4.7	9.0	10.0	4.7	4.6
All retail trade corporations[5]	12.3	13.3	29.1	9.6	NA	6.9	7.4	18.7	5.0	NA
All wholesale trade corporations[5]	10.2	9.8	8.3	6.9	8.7	5.0	5.7	3.3	3.6	4.9

[1]Based on profit figures which include net income (loss) and equity in earnings (losses) of nonconsolidated subsidiaries, net of foreign taxes.

[2]Some of the rates in this column have been revised since their first appearance. See footnotes to Tables 1.0 — 47.1.

[3]Tobacco industry data have been collapsed into food industry data. Major merger and acquisition activity resulted in the reclassification of a significant portion of gross receipts and assets from tobacco to food. The remainder, composed of data from highly specialized tobacco manufacturers, is too small to be considered publishable as a separate industry category.

[4]Included in major industry above.

[5]Mining, wholesale and retail trade data are representative of the quarterly results of companies in those divisions drawn into the sample in the fall of 1990 with assets over $50 million. Data for manufacturing corporations represent the quarterly results of companies with assets over $250,000.

Source: U.S. Department of Commerce, *Quarterly Financial Report, Second Quarter 1991.*

Figure 3.1
Current Market Perspective Chart Illustrated

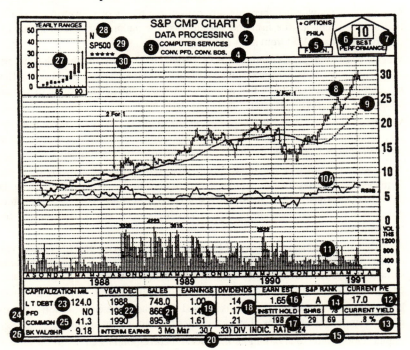

Source: Courtesy Standard & Poor's/Trendline.

FUNDAMENTAL VALUES SHOWN ON TRENDLINE CHARTS

As stated above, *Current Market Perspectives* charts provide an abundance of fundamental information, as well as several purely technical indicators, for each of the 1,476 stocks reviewed monthly by the weekly range chart service. Figure 3.1 provides a sample of the data provided on this set of charts, so each is described in the following list to key them with the numbers marked on the illustrative figure. These should be studied carefully before proceeding to Chapters 4 and 5.

1. The company's name and ticker symbol are shown at the top of the chart. Brokerage firms trade the stocks on the basis of the ticker symbol, so its ready knowledge saves time in transmitting orders.

2. The industry group (one of seventy-one categories developed by Standard & Poor's Corporation) aids in the evaluation of comparable companies by permitting us to compare stocks of firms from the same major group.

3. A brief corporate description lists the major products or services provided by the

reviewed firm, and thus permits easy detection of limited product versus diversified firms.

4. This item shows whether there are any convertible bonds or convertible preferred issues outstanding for the firm and permits easy estimation of potential dilution to earnings per share (E/S) from such conversion.

5. Weekly price ranges and closing prices (horizontal tick), adjusted for stock splits and major stock dividends, are shown for about four years on each chart. Technicians draw in trend lines to detect stocks that appear to be timely purchases or those that might be nearing the top of their approximate near-term price.

6. Volume of trading for the week appears on the graph immediately below the price range. Rising prices on heavy volume is considered bullish, whereas falling prices on heavy volume is interpreted as distribution of the stock by wise investors.

7. The relative performance ranking by decile groups are provided, showing price performance for the latest twelve months. The reviewer can then tell in which decile the stock has performed. The aggressive investor is likely to concentrate his or her stock holdings in issues that are showing high, relative price performance, since trends tend to continue for several years for many stocks.

8. A yearly range chart shows highs and lows for the past ten years plus the current year to date. Past highs usually serve as resistant tops of a move, whereas past bottoms show strong support in stock declines. Thus some traders attempt to buy stock at or near previous low prices and to trade out of them when approaching past high prices.

9. Best performance in trendline group is marked below its decile classification. Industry giants often lead their groups of stocks in price turnaround situations.

10. Capitalization is the total of long-term debts and corresponding equity in the form of preferred and common shares, expressed in millions of dollars. The balance between debt and equity permits the reviewer to estimate the degree of financial leverage being utilized by the firm and to recognize that a heavily financially leveraged firm has much more volatile E/S and common stock prices than do firms with an almost all equity base.

11. Long-term debt matures more than one year ahead of the financial statement. This classification contains bonds, mortgages, term loans from financial institutions, deferred compensation, capitalized leasing payments, and so on. Although the interest on debt is a deductible income tax item (dividends on preferred or common are not), the excessive use of debt has led to bankruptcy for many careless corporate managers.

12. Any preferred stock, stated in millions of outstanding shares, is shown. Such stocks rank behind debt but ahead of common shareholders in case of liquidation or in the periodic servicing with interest or dividend payments.

13. Common shares outstanding, in millions, are shown net of any treasury stock (reacquired shares). Large institutional holders of shares will often limit their purchases of shares to firms with a minimum number of outstanding shares, such as 10 million. Weekly trading volume, shown on the base of the chart, provides the chart reviewer of the ease or difficulty of trading large blocks of stocks over a short time horizon.

14. Book value per share, or the assets less debts and claims by preferred holders, divided by the number of common shares outstanding, is provided. This figure is analogous to net asset backing per common share, with assets carried at historical costs less

possible write-offs. Bank and utility shares normally trade from about 1 to 1.50 times book value per share, whereas prudent investors may not wish to pay more than some multiple of book value per common share, such as four times such value, for common stock.

15. Revenues and key operating data are shown for the last three or four years. Most fiscal years end with a month or quarter, although some retail trade firms may set thirteen, four-week periods in a fiscal year in order to present better sales and profit comparisons. Thus easy comparison of trends in sales, earnings and dividends may be made.

16. Sales (of goods), revenues (from services), or income (e.g., from interest, for financial institutions) are shown.

17. Earnings are shown in dollars per common share, generally stated on a primary basis and may include discontinued operations, while excluding extraordinary items. The figures for investment companies reflect net asset value (NAV) per share (or NAV or net liquidation value per share at recent asset valuations). No attempt is made for this calculation to show possible dilution from exercise of options or warrants or conversion of convertibles. Rising earnings per share usually cause stock prices to advance, although prices may move in anticipation of such future positive earnings changes.

18. The dividends, stated in dollars per share, are shown for the previous fiscal years. Those for the current calendar year reflect the amount of dividends per share that are expected for the current year. This comparison permits the chart user to estimate the rising trend in dividends and to estimate future increases.

19. An earnings estimate is S & P's latest forecast of anticipated earnings per share for the current fiscal year. The market reacts favorably to overachievement of estimates but declines when disappointing quarterly earnings per share are published.

20. The number of institutions currently holding the stock, the number of shares held by these institutions, and the percentage of such holdings are shown. Ideally, a stock should be bought that is being accumulated by institutions rather than for one being distributed, since large holders provide substantial demand or supply for an issue being accumulated or sold off, respectively.

21. S & P earnings and dividend rankings, which measure the growth and stability of earnings and dividends, are shown. This ranking is generally one of seven, plus non-ranked (n.r.) (or A+, A, A−, etc., and nonranked due to unusual earning factors). Stocks of utilities and retail trade firms with stable earnings and continuous growth in E/S rank high, A+ or A, whereas speculative shares fall near the bottom of the ranking array.

22. Current P-E (price-earnings) ratio is the relationship between the latest price and the last twelve months of reported earnings per share. Forecasted E/S are sometimes used in making this calculation. A prudent investor concentrates in reasonably priced stocks and avoids those trading at excessive P-E levels compared to their past levels and in comparison with other groups of stocks.

23. Current yield is the percentage relationship between the dividends paid in the past twelve months and the latest price per share of common stock. Defensive investors, especially, prefer stocks with average or above average dividend yields.

24. Interim earnings provide comparisons for one or several quarters for the current fiscal

year with comparable quarters of the previous fiscal year (shown in parentheses). This comparison eliminates the seasonality of reported earnings.

25. Dividend indicated rate is a projection of expected dividends to be declared over the next twelve months, permitting the viewer to estimate the growth in dividend payments.

26. The thirty-week moving average is the mean average weekly closing price for the past thirty weeks and tends to smooth out week-to-week fluctuations. This average serves as a support and resistance level (or approximate pullback or price advance zone).

27. A. The industry group's relative strength is a solid line on the chart and represents the relative strength of the stock compared with the average of all other stocks in the same industry group. An upward sloping line means that the stock is doing better than others in its industry, or vice versa, and its usage permits one to buy stocks with above average market momentum.

27. B. Relative strength ratio (RSR) shows how a stock is acting compared to the market as a whole. The stock's thirty-week moving average is compared to that for the S & P average of 500 stocks in order to determine this ratio. Its interpretation is similar to that in 27A.

28. Option exchanges and months of expiration for options are shown in this space. The data are useful to stock buyers that may wish to hedge their portfolio position with put options or to sell options on stocks that they hold.

An example of the data appearing on a *Current Market Perspectives* chart appears in Figure 3.1.

Trendline Corporation recently began to publish the *Chart Guide* on a monthly mailout basis that provides weekly bar charts on about 4,400 stocks, including virtually all NYSE and AMEX stocks and some that are heavily traded in the OTC markets. An example of the items that appear on each of these charts is shown in Figure 3.2, which closely parallels the items shown on the *Current Market Perspectives* chart illustrated in Figure 3.1. A battery of numbers has been added to the *Chart Guide,* shown in Figure 3.2 as a series of numbers (i.e., 79, 56, 66 and −4, 22, and 33). The top numbers show that the issue outperformed 79% of the charted stocks over the last fifty-two weeks, 56% over the last quarter, and 66% over the past four weeks. The lower series of numbers refers to its change in relative strength measurement, or suggests that the stock fell by 4% over the past fifty-two weeks, increased by twenty-two points in its thirteen-week ranking and rose by thirty-three points in the past four weeks. When a stock rises in relative strength, it suggests that the issue is doing better than its reference market average (S & P 500 index is normally used) and is expected to be a candidate for gaining faster in market value than other stocks in its industry that show poorer relative strength. Other information on the chart appears similar to those described for the longer-term vertical bar charts, *Current Market Perspectives*. The reader is urged to study the exhibit in Figure 3.2 carefully before studying Chapters 4 and 5.

Figure 3.2
Illustration of the *Chart Guide*

A wealth of market information on over 4,400 stocks at your fingertips!

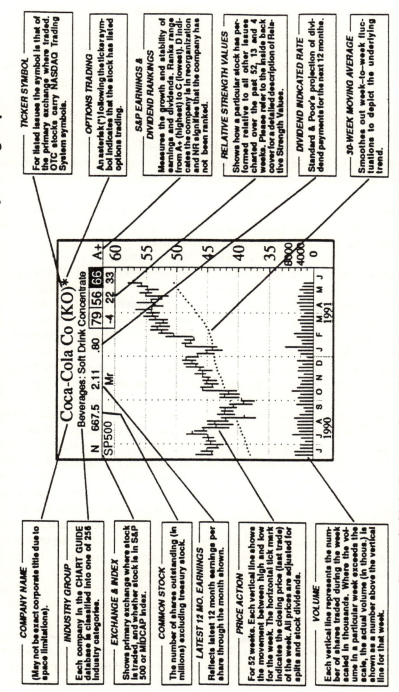

COMPANY NAME
(May not be exact corporate title due to space limitations).

INDUSTRY GROUP
Each company in the CHART GUIDE database is classified into one of 256 industry categories.

EXCHANGE & INDEX
Shows primary exchange where stock is traded, and whether stock is in S&P 500 or MidCAP Index.

COMMON STOCK
The number of shares outstanding (in millions) excluding treasury stock.

LATEST 12 MO. EARNINGS
Reflects latest 12 month earnings per share through the month shown.

PRICE ACTION
For 52 weeks. Each vertical line shows the movement between high and low for the week. The horizontal tick mark indicates the closing price (last trade) of the week. All prices are adjusted for splits and stock dividends.

VOLUME
Each vertical line represents the number of shares traded during the week scaled in thousands. Where the volume in a particular week exceeds the scale, the actual volume (in thous.) is shown as a number above the vertical line for that week.

TICKER SYMBOL
For listed issues the symbol is that of the primary exchange where traded. OTC stocks carry NASDAQ Trading System symbols.

OPTIONS TRADING
An asterisk (*) following the ticker symbol indicates that the stock has listed options trading.

S&P EARNINGS & DIVIDEND RANKINGS
Measure the growth and stability of earnings and dividends. Ranks range from A+ (highest) to C (lowest). D indicates the company is in reorganization and NR signifies that the company has not been ranked.

RELATIVE STRENGTH VALUES
Shows how a particular stock has performed relative to all other issues charted over the past 52, 13 and 4 weeks. Please refer to the inside back cover for a detailed description of Relative Strength Values.

DIVIDEND INDICATED RATE
Standard & Poor's projection of dividend payments for the next 12 months.

30-WEEK MOVING AVERAGE
Smooths out week-to-week fluctuations to depict the underlying trend.

Also see inside back cover and page 2 for further information on How To Use Chart Guide.

Source: Courtesy Standard & Poor's/Trendline.

ADDITIONAL FUNDAMENTAL CONSIDERATIONS

Most stock fundamentalists attempt to determine by using one or several quantitative models, an underlying or intrinsic value for a common share, comparing this "value" to the price of the stock to gauge its underpricing or overpricing in the market. The most popular of these models are the dividend growth model (illustrated in Chapter 1), the price-earning model, the cash-flow per share model, and the Benjamin Graham intrinsic value model. Each of these are described very briefly.

As described in Chapter 1, the dividend growth model assumes that the present value of an infinite stream of dividends will be determined, using a calculated required rate of return, the current dividend per share level, and the forecasted annual growth in dividends per year. A constant growth model, or one with several different growth rates for specified time periods, can be used. Investment calculators (i.e., on PC disks) are designed and included with leading investment textbooks so as to facilitate these computations.

Let us illustrate how the present value of anticipated future dividends on a share of stock is determined. The capital asset pricing model, illustrated in Chapter 1, suggests that a stockholder expects a risk free rate of return, such as the six-month Treasury bill rate, plus a risk premium multiplied by a measurement of risk for the stock. The risk measurement ordinarily used is beta, or the relative volatility in price of a share compared to moves in some popular stock average, such as the S & P average of 500 stocks. Beta for a stock is the slope of a regression line from "regressing" monthly price changes for a given stock on changes in the reference index to stock prices. (Note that betas shift over time, as is shown in Table 9.2, and should be used with caution.) In a market where the T-bill yield rate is 5.0%, the justified discount rate for forecasted cash dividends is 5.0% plus a market risk premium $\times$ beta on the stock. During the period from 1926 to 1989, the market's geometric mean return premium on common stock has been about 6.7% above the average T-bill rate. Thus an appropriate discount rate appears to be about 5% plus (6.7%) (beta)—assume 1.00—or 11.7% on an average stock. Should that stock be paying an $0.80 annual dividend with an historical and expected future growth rate of 7.0%, the stock should have a value of $0.80/ (0.117 − 0.07) or $0.80/0.047 or about $17, assuming the rate of growth will continue indefinitely. This "indicated value" would then be compared to the market price to see whether the stock is overpriced or underpriced. This process would continue for a large number of companies, including in the stock portfolio those issues that appear to be the most underpriced. As prices of the individual issues move above their estimated values, they are liquidated and replaced with other worthy issues.

The average price-earnings multiplier is sometimes used as a guide in determining whether to buy or to liquidate a stock. For example, suppose that the P-E ratio for a given company is usually about 90% of the market average, such as that of the NYSE. If it drops to 80% or less of its current (or forecasted for the next twelve months) P-E ratio, it might be said to be underpriced adequately for purchase, or at the very least, it would be rated as a hold for the stock portfolio. Should the P-E ratio rise much above this historical high of 90% of market average, it might be judged a candidate for liquidation.

Value Line, Inc., in its *Value Line Investment Survey,* suggests that there is a better regression fit between cash flow per share and its historical per share price than between other variables (such as earnings per share or dividends per share and the per share price) for most firms reviewed. If, for example, the "cash flow per share" *value line* is 7.0× and the stock is trading much below this forecasted figure for the next year, it would be interpreted as a buy by Value Line. Thus stocks with prices below this *value line* (on the *Value Line* charts) would be buys, whereas those trading above this bold or broken line would be somewhat overpriced in the market. The broken line is extended several years into the future, based on historically computed multiples but projected cash flows per share.

Benjamin Graham, in his several editions of *Security Analysis,* gave evidence to support an intrinsic value stock model that presented the growth in dividends per share, the actual earnings per share, the actual dividends per share, and the book value per share as having about equal weight. The source suggested that a stock without growth should trade at about 8.5 times earnings per share. One with growth prospects might justify a multiplier of 8.5× plus two times this growth factor in earnings per share for the next seven to ten years. The writers also suggested that a growth factor in excess of about 20% not be assumed. In the GDC model this multiplier would be weighted with actual cash dividends and 1/3 the earnings per share. These three factors then should be weighted with 75%, whereas book value per share should be weighted with 25%. In our previous illustration, let us assume a growth rate of 7%, a dividend of $1.00 per share yearly, and an earnings per share of $2.00. Assume book value per share is $20. The calculated *GDC intrinsic value* would be as follows:

Multiplier justified = 8.5 + 2(7) = 22.5×

Intrinsic value = 22.5 [$1 + 1/3($2)] × 0.75 = $28.18

and the book value contribution of ($20 × 0.25) = $4

so that the total "intrinsic value" is $28.18 + $4 or $32.18 per share.

Now, assuming that the price per share of the stock is $27, the stock appears to be underpriced by about $5 per share, or roughly 17%. We would make similar calculations for several stocks in the industries that we wish to hold in our stock portfolio, selecting those for purchase that appear to be the most underpriced. Studies made by these authors suggest that the GDC model appears to be superior to most other models in selecting overpriced and underpriced stock issues.

Rather than make these calculations by hand, the financial analyst may wish to employ the use of some up-to-date electronic data processing (EDP) data base and screen out those issues appearing to meet these preset undervaluations.

DETECTING TEMPORARILY OUT-OF-FAVOR STOCKS

Although the financial literature is generally supportive of a (reasonably) efficient market pricing system, certain market anomalies appear to exist. Some of these may be based on fundamental measurements, whereas others are technical or special situation events. The small firm effect, the low P-E ratio stocks, the month of the year, the days of the month, and so forth are well documented as providing above average returns from market averages. These will be described briefly.

Ibbotson's study, cited in Chapter 2, suggests that the geometric mean average returns on small companies' stocks from 1926 to 1989 was about 2% yearly above the average return on NYSE issues. Perhaps the smaller companies have heavier debt usage, are less well known, or are under lesser accumulation by financial institutions than are the shares from larger firms. However, stocks in smaller firms, if bought and held for lengthy time periods, usually do grow in values and generate returns that exceed those of the popular averages but are more volatile in bear and bull markets, as shown by their reported standard deviations of total returns and higher betas, generally.

Stocks trading at below average P-E ratios that are held for a year or longer and then sold when they are no longer trading at a below average P-E ratio, also usually outperform the returns on the total market. For example, if the five of the thirty Dow Jones Industrial Average (DJIA) stocks trading at the lowest P-E ratios (say in March of each year) are bought and held for one year and then liquidated so as to acquire other stocks that may have moved into this lower quintile of P/Es, the long-term annualized gain is about 2–3% higher on the low P-E stocks than on the average for the DJIA.

A substantial percentage of total upside price movement in stocks appear to occur in the first month of each quarter. January is usually the best trading month, followed by April, July, and October. The year-end tax selling pressure often occurs from about mid-November to mid-December. To a degree, the last three or four days of each month and the first three or four days of the month usually have upside price moves followed with little upside gains (based on market averages) during the balance of the month. Mondays are often weak in the market with some strength being shown on Tuesday to Thursday and significant upside gains usually occurring on Fridays. Thus in bull markets, one might buy shares about an hour before market closing on Mondays and sell shares near the close on Fridays to maximize short-term profit taking. Opposite patterns of price movements often occur during bear markets.

Stock prices usually spike up the day of and for about two days following the release of an unexpectedly large increase in reported earnings per share. Most of this increase occurs within the first three hours after the release of the information. In addition, NYSE and American Stock Exchange (ASE) stocks provide relatively high average market-adjusted returns on the payment dates of quarterly cash dividends and for several subsequent trading days. Issues with poorer than expected E/S figures usually decline for a few days following such news releases. Stocks that reduce the actual amounts of cash dividends, or terminate them entirely, are usually penalized with lower prices for the shares.

There appears to be a substantial correlation between projected future earnings growth rate and subsequent equity return of individual firms, according to several stock market studies. In addition, a long series of real per share earnings helps to forecast future dividends. Forecasts are generally more accurate for large- and intermediate-sized firms than for small firms, however, perhaps accounting for a portion of the small firm effect (i.e., investors accept such forecasts with a higher degree of skepticism).

Initial public offerings (IPOs) usually underperform the overall market when stocks are held for a year or longer, suggesting that IPOs are a bull-market phenomenon and that the issues, in general, are often somewhat overpriced when coming to the market.

Many of the preceding, market-tested opinions are reviewed with data base statistical studies in Chapters 9 and 10.

OBSCURE COMPANIES

Many enterprising portfolio managers subscribe to alternative sources of financial literature that regularly review a large number of firms, including small and obscure firms. During the past few years, many investment company management groups have designed portfolios of emerging firms. These often perform better in the market place than do portfolios of more mature firms. However, it is not too uncommon for such stocks to run up very rapidly in early stages of a bull market, only to fall back (or consolidate) and sell down by one third to a half of the previous gain during the second stages of the bull market. Many industry specialized or emerging firm mutual funds that perform best in one year will often perform near the bottom of their categories in the following year. These obscure firms are sometimes referred to as being in "the shadow of Wall Street," and a text describing their places in the markets has recently been written.[1]

It is these obscure companies that often move the trading of their stocks from the over-the-counter market to one of the major exchanges for trading. Although prices may rise a few days after exchange listing, they usually fall back to or below such levels after a few weeks.

Some independent financial analysts, with data banks of financial information, regularly monitor large numbers of small, relatively obscure firms, providing their names and some key financial information to newsletter subscribers (for a price).

STOCKS WITH QUICK PROFIT POTENTIALS

Some fundamental approaches exist for determining stocks with fast price runup probabilities. These are reviewed briefly.

Stocks with very rapid increases in reported E/S usually gain in price the day of the earning report and for about two additional days. In a series of upward waves (three are usual) the stock rises for about eight or nine weeks. The stock price then consolidates about half the previous advance for the next four or five weeks and repeats the cycle so long as the stock's E/S continues to grow at such high rates. A well-above-average annual rate of growth in interim earnings per share is generally needed for this pattern to occur.

Stocks with below average price-earnings multiples but with an above average rate of growth in earnings per share will usually move to a level of somewhat above average P-E ratio over about a two-year period. Above average P-E stocks are vulnerable to large price sell-offs if growth in reported earnings is interrupted.

Other situations usually lead to above average performing stocks. Candidates for stock splits (those that have doubled or tripled in price over the past year or two), those that are candidates for mergers (those trading for less than book value per share but with growth potential), and those that make a cash tender offer for a significant portion of their outstanding shares are also likely to rise more than the general stock price level. Manufacturing firms with a growing backlog of orders often build in an above average profit margin. As sales are generated, profits increase even more rapidly, pushing the stock to higher price levels. During distressed economic times, profit margins narrow, E/S declines, and prices decline even more.

Most stocks in a given industry tend to move in the same direction, although the financially strong stocks often move first. Locating laggards in a sought-after industry, then, is another way of catching a rapid move in price for shares.

Several technical strengths may become apparent on a stock's chart that suggest a near-term price runup, and these are now discussed briefly. A stock with a growing relative strength index, compared to its industry group, is usually an above average price performer. A stock with heavy relative trading volume and an upside closing in price suggests that demand for the stock is about to overcome its price at that level. Thus it is about to move to a higher price. Stocks with long consolidation patterns that make a break through several previous upward spikes are likely to run upward in price. Stocks with unusually large short-interest ratios (say above about five days of usual trading volume) are candidates for large upside runs once they rise into the area where stop loss buy orders are likely to be executed. Stocks of secondary-tier quality in industries under heavy financial institution (mutual funds and pension accounts) accumulation are likely to be bought in heavier amounts, thus causing a major upward adjustment in price. Many of these technical approaches are illustrated with chart pattern configurations in Chapters 4 and 5.

SUMMARY

Some stock analysts are pure technicians, using charts to forecast stock movements, whereas others subscribe to the fundamental approach and use trends in sales, earnings, and dividends to estimate the value of common shares. Both technical and fundamental information are provided on leading vertical bar charts, such as those published monthly by Trendline Corporation, a division of S & P Corporation.

Comparative financial statement analysis may be accomplished by comparing percentage statements and key financial ratios with a firm to that of its industry. Important sources of statements for industries appear in *Quarterly Financial Report,* distributed by the Department of Commerce, and those provided quarterly by Value Line or S & P in their industry surveys. Dun & Bradstreet and Morris Associates provides key financial ratios on several hundred lines of business.

Important key ratios, and their usefulness to the security analyst, appear in several leading stock market services and are illustrated in this chapter. Both listed and OTC stock services are reviewed.

Last of all, we review several ways that fundamentalists attempt to determine the *value* of a stock so as to compare this computed value to the price, hoping to discover those that they feel to be mispriced in the short run. Popular models include the dividend discount model, the price-earning ratio model, the cash flow per share model, and the intrinsic value model.

NOTE

1. P. Strebel and S. Carvell, *In the Shadow of Wall Street* (Englewood Cliffs, NJ: Prentice-Hall, 1988).

Chapter 4

BASICS OF VERTICAL BAR CHARTING

CONSTRUCTING VERTICAL BAR CHARTS

Before beginning to construct a vertical bar chart with the price movements for a common stock, the preparer should determine whether the chart should be completed on arithmetic or semi-log paper and whether to make the recordings daily, weekly, monthly or yearly. Some preparers also add other technical features, such as a ten-week or thirty-week moving average (50, 100, or 200 days on daily graphs), and relative strength of the issue compared to a market average such as the Standard & Poor's average of 500 stocks. Some users prefer daily graphs, whereas others prefer weekly or monthly ones.

Trendline Corporation, a subsidiary of Standard & Poor's Corporation, provides four types of vertical bar charts to its subscribers: *Daily Basis Stock Charts* (published weekly); *Current Market Perspectives* (weekly graphs, published at mid-month, on about 1,472 issues); *OTC Chart Manual* (published bimonthly on about 600 OTC issues and utilizing weekly bar charts); and *Chart Guide* (with its weekly range charts on most actively traded NYSE, ASE, and OTC issues). Some of these were introduced in Chapter 3 and other types of charts are used in this and the following chapter to illustrate various chart patterns. Mansfield, another leading producer of vertical bar charts, uses the weekly bar charts on an arithmetic scale, whereas John Magee and some other chart services provide charts compiled on semi-log paper.

Very short term traders generally prefer the daily basis stock charts, whereas intermediate-term stock holders often prefer the vertical bar charts prepared on a weekly basis. Recent past history of stock highs and lows are often shown on an inset with range graphs for the past ten years, usually shown on an annual basis. Monthly bar graphs are provided by such well-known investment services as Value Line (semi-log scale), Moody's Investor's Service in *Widely Held Common Stocks,* and S & P in *Corporate Reports.* Daily and weekly bar graphs are usually constructed to show the high, low and closing price for the period (day or week). The volume of trading for the period is shown immediately below the recording for the price.

RECOGNIZING BAR CHART PATTERNS

An example of the recording of the price range and volume of trading is shown in Figure 4.1. After several months of data are recorded, a trained technician can usually interpret certain strengths and weaknesses from the charts. Recognizable patterns can more readily be seen if the employer uses a pencil or ball point pen to draw in lines connecting important highs or lows or to emphasize rounded bottoms or tops. For convenience, the price and volume of trading scales are sometimes shown on the right or left margin of the bar chart.

In Figure 4.1, selected bullish formations are shown in the top section. This includes the saucer, the rising trend, an inverted head and shoulders, pennants, and a flag. Some uncertainty patterns are shown in the center section, including a coil or symmetrical triangle, a rectangle, a box, and a diamond. Other uncertainty patterns are triangles, illustrated at the bottom of Figure 4.1 or rising or descending wedges. Bearish patterns, not illustrated, are about the same as bullish patterns only up side down. The construction and interpretation of the more important of these are described in the sections that follow.

HOW TO DRAW TRENDLINES PROPERLY

Some users of long-term vertical bar charts merely draw in lines across major tops of downtrends and across major bottoms of rising trends in stocks to determine the trend base along which the issue trades. Stocks with little swing in profits from a boom period to a recession period (a growth stock, for example) may remain in a growth channel for several years. Cyclical stocks, those with above average relative price volatility, often move upward by 200 or 300% during a bull market only to retrace one half to three fourths of the move in the following bear market. For this type of stock, the trend channel is hardly so useful as the other (more or less) repeat patterns that usually appear on vertical bar charts.

In a rising trend, two points are needed to draw in a rising trend, but a third point is needed to verify that the stock is, indeed, following a definite trend line. A straight line connecting the intermediate tops can then be drawn in to form a channel. The channel usually appears with approximately parallel upper and lower trendlines. For several additional moves (up and back) the price of the stock often remains within the trend channel. Some stock traders buy the stock as it falls near the baseline and sell the issue when it approaches the (assumed)

Figure 4.1
Recognizing Important Bar Chart Patterns

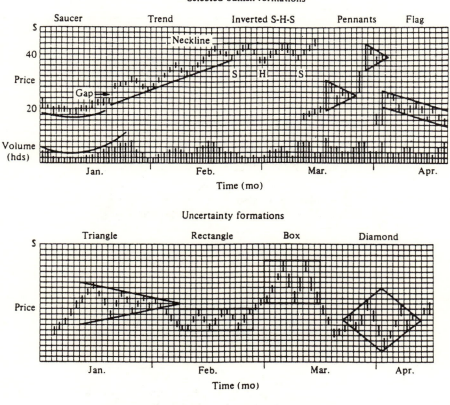

Selected bullish formations

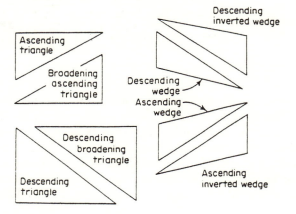

Figure 4.2
Trend Channels Illustrated

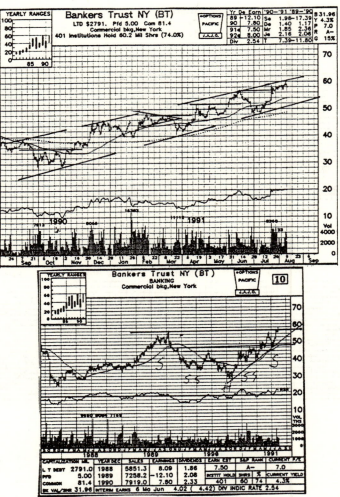

Source: Courtesy Standard & Poor's/Trendline.

top of the trend channel. Sooner or later, the price action of the stock will carry the issue out of the channel at the top or bottom, but this breakout is usually suggested by unusual strength or weakness and the formation of breakout patterns.

A trend channel is shown in the left top panel of Figure 4.2 on the daily basis chart for Bankers Trust NY. The first base point is in October at about $30; the second is in March at about $41; and one might assume that the stock would pull back to about $50 in another three or four months. This confirmation was actually made, with a pull back to about $49. The reader should note that the intermediate tops are about parallel to the base.

Immediately below the daily basis chart on Bankers Trust NY is the weekly basis chart. Note that the trend line, from September, 1989 through June of 1991, rallies about to 59, or a previous top reached in late 1988, and again in October, 1989. A glance at the annual bar chart at the upper left of the weekly range chart shows that 60 was the all-time recent high on the stock. If the stock breaks above $60 on this move, by a point or two, it is likely to gain another 50% (i.e., the depth of the pattern, or from 30 to 60) and move toward $90 per share.

Two types of trend channels are illustrated in Figure 4.2. For the *Daily Basis Chart* on Bankers Trust, the stock appears to be moving upward in an orderly trend, pulling back approximately to the 200-day moving average and to the base trend line. Tops also seem to stall as they approach the top of the trend channel. On a longer-term basis, the stock (bottom pannel of Figure 4.2) appears to be in a sidewise pattern with a top at about 60 and a bottom at about 30. A short-term trader might buy the stock for the ten-point move (on the daily basis chart), while a longer-term investor might take a position at about 30, hold for about two years, and sell out for about 60. Thus the short-term trader has an opportunity of about two trades per year while the cyclical buyer buys and holds for about two years and then looks for another buying opportunity.

As additional practice, let us draw in trend lines on the four stock charts that appear in Figure 4.3. For example, A. L. Labs has a slightly broadening trend channel. Since a great deal of recent trading took place between 18 and about 29, several moves within these boundaries will likely be needed before the stock breaks out of this range. The left, lower chart is for Boeing. A very tight trend channel occurred from late 1988 through March 1990. The stock then broke from the top of the channel before falling back into and through it. It is likely to pull back to about 40 before making another upside run. Aon Corp stock formed a broad channel during 1990–1992. It rose well above the trend baseline and might pull back to it, especially in some market sell-off. Volume patterns tend to support this hypothesis, and the relative strength line had turned downward. The chart on Broken Hill Properties ADR remained in a rising trend channel for about three years and then broke from the top. It made a new, all time top with the break above 40, so it is likely to run to the upper 50s before consolidating back to about 40. Patterns that appear within the trend channels often give clues to approximate estimated moves.

IDENTIFYING MEANINGFUL VERTICAL
BAR CHART PATTERNS

Some chart patterns appear very often on vertical bar charts and are reasonably accurate in their forecasting ability about 80 to 85% of the time (according to some technical estimates). The reader should refer again to the patterns that appear in the top panel of Figure 4.1. A rounded bottom, or saucer, appears first,

Figure 4.3
Trendlines Illustrated

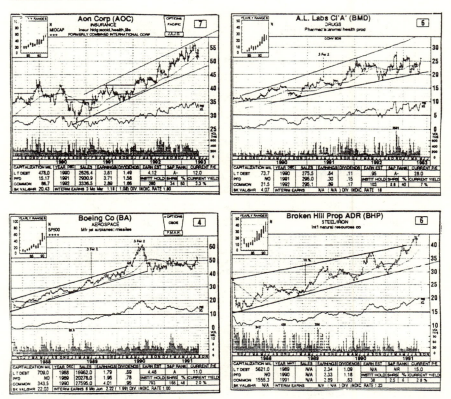

Source: Courtesy Standard & Poor's/Trendline.

followed by a gap in trading, a wave-like trend line, a horizontal trend with a somewhat deeper center penetration that is popularly referred to as an inverted head and shoulders. Shown to the right of the chart are two small triangles, or pennants, and a flag. These pennants and flags are usually formed over a few days or weeks and are often just small pauses, or brief consolidations, within a broader move. The inexperienced technician should now study these patterns carefully so that they may be identified as they appear on a daily basis or weekly basis range chart.

In the center section of Figure 4.1, a symmetrical triangle (often called a coil), a rectangle with a topside breakout, a box, and a diamond are shown. These patterns are usually classified as uncertainty patterns inasmuch as their direction of breakout is in doubt until breakout occurs. Still other forms of uncertainty patterns appear in the lower section of Figure 4.1. The patterns are merely descriptive names of their appearances as lines are drawn across major tops and bottoms plus a vertical line to join the two. These uncertainty patterns usually take the form of triangles (narrowing, broadening, ascending, descending, or symmetrical) and wedges (which have both legs or drawn-in trend lines moving in the same direction).

Most instructors or authors of published works on vertical bar chart theory suggest that the user concentrate only on the bullish patterns in a strong market and forget the uncertainty patterns. Attempting to make a profit on a long stock investment in a bear (weak or falling) market is analogous to swimming against the tide of a strong river. One, ideally, should be long in a bull market and short (or at least neutral with funds invested in safe, liquid assets such as Treasury bills or money market shares) in a bear market. A trader wishes to buy low and sell high in a strong market and to withdraw to the sidelines when the strong market has approximately run its course. A later chapter addresses this issue.

Figure 4.1 identifies the five most reliable bullish stock patterns: the saucer base (or rounded bottom), the rising trend, the inverted head and shoulders (three waves of prices with the center one having a deeper penetration than the right and left ones, and the rallies being to about the same level), gap(s) on the upside, small pennants, and flags. Flip the patterns upside down and they become bearish patterns, which are commonly referred to as rounded top (or inverted saucer), the downtrend (with the trendline drawn across tops), the topside head and shoulders, the down pennants, and the down flags (as the staff points down), and downside gaps. Naturally, bullish patterns appear very frequently for a few months following a bear market bottom, although some continue to be formed for laggards in the market over the economic upswing in the economy. The bearish patterns begin to appear after an extended price move in groups of stocks and in abundance when a market begins to tire and to turn from a strong to a weak bearish market. A rule of thumb is that a stock will usually move as far above (below) a breakout point as its deepest penetration before the breakout.

In addition to the obvious trends or trend channels shown in Figures 4.2 and 4.3, let us study the charts for possible bullish patterns. You may wish to turn back to Figure 4.2 on Bankers Trust NY. A saucer pattern was formed in June–July 1991. The depth of the pattern was from about 49 to 60, or $11. One would expect the stock to move to about $70 in the short run (maybe within three months) after this breakout. On a longer term basis, the stock had formed a deep pattern over 1987–1991 with a bottom of about 23 and a top at 60. This provides a long-term target price of 60 + 37 or to about 97. In the weekly range chart at the bottom of Figure 4.2, the inverted shoulder within another inverted head and shoulders has a top neckline (drawn in at $58) from $28 to $58 (or thirty units deep). The measured, or estimated, move from this configuration is $58 + $30 or to about $88.

Resistance and support lines will sometime halt a rally or decline. *Resistance* is that area where the supply of stock is expected to increase, whereas *support* is that price or price zone where price support is likely to occur. Substantial resistance, and sell-offs, are usually engendered at target prices, those divisible by 10, and those divisible by 11. Moving averages and the base trend line offer other points of support (or resistance). The stock is likely to be a candidate for a stock split as it approaches the $90 or $100 range.

Several bullish patterns appear in Figure 4.3. The patterns, other than the rising trend, are not very pronounced on A.L. Labs. For the Aon Corp chart, three bullish patterns are marked. A saucer appeared in late 1988 with a depth of $4.50. The stock broke from this pattern and moved about $5 above this level. In early 1991, the stock broke from an inverted head and shoulders with a neckline at $36, a depth of the pattern to $27, and an indicated move to $45. The stock first moved to $42, consolidated, and then moved to $45 before consolidating again. It continued to move up at a somewhat accelerated pace. A saucer is shown on the Boeing stock chart in early 1989. A rounded top or topside head and shoulders appeared in mid–1990, suggesting that the stock price had topped out. It declined back and below the base trend line. On the chart for Broken Hill, several saucers are present. One occurred in 1989, another in 1990, and a third in 1991. In each instance, the approximate forecasted move was reached. Note the upside gaps in 1990 on the chart pattern. A breakaway gap occurred in May 1990 at $28; a measuring gap occurred in July at $32, suggesting that the stock had about $4 more advance to move. It did stall at $37–$38, forming an exhaustion gap, and moved downward to $29. The depths of patterns, then, as well as the occurrence of measuring gaps, are usually trustworthy means for estimating a future price move.

WAVE THEORY AND ITS ROLE IN PORTFOLIO MANAGEMENT

Chapter 2 discussed the major swings in the economy in the United States (and the worldwide economy). Business tends to move from strong to weak over a period of several years. The average length of the business swing in the United States has tended to be about four years since about 1940, although two business upswings were closer to seven years in duration. The stock market also tends to swing from a weak, bear market to a bull market and back to a bear market over about a four-year time period. Falling interest rates tend to send stock prices higher, whereas rising rates tend to depress stock and bond prices. This repeat in patterns has significance for the asset portfolio manager who wishes to pursue an active approach in the asset allocation process (i.e., switching from stocks to T-bills when bear markets appear imminent and back again when the stock prices appear to have reached approximate bottom).

Major moves in the economy (and in stock market averages) seldom occur without some pause. Three upside waves often occur with two or four shorter waves on the pullback. Each of these major waves may also be divided with intermediate waves (usually odd numbers on the upside and even numbers on the downside). Thus a major bull market may be in three (or nine) upside waves, whereas consolidations are more often than not made with even numbers of sell-off moves (two in a brief consolidation of 5 to 10% and four in a major bear

Figure 4.4
Stock Moves in Similar Legs

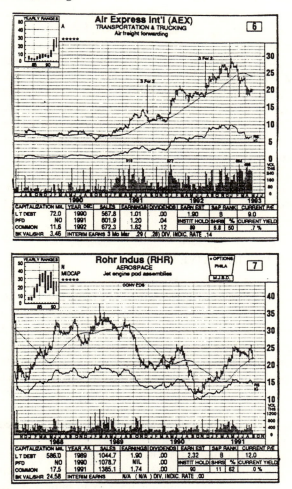

Source: Courtesy Standard & Poor's/Trendline.

market that sends stock prices lower by 20 to 40%). These moves are reviewed in detail in *Elliot's Wave Theory.*

These waves in stock market action can best be seen on a long-term chart of some popular average, such as the one illustrated in Chapter 8 for the Dow Jones Industrial Average and the S & P Average of 500 Stocks. However, this wavelike price action sometimes occurs on individual stocks, especially cyclical stocks.

We now illustrate in Figure 4.4 how legs appear on the upside on the chart for Air Express and on the downside for the stock chart on Rohr Industries. Air Express moved from 5 to about 14 in one leg; consolidated for about five months, and then moved from 11 to 21. It then consolidated for about six months and moved from 18 to 29. Note that each of these legs were close to $10 in length. The stock then formed a major bearish pattern and began to decline. Rohr Industries common formed a major top in 1988–89, falling from 37 to 27.5 in one move; rallying to about 33–34, and then sliding to 19. It then rallied about half of the previous fall, and then fell in two additional legs from 26 to 22 and then from 24 to 12. At this point, the relative strength line had turned up; the stock was down by over 65% from its high of two years before, and could safely be bought for a return to the previous zone of heavy trading, $25–$26. The stock attained this level, and pulled back to the thirty-week moving average. A technician would expect, at this point, for the stock to consolidate to about 18–19 and then make another run on 25. If it breaks through, its next move will be to 30–32 and so on. Note that the major pullback occurred in four legs of almost equal length. A short-term trader might try to scalp the stock for short, upside moves, or a short-seller or a seller of options might try to benefit from expected price declines.

UNDERSTANDING RELATIVE STRENGTH

Relative strength of a stock, compared to the overall market, may be detected on *Current Market Perspective* charts in two ways. The first of these is the decile (ten highest to one lowest) for price performance during the past twelve months, as marked in the upper right corner of each chart. The second method tracks weekly changes in the price of the stock on a relative basis to the S & P 500 stock average (shown as the RSR S & P line). Most stocks break out on their relative strength line before making a breakout on the price chart. This relative strength indicator can be seen in Figure 4.5 for Allied Products in November 1985, prior to the stock price breakout in late December of that year. Weakness in the relative strength of the stock first appeared in May 1986 and was confirmed in August of that year before a major sell-off in price.

In the bottom panel of Figure 4.5, relative strength on American Express began to be noted in late 1983 when a rounded bottom was being formed. The line strengthened about two or three months prior to an upturn in price. The stock moved from about a base of 30 to 80 per share before topping out. The relative strength line indicated a pullback at 70 (and actually fell in price to about 55 per share) before moving to 80. The relative strength line (at that point in time) was not showing strength, so an investor would have been warned (by this S & P RSR) to take profits and to seek another stock suggesting better market strength.

SIGNIFICANCE OF THE MOVING AVERAGE LINES

The *Daily Basis Charts* usually depict two moving average lines. The one with close dots is the 100-day moving average line, which usually marks intermediate moves in a stock. The wider spaced dots appear for the 200-day moving average,

Figure 4.5
Relative Strength Ratio Illustrated

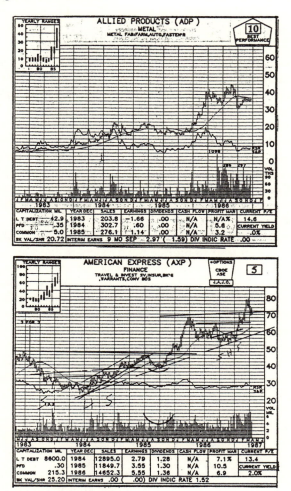

Source: Courtesy Standard & Poor's/Trendline.

which is usually the major support (or resistance) level for the stock. Both are used by the technician.

The thirty-week moving average is recorded on the weekly range charts and is interpreted in about the same way as the 200-day moving average on the daily basis chart. Technicians who use the longer-term, weekly range chart are more interested in intermediate swings than in short-term trades, and thus the ten- or twenty-week moving average is of lesser importance. However, in widely swinging options or commodity future contracts, three-, five-, and nine-day averages are sometimes used to design option trading strategies.

REVIEWING WHAT WE LEARNED

Technicians use several methods to forecast the price objective from a given chart formation. On a trendline, a base trend is drawn in connecting two major bottoms. A parallel line can be drawn which touches the top of the intervening rally. Two additional points are needed to confirm the trend—a third along the rising base and a second along the rising top. Many stocks move within price channels for extended time periods, sometimes for a year or two and sometimes for more than a decade on growth stocks with about average price volatility.

The forecasted move from most completed vertical bar chart patterns is the depth of the pattern. That is, a saucer with a neckline (imaginary line drawn in at two rally peaks) of 20 and the deepest penetration at 10 suggests that the stock should, upon breaking the line of resistance of 20, move to about the 30 level. However, the forecasted move should consider the likely zone where heavy supply of the stock is likely to occur. This zone of supply is often referred to as a resistant line or zone. Resistance is a line of previous trading for the issue, but on many stocks it tends to form at price levels divisible by 5, 10, or 11. Round figures, such as 16, 24, or 28 tend to provide minor support. Previous tops, zones of recent heavy trading, the base or overhead trendline, and the moving average also tend to be resistance levels when a stock is trading below them but become support once they have been broken on heavy trading volume. Numbers that are the squares of other numbers (i.e., 4, 9, 16, 25, 36, 49, 64, etc.) also tend to be support and resistant levels.

Wave theory of chart action, described briefly here, holds that stock prices often move up in odd numbers of runs but downward in even numbers. In total, this may be correct, but the past action of a given chart may suggest that it has two major moves upward, then consolidates, and moves up again in two additional legs. The short legs are often divided by flags or pennants (small continuation patterns, usually), or by the described broader-based bullish patterns. Downside moves, more often than not, are in two legs for consolidation moves but four downside legs with a brief consolidation after legs one and three but an extended rising trend as a center consolidation that occurs about half-way down an extended price drop. This is what has become known as a bull trap, as rising bottoms and tops make one think that the issue is strong, when in fact, it is only retracing a portion of its previous loss. The relative strength line or a weak advanced-decline line may suggest that the market has farther to decline, a subject described in greater detail in Chapter 8.

ESTIMATING MOVES WITH GAPS

A gap is an absence of trading, and they usually occur in three forms: a breakaway gap, one or more measuring gaps about one half the distance up an advance, and an exhaustion gap. Some technicians use the location of gaps to estimate the approximate extent of an expected move. A breakaway gap occurs within the base

Figure 4.6
Support and Resistance Levels Illustrated

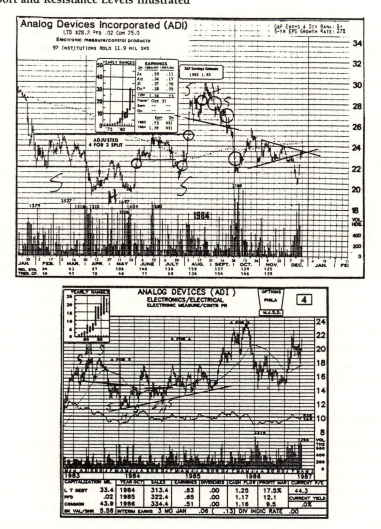

Source: Courtesy Standard & Poor's/Trendline.

pattern or at its breakout point (the neckline), the measuring gap occurs about 40–50% up the entire move, and an exhaustion gap appears just prior to the top of the formation and its turndown and retreat. Gaps, as their names imply, are absences of trading, and occur more on daily basis stock charts than on weekly or monthly basis charts. However, gaps sometimes do occur from Friday's close to Monday's opening price and would thus be recorded on the weekly range chart.

We now review the chart on Analogue Devices (Figure 4.6) for measuring gaps. On the daily basis chart (top panel), a gap appeared two times at 22; a measuring gap occurred at 25; and an exhaustion gap occurred at about 28 ½. Some stocks tend to pull back (after a gap) and fill the gap, whereas others do not. Most gaps are only partially filled on the pullback, but this provides a good buying position for watchful stock buyers. The gaps are hardly obvious on the weekly range chart as weekly range is recorded and the gaps on ADI occurred within the week rather than on the weekend.

ACTION AND REACTION

The swing rule of "reaction = action" or the move below a pivot point is about equal to the move above the point applies to most bullish patterns, bearish patterns, and the coil (or symmetrical triangle). An experienced technician remembers all of these usual target rules and considers them before taking a position in an individual stock issue. This swing rule is illustrated on Analog Devices' daily basis chart. The inverted head and shoulder formed in early 1984 had a neckline at 25 and a bottom at 19½, suggesting a move to about 30. This was reached before the stock retreated. A coil occurred in November 1984. The stock fell from 23 (center of the coil) to 20½ before rallying back through the coil. The estimated target is to about 25½. Note that this was a previous top. A pullback to previous support (about 22) would be expected, an inverted head and shoulders might then be formed, and then the stock would move higher. Over the 1983–1986 period, the stock had several stock splits (shown on the weekly range chart), so exact moves are tough to estimate. However, the inverted head and shoulders (H & S) that appeared on the daily basis chart can clearly be seen in late 1984 on the longer-term, weekly range chart.

SUPERMOVING STOCKS

Most common stock supermovers occur during early turnarounds from bear markets to bull markets, with changing fiscal or monetary action that might favorably or unfavorably affect a certain sector or a few industries, or during frenzied merger activity. Hot issues market is a term that applies when many intermediate-sized companies are first going public. An oversubscribed issue, especially when the stock is offered at a price-earnings level somewhat below its industry group, will often become a supermover, doubling or tripling in price over a period of a few weeks. A vertical bar chartist seeks chart patterns with very deep formations, or perhaps stocks that have had long, narrow base formation for several years with very little, near-term (say the last eight years) overhead supply (or resistance) in evidence on the long-term bar chart.

One of the earliest keys to a breakout from a narrow trading range is an early upturn in the relative strength ratio (shown on the base of the price chart as RSR), which tells how a stock is acting compared to its own past performance and that of the market as a whole. The RSR also usually turns down while the stock is continuing to rally to new highs, signaling that the stock is no longer a favorite and is likely to soon come under heavy selling pressure. The formation of a bearish pattern merely reinforces the early warning of stock weakness (i.e., downturn in RSR). Stock price declines usually occur more rapidly than do stock rallies, so short sellers of stocks, or those that use put contracts (a contract to sell 100 shares for a specified time period, such as three months, at a set striking price) may benefit from this trading strategy. Portfolio managers might take the short side of a market basket financial future (S & P, Value Line, NYSE, etc.), hoping to capture profits in the future about equivalent to book losses suffered on its diversified stock portfolio.

USING LIMITED ORDERS OR STOP LOSS ORDERS

Registered exchanges permit the use of limited orders as to price. These may be entered for the balance of a trading session, the week, the month, or as good until canceled. Profits earned on a stock trade (or from a stock option, future, or commodity future) will oftentimes disappear just as quickly. Prudence suggests that profits be permitted to run, but that the capital invested and a portion of the profits having been generated by a favorable price move be recognized (taken or booked) by the trader. Stop sell orders, for long purchases, should be set just below major zones of support. These zones include previous bottoms, the moving average, the trendline base, and the like, as described. When the price breaks through this (expected) support zone, it usually falls to the next one. To safeguard a short sale against a runaway upside move, stop buy orders should be placed just above resistant zones (or previous tops; numbers divisible by 5, 10, or 11; the moving average; or the trendline). A break through this level may cause the price to catapult very quickly to the next resistance zone, causing bears (those with short positions) to scurry for cover (or buy back in to cover previous short positions), thus sending prices higher as buying comes into the market.

Figure 4.7 illustrates several zones of resistance (or support) for Air & Water and for BJ Services. Note that upside runs on Air & Water tended to stall at 22, 25, and 30, whereas resistance appeared just above and below 25, again at 20, and still again at 15. Limited orders to sell the stock as it rallied from below to these positions probably accounted for the further selldowns. On BJ Services, the stock (an initial public offering at 20) stalled at 28, found support at 22 and 19–20, and then moved to almost 30. It then declined in several waves to 10 before rallying in three legs back toward its previous high. In a strong market for this industry, the stock might stall at 30, pull back to about the 20–22 area, and then move even higher, possibly to 50. Several bullish, enforcing patterns would probably be formed during the advance. A prudent trader should protect a portion of book gains with stop loss orders.

Figure 4.7
Support and Resistance Zones

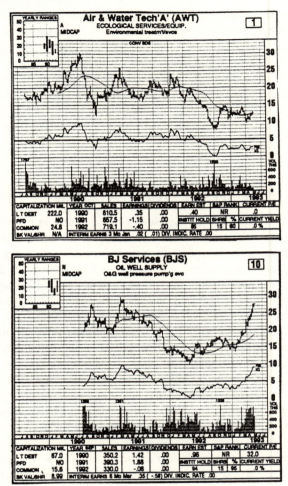

Source: Courtesy Standard & Poor's/Trendline.

BAR CHART PATTERNS FURTHER ILLUSTRATED

Several additional charts have been clipped from Trendline's various vertical bar chart services to illustrate the preceding suppositions. We have drawn in lines to identify important trendlines, continuation patterns, and reversal patterns. In some instances, daily graphs and weekly bar charts are provided on the same issue so that the reader may recognize similarities and differences in their appearance and usefulness to stock traders.

Figure 4.8 provides daily basis charts on Ethyl Corp (EY) and on FMC. Some

Figure 4.8
Gaps Illustrated on Daily Basis Charts

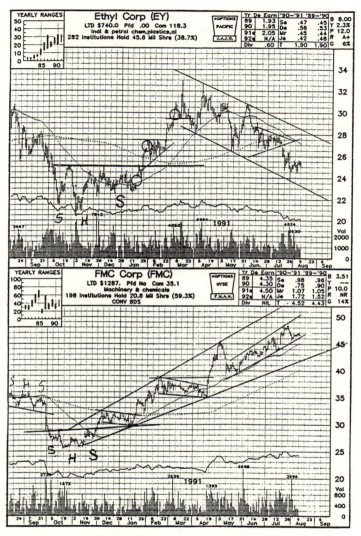

Source: Courtesy Standard & Poor's/Trendline.

interesting patterns appear on the two charts for late 1990 and early 1991. On
the Ethyl chart, the stock is in a steep decline, after attempting a 1990 break
through the previous high of about 31 set in 1987. An inverted head and shoulders (base) was formed with a neckline at 25 and the lowest level at 21. A breakout
was followed by a pullback to 25 and then a fast run to 33. The stock did not
have the strength to hold this level, though, and began a six month decline to

about 24–25. This weakness might have been anticipated had one remembered the usual location of gaps, breakaway, measuring, and exhaustion gaps, and the fact that the firm's stock price almost always fills gaps. Something magically seemed to be drawing the stock back to the 23 ½–24 range to fill that unfilled gap. Moreover, the RSR (relative strength ratio) was slightly weaker when the price was at 31 in February 1991 then at the same level in August 1990. The move was made in four legs.

The lower portion of Figure 4.8, the chart on FMC, has several interesting patterns. A break through the neckline of the small head and shoulders top, with weakness being shown in the RSR and the stock trading below its 100- and 200-day moving average, suggested that it would decline further. Consolidation between 26 and 29 occurred in October and November, with an upside break above the neckline. A narrow inverted H & S was formed with a breakaway gap at 27–28 in November 1990. The stock moved into an uptrend, with several consolidations along the way. A measuring gap occurred at 35. A downside gap occurred in early May 1991 at 42. The small trend channel (inside the larger one) suggests that the stock will likely break down and fall back to the base trend channel. It should probably be bought at the base trendline or at the support of the 200-day moving average. The RSI (Relative Strength Index) index is showing strength, so support around 42 is likely.

Four graphs are provided in Figure 4.9. The daily basis chart on VAR also provides interesting annual price levels from 1980 to 1990, showing that the stock fell from 60 (approximate) to 20. The daily chart shows a compound inverted head and shoulders (two shoulders on each side of the head), which was occurring in late October 1990. An upward break through the previous intermediate high of 33–34 occurred with vigor, producing several small gaps. The stock moved up very rapidly, after breaking through the moving averages, but ran into substantial overhead supply at 48–50, falling back to the upper 30s. The downturn in the RSR and the 100-day moving average suggests that the short term direction of the stock is downside. The target, after breaking through the support line (neckline) at 41, is $(50 - 41) = 9$. And $41 - 9$ produces a target of about 32. One might anticipate that another broad-based pattern would begin to form at about 32–33, a usual support level. Or perhaps the stock merely wishes to return and fill the gaps left at 31, 32, and 33?

The bottom of Figure 4.9 provides some weekly range charts from the Trendline *OTC Chart Book*. Three well-formed patterns can be seen on the charts for AMBR (a saucer with a breakout at about 3.75), a well formed trendline for AMED, and a reversal pattern and support levels at about 8 and again at 6 ½ on AMCA.

As added experience, the reader should review the charts in Figure 4.10 for strong patterns and weak patterns, labeling those that can be identified. Remember that charting is more of an art than a science, so sharpen your pencil and your eyesight and make your predictions as to future price movement by the issues. You should see a head and shoulders pattern on AW, a V bottom and rising trend on AWK, a trend reversal on AMWD, an inverted head and shoulders

Figure 4.9
Recognizing Important Reversal Patterns

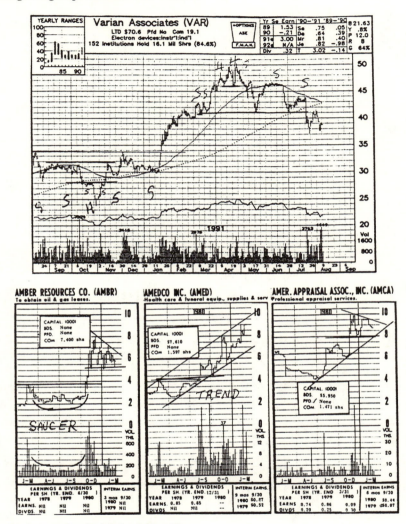

Source: Courtesy Standard & Poor's/Trendline.

bottom on Amerada Hess, a trend reversal on AINVS, a downtrend on FUND, a downtrend and attempted but aborted rally on AWALQ, a huge downside gap on AHR (perhaps an aborted merger), a rounded bottom or saucer on ACR, a rounded top on AIT, a saucer and upside gap on AMTR, two legs and an intermediate rally on AMN, an inverted head and shoulders bottom on ADD, another on AME, a rising trend on AMV, a rounded bottom on AMGN, followed by a

Figure 4.10
Some Bar Charts for Review

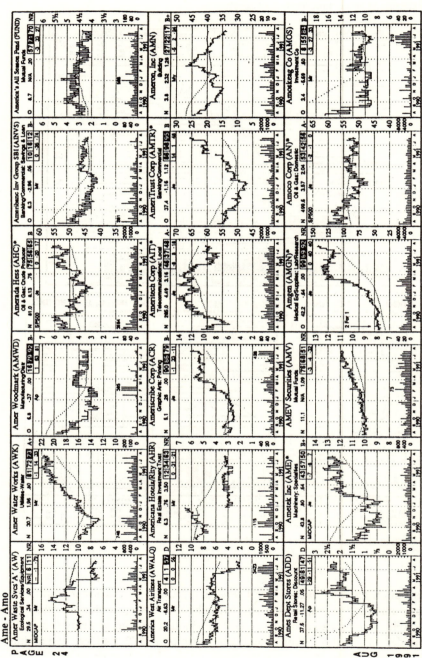

Source: Courtesy Standard & Poor's/Trendline.

small saucer, the beginning of a rectangle base on AN, and the partial completion of an inverted head and shoulders on AMOS.

In Chapter 5, we discover how vertical bar charts can be incorporated into the asset allocation process for that portion of a financial portfolio committed to common shares.

SUMMARY

Vertical bar charts can be prepared using different time periods for the price range shown by each vertical bar. Some technicians use daily or weekly graphs, and still others prefer to use them on a monthly or yearly basis. Each are useful in their own ways.

Some technicians attempt to buy stocks as they approach their base trendline, drawn in along major bottoms and tops, and to sell the issue as it approaches the top trend line. Still others attempt to identify meaningful patterns on the charts.

Some stock patterns show strength and others show weakness or are considered to be uncertainty configurations. Strong ones include rising trends, inverted head and shoulders, saucers and upside gaps. The opposite to these are bearish. Uncertainty patterns usually form patterns such as triangles, wedges, or rectangles.

The technician uses several ways to forecast the expected move from a stock, including from bottom to top of a trend channel, the depth of a pattern from bottom to break above a previous intermediate high, location of gaps, and the equal leg theory of odd number of legs up and even number of legs down. Many daily, weekly, and yearly graphs are shown as illustrations.

Chapter 5

DEVELOPING TRADING STRATEGIES WITH BAR CHARTS

The theory of bull and bear markets (the first technical usage of stock prices) dates back for more than 100 years to the work of Charles Dow, Hamilton, and his associates that established the *Wall Street Journal,* and began to develop a stock market average that might be used as an indicator of the overall direction of the stock market trend. The bull (bear) market theory merely suggests that rising trends of tops and bottoms are bullish, whereas falling ones are bearish. Today, the Dow Jones Industrial Average of thirty industrial stocks, and its counterparts of twenty transportation, fifteen utility, and sixty-five composite stocks, are well known. Many financial analysts and portfolio managers place much importance on the direction of movement for these popular simple price averages. Still others prefer to use the broader based S & P average of 500 stocks, the NYSE stock index of about all common issues that trade on that exchange, or the Wilshire 5,000 average (the NYSE, ASE, and leading OTC stocks). Some technicians use the transportation average as a confirmation for moves in the DJIA, whereas others prefer to use the cumulative advance-decline line as an indicator of broad strength (or liquidation) in the overall stock market.

In its various stock services, Trendline Corporation provides graphs of several important stock averages. Figure 5.1 shows from 1980 through late 1991 averages for the DJIA, S & P 500, and the cumulative advance-decline (AD) line. The latter is a cumulative differential between the weekly advances and declines from March 28, 1931. Some technicians have begun to use this AD line as a confirming tool with the stock averages. Rising tops and rising bottoms are held to be bullish, whereas falling tops and bottoms in the averages are signs of weaknesses.

Patterns occur on the graphs for stock market averages, and are interpreted in

Figure 5.1
Cyclical Swings Illustrated on Group Stock Averages

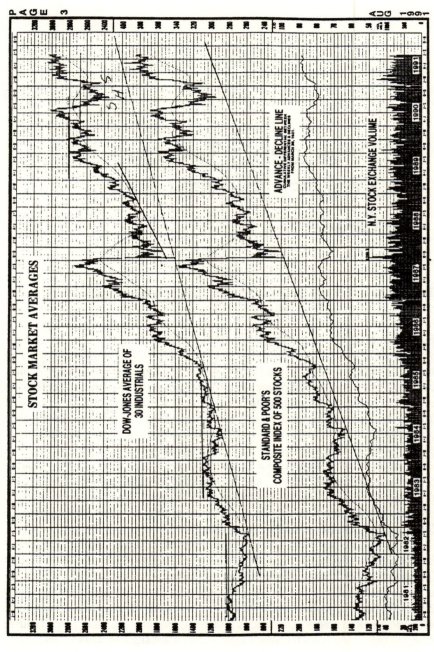
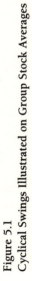

Source: Courtesy Standard & Poor's/Trendline.

the same way as for individual stocks. A review of the chart on the DJIA in 1981–1982 shows a saucer with a breakout level of about 1,120. Depth of the pattern would be used as a rough guide to the expected top. This was reached approximately in late 1983. An inverted head and shoulders was formed, with a breakout at about 1,300. This suggested a move of roughly 200 points, which was achieved in January 1986. The economy was recovering from a deep recession in the mid–1980s, and the stock market averages had been trapped from 1966 to 1982 (sixteen years) between about 750 and 1,050. When the breakout came, it came with vigor. The market exploded, rising to about 2,700 on the popular DJIA. Prices in the broader based S & P 500 moved in tandem. Program trading (automatic sales of large blocks of stocks through limited orders) received the blame for the market's breakdown in September and October 1987. In one day, the DJIA sank more than 500 points, or about 22% of its value. In reality, the market was only (very sharply) retracing about one-half to two-thirds of its previous lofty advance. Roughly a five-quarter, rising trend channel formed in late 1987 and all of 1988. Stocks moved to the magic 3,000 level on the DJIA before encountering substantial resistance. At that point, Iraq captured Kuwait, Operations Desert Shield and Desert Storm followed, and the market sank below 2,400. Weakness in the overall U.S. economy occurred. The DJIA then formed an inverted head and shoulders base, the advance-decline line and moving average turned up, and the stock average again moved above the 3,000 level. The S & P average of 500 stocks moved parallel to the DJIA and began to set new high records on each new advance. Where will the market go from this level? Probably up-and-back, up-and-back, and so forth.

The bold investor (or speculator) must take positions in stocks long before the fundamentals turn strong. In the summer of 1991, the market had already advanced roughly 30%, some issues (especially in medical care) had doubled or tripled, and many economists were still arguing that we were locked into a prolonged recession. The Federal Reserve authorities, however, had been pursuing a policy of easy money for several months. Short-term interest rates had fallen from about the 8% level a year earlier to below 6% by the mid-summer of 1991 (and continued to drop to 3% by July 1993). Business loan rates, and certainly not consumer rates, had not declined so much. Banks were attempting to restore their financial strength and safeguard against widespread losses as had been occurring for several years in the Savings and Loan industry. The leading indicators, including stock market prices, had been moving upward for several months, thus pointing to a healthier economy for the next year or two. The aborted coup in the U.S.S.R. and the hoped-for increase in world trade brought about wide daily fluctuations in stock averages. A review of the chart on the DJIA and S & P 500 index suggests that the former might move to about 3,650–3,700, while the S & P should climb to about 460. The swing rule would suggest a move from 2,350 on the DJIA above 3,000 should carry the market to about 3,750, which is about a 60% advance from the market bottom, about average for the historical moves. Retracement of half this advance to about 3,000 might then be expected.

These levels are merely conjecture, of course, and world events could occur that would disrupt expected stock average moves. However, only time will tell.

BUYING AT LOW PRICES, SELLING AT HIGH PRICES

The objective of a rational speculator or investor in stocks is to earn an above average profit from his or her endeavors. Thus one must sharpen trading skills in applying fundamental or technical tools so as to do this. A speculator (or investor) will have greater success in selecting individual stocks if he or she follows the general trend of the market. That is, stocks should be purchased long when the averages are in an uptrend. When there is a strong bear market, few individual stocks perform as one might usually expect from chart theory. Chapter 4 illustrated the usual trustworthy patterns that appear on vertical bar charts. A serious trader might buy a stock that is on the base trendline and attempt to sell it as it approaches the top of the trend channel. Other stocks might be bought as they break out of a broad consolidation pattern, such as an inverted head and shoulders pattern or a rounded bottom and breaks through the previous top(s).

It is sometimes fruitful to assess groups of stocks and to concentrate in those that appear to be under accumulation by institutional and other large buyers. Identifying timely groups of stocks is relatively easy when using *Current Market Perspectives,* as the service provides about sixty graphs on industry groups.

An attractive feature of Trendline is the inclusion of five-year, weekly graphs for transportation, utility, the AMEX, NYSE, and NASDAQ composite averages. One master graph shows how the issues included in this service have performed over the past twelve months. Some eight pages also show vertical bar charts for each of the roughly sixty industry groups reviewed by S & P in this service. Thus a bold speculator might select one or two issues from each of several industries that appear to be rising more quickly than other groups of stocks. Four of these industry group charts are provided in Figure 5.2 for review. The reviewer should notice that most of these are forming what appears to be inverted head and shoulders patterns or saucer base patterns in late 1991. Even in a strong, bull market, a few groups of stocks are being liquidated by their holders and refuse to advance in price. Still others tend to advance upward in price several times as rapidly as the market as a whole. The high-performance stock buyer hopes to outperform the market as a whole, so often concentrates his or her holdings in those issues that are under accumulation by institutions.

The graphs of Consolidated Edison in Figure 5.3 provide some insight into how a short-term trader might buy low and sell high. The short-term speculator would choose the daily graph (top panel), whereas the intermediate-term holder should use the longer graph (bottom pannel). One trend-buying strategy is to accumulate the stock as it approaches the base trendline. The stock should be sold as it approaches the top of the trend channel. Over a twelve month period, ED moved up and back almost three times within the channel. The yearly range chart for the stock suggests that the issue often pulls back just above 20 (say to

Figure 5.2
Yearly Performance of S & P Stock Groups

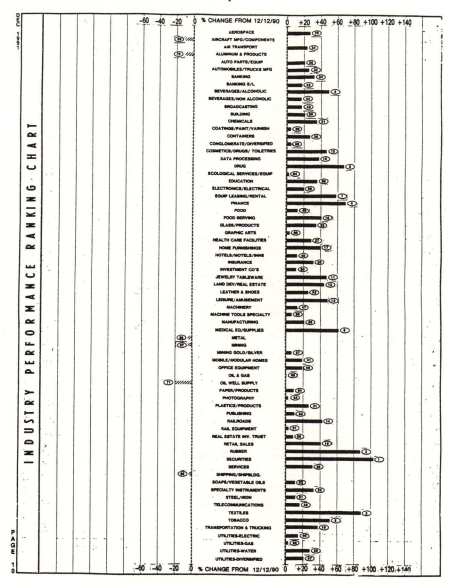

Source: Courtesy Standard & Poor's/Trendline.

Figure 5.3
Recognizing Buy-Low, Sell-High Opportunities

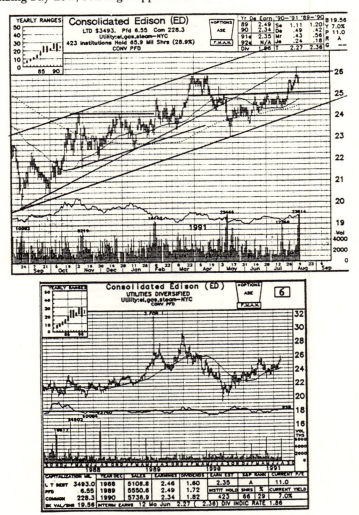

Source: Courtesy Standard & Poor's/Trendline.

20 ½ or 20 ¾ and then rises by about $4 per share). On a longer-term basis, a strong support appears at about 20 with substantial resistance at 26 and 30 per share. Once a stock moves to an all time high, there is no overhead supply, and the stock is likely to run up in price at an accelerated rate. Electric utility stocks have low market volatility, and might not be a choice for a trading vehicle, but the pattern does illustrate how trend channels, support, and resistance levels might be detected on the vertical bar charts.

IDENTIFYING UNUSUALLY LARGE PRICE MOVES

Not only must one be concerned with the groups of stocks to hold (in an overall strong market), but selecting leaders in the groups will provide more profits than being stuck in a stock that refuses to move. These leaders are usually the largest few stocks that operate in a given industry, especially if they have some ability to resist sales and profit declines during economic slumps. Growth industries are often under strong, early accumulation by performance-minded mutual fund and pension fund managers and are early and large movers in price during early stages of a bull market. As stated, stocks that break above previous high prices often are rapid movers. Those that break from very deep or wide consolidation patterns also have substantial runups. Several of these concepts are illustrated in Figures 5.4 and 5.5 for four stocks.

Figure 5.4 compares price action on Atlantic Southeast Air and Consolidated Rail, two transportation issues. Note that the two stocks performed in the tenth and ninth deciles for the past twelve months as compared to the S & P average of 500 stocks. Moreover, each broke above their long consolidation tops. The previous top of ASAI was about 16 per share (in 1985). Once it broke this level, it was able to move to 20–22 before consolidating back into the formation. When this new top was breached, it moved very quickly from 22 to 37 per share (in about six months). The per share price of Consolidated Rail has been to 40 in late 1987. Its pullback to 20 suggested a move upward of at least 40 points. It did run into resistance at 50, but formed a consolidation pattern, an inverted head and shoulders configuration with a depth of $52 - 32 = 20$, which provided a target of 72 once the stock had broken the previous top of 52. This target was approximately attained by late 1991.

Two gold mining issues are reflected in Figure 5.5. When gold prices are advancing, the prices of gold mining shares are often rising about as rapidly. The chart reviewer should note that the previous high price of WDRIY was at about 75 per share (having come from a bottom at about 18 per share) This depth of pattern is about $60, so an advance to the 120–130 range was likely after a strong breakout. The stock actually stalled at 120. A bullish saucer pattern that occurred in 1980 was about $35 deep, with a neckline at 90, suggesting a move to about $125 after a breakout. Although actual moves did not quite attain their targets, downside gaps suggested at about 110 that the issue should be liquidated. The lower panel of the figure shows a topside breakout for WHLDY at 60 (with a saucer bottom at about 12 per share). This predicted a move above $110 per share. A price of about $118 was actually set on four different days before the stock began to decline back to the support level at 60.

SELLING AND SHORT SELLING

Knowing when to sell a stock is more of an art than determining the price at which to buy the issue. The swing rule from a symmetrical coil or triangle, the

Figure 5.4
Recognizing Large Price Move Potentials

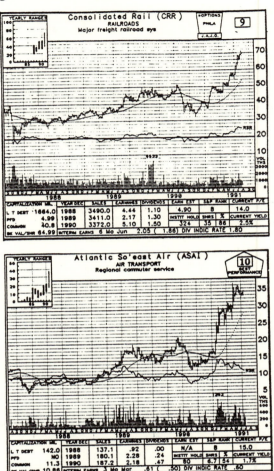

Source: Courtesy Standard & Poor's/Trendline.

depth of a saucer or inverted head and shoulders bottom, or the width of a rectangle are rules often followed in setting a selling target. Other resistance points (or zones) suggested in Chapter 4 are sometimes used with good results. Remember that numbers divisible by five are major resistance (or support if below an issue's price). Base trend line usually offers a bounce (support), whereas the upper trend channel tends to be a resistance zone. The thirty-week moving average is an intermediate zone of support (resistance), whereas the shorter-term moving averages are used for minor support or resistance points. Previous tops and bot-

Figure 5.5
Using Annual Price Ranges to Forecast Moves

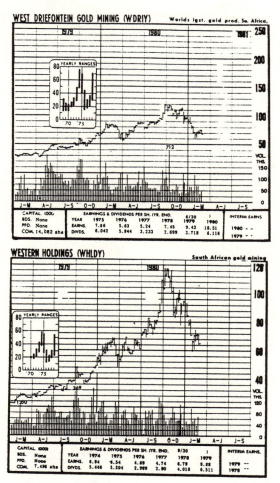

Source: Courtesy Standard & Poor's/Trendline.

toms are also zones of support/resistance and are often used to modify the position of sale by the astute technician.

Institutional investors are not permitted short sales, although they may trade in puts, calls, and financial futures contracts on groups of stocks, a topic covered in the last chapter of the book. An individual who feels that a bull market is coming to a close is wise to sell enough shares to pay off any margin (so as to eliminate unwarranted financial leverage during a bear market). Other shares should be watched carefully to detect a pending major change in direction (from

Figure 5.6
Recognizing Short Sale Opportunities

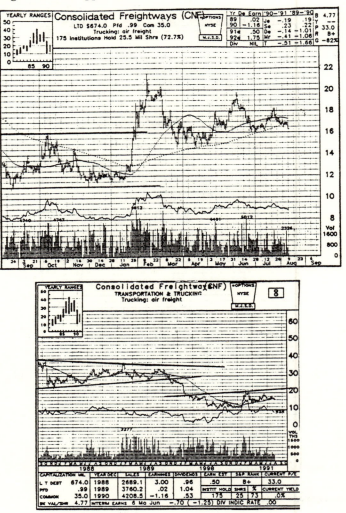

Source: Courtesy Standard & Poor's/Trendline.

strong to weak). The relative strength to S & P average line on the *Current Market Perspective* charts are especially useful in this technique.

Stocks usually fall more rapidly in a bear market than the rate of advance in a tiring bull market. Some risk-taking individuals attempt to move from a long position in stocks to a short position. That is, they reverse the process, short sell shares, and hope to cover their short position at lower prices at some future date. Stocks are loaned by the brokerage firm to make delivery to the accounts buying from the short seller. The short seller must make up any dividends paid on the shorted shares, but the market automatically adjusts to this payment on the day the stock trades ex-dividends.

A downside breakout from an extended consolidation pattern offers little upside risk to the short seller. For example, consider the symmetrical coil on CNF in Figure 5.6. The moving average had begun to decline in about March of 1989, as did the relative strength ratio. A short in the 29–30 range would have anticipated a move in the stock of about 16, or to roughly 13–14 range. The stock, in several legs, did move to and somewhat below this projected price level. The RSR line turned strong in 1990, however, so the astute trader should have taken steps to cover his or her shorted position, perhaps at about 12–14 per share. Thus a gain of more than 50% over a twelve-month time period was possible from a short in this stock. However, a word of caution is in order, as stocks that decline rapidly also sometimes rally vigorously once a broad-based bottom is broken on the upside. Note the daily basis chart on CNF for 1990–1991. The relative strength line turned up in late January 1990, and the stock moved up sharply from 12 to 21 ½. The moving average lines were broken with vigor, another sign that the previous short should be covered if still outstanding. A break from the top of the formation at 16 suggested a rapid run in the stock from 16 minus 11 to about 16 plus 5 or to 21. This move was achieved in less than three weeks. A portion of the fast run-up in price might have been caused by shorts scurrying to cover their previously shorted positions.

The term "reaction is equal to action" is illustrated by several moves on EFU in Figure 5.7. The daily basis chart is an excellent tool for perfecting short sales, but the longer-term weekly range chart might point out some impending danger zones. In October 1990, the stock gapped through two previous tops at 26 ½. The depth of the pattern from 23 ½ suggested that it would move to about 29. This was attained, and then the stock fell back through the formation, approximating the depth of the pattern from 26 ⅝ to 29 on its downside swing to 24 ¾. Highly volatile stocks, such as Eastern Enterprises, are choice candidates for the accomplished short seller of shares. However, few technicians are foolish enough to attempt major short sales in strong bull markets. Thus, for maximum profit taking on stock trading, one should attempt to trade with the overall direction in the market—long positions in advancing markets, and withdrawal or short sales in weak, falling markets.

ESTIMATING PRICE MOVES

Price moves are estimated in a number of ways, including depth of bullish and bearish patterns, movement between major trend channels, approximate equal leg length, and placement of gaps. Each of these will be illustrated in the charts that follow.

Figure 5.8 provides charts on Andrew Corp. and Advanta Corp., two relatively widely swinging issues. On the ANDW issue, a saucer occurred in late 1987–

Figure 5.7
Using the Swing Rule with Longs and Shorts

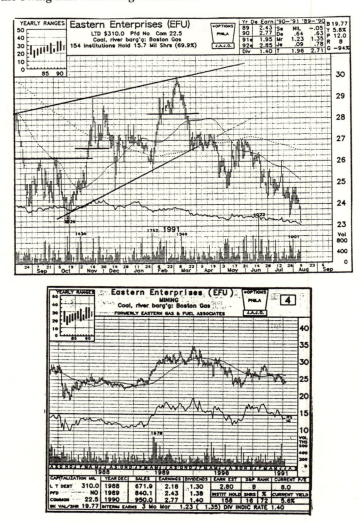

Source: Courtesy Standard & Poor's/Trendline.

1988 with a top at 17 ½ and a bottom at 11, suggesting a move to 24. After a breakout, the stock moved to 26, with a few advances and declines. A rounded top with a neckline at 21 (many technicians suggest that an interday or interweek low be discarded if the stock closes above that level) suggested a move to about 16. The actual move was to 15 ½. Another saucer in 1990 suggested a breakout at 25 (neckline) and a move to 36. This price objective was reached in April 1991. The stock appears to be pulling back toward the moving average, and perhaps to

Figure 5.8
Recognizing Rounded Tops and Bottoms (Saucers)

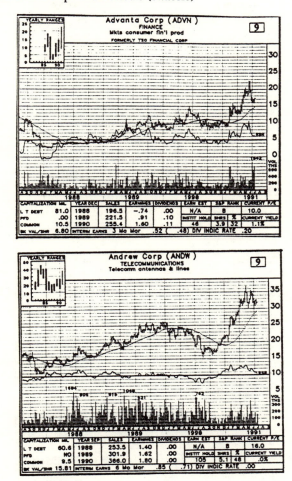

Source: Courtesy Standard & Poor's/Trendline.

support at the 25–26 level. ADVN had a long saucer pattern in 1988 and 1989 with a neckline at 11 per share. The low price of about 3 per share suggested that the stock could move to 19. A small, inverted head and shoulders (base in 1990 suggested a move from about 13 to 18). The stock formed another saucer pattern with a projected move of 7 points from a breakout at 15. The actual move was a plus 7, or to 22 per share. Although depths of reversal patterns do not give pinpoint accuracy in their forecasting ability, they do, nevertheless, provide a useful starting point for assessing probable zones of resistance for the issue (price, previous tops, moving averages, etc.).

Figure 5.9
Trading from Base to Upper Trend Channels

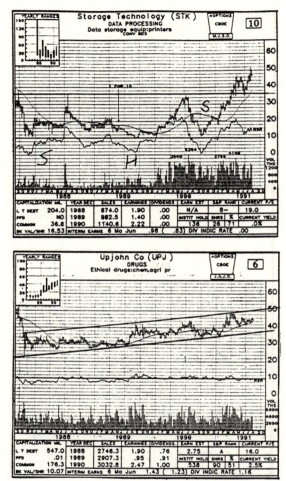

Source: Courtesy Standard & Poor's/Trendline.

As suggested, some stocks do remain within orderly trend channels for several years. Two examples of this are provided in Figure 5.9 for Storage Technology and Upjohn Company. STK was moving in a sidewise trend from late 1987 through late 1990 (before a topside breakout). A long (3 ½ year) inverted head and shoulders bottom appears within a broad rectangle base. With a bottom at 10 and a top at 36, the projected price attainment of the stock is 62. The stock reached 52 within about four months after a neckline breakout, but may need to consolidate to 40 before continuing its upward movement. Upjohn, a growth company in the ethical drug industry, moved upward from late 1987 through late 1991 within a narrow trend channel. An appropriate trading strategy for the stock might have been to buy the stock on the base trend line and to sell it with about a ten-point gain.

Lengths of legs are sometimes used as a selling guide for fast action common shares. Daily basis vertical bar charts are more useful with this endeavor (usually) than are weekly range charts. American Family and Analog Devices charts are provided in Figure 5.10, which illustrates leg action. The first leg of AFL might be measured from 12 ½ to 19, the second from 18 to 25, and the last from 21 to 27. The major legs occurred on the upside followed by two consolidation legs (27 to 21 ½ and from 23 ½ to 20 ½). The last leg in a sequence is often somewhat shorter than its predecessors. The major legs on the chart of ADI are subdivided into two approximately equal parts. A leg from 5 ½ to 7 ½ was followed by another that moved from 6 ½ to 9 ¼. The last was from 8 ½ to 12 ⅞. A downside gap at 11 ½ suggested that the stock was ready to plummet. A topside head and shoulders preceded a major decline to the 7 ½ price level. Although the moving average lines offered a few weeks of support (at about 11 and 9 ½, respectively), the stock eased on through them as reported earnings per share were disappointing.

Locations of gaps are sometimes used in estimating the overall move of a stock that tends to gap. This is often done on thinly traded issues of stocks. In Figure 5.11, KLM Royal Dutch Air gapped at 11 ½, again at 14, and again at 16. The measuring gap (center one at 14) is usually about 40 to 50% of the distance from the breakaway gap and the total move attainment. A gap at 15, another at 14 ½, and another at 13 ½ occurred on the downward pullback. Gaps are also present on the stock for CDN at 18, at 24, and again at 32. Gaps on the downside occurred at 32–28, at 24, and at 17. The stock that rises rapidly often declines in a similar downside pattern roughly parallel to the previous upward move.

Other things being equal, a very broad consolidation pattern (a rectangle base, for example) will often provide a more extended move (relative to the depth of the pattern) than will a move from a deep saucer. This is illustrated in the next two chapters that deal with point and figure (P & F) charts and its method of estimating a move from a P & F configuration.

Although a fundamentalist might insist that the earnings for a stock turn from weak to strong before taking a position, many risk-prone speculators using daily basis charts disregard the fundamentals if a very strong technical pattern exists. The chart on Goodyear Tire in Figure 5.12 illustrates this point. Despite weak earnings in 1990 and 1991, the stock broke out from 25 (saucer with a depth of 12). The forecasted move was into the upper 30s, which was attained about four months after the breakout (despite the poor earnings record). Also illustrated in the chart is Willcox & Gibbs, which shows a move from 6 to 15 in three or four legs, a decline to 10 in two major legs, a breakout at 15 and run to 20, before splitting and then returning to the (adjusted) six per share level. The stock fell in four relatively similar legs. The relative strength ratio line was a key to buying, holding, or selling the issue.

Figure 5.10
Moves in Upside and Downside Legs Illustrated

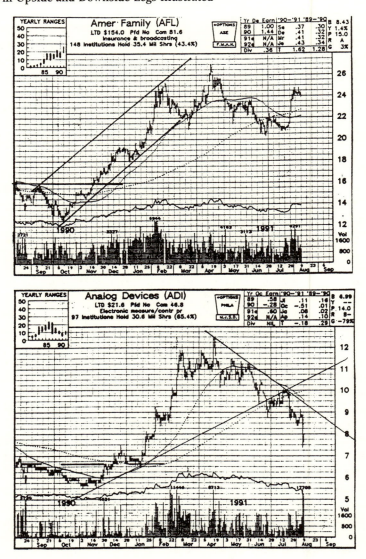

Source: Courtesy Standard & Poor's/Trendline.

PUTTING THE VERTICAL BAR CHART STRATEGY TOGETHER

No tool of investing is perfect and without its flaws. An astute technician attempts to locate strong performing issues within strong performing industries (or sectors) and to trade with the tide (bull or bear market). The idea is to buy low

Figure 5.11
Using Gaps to Estimate Price Moves

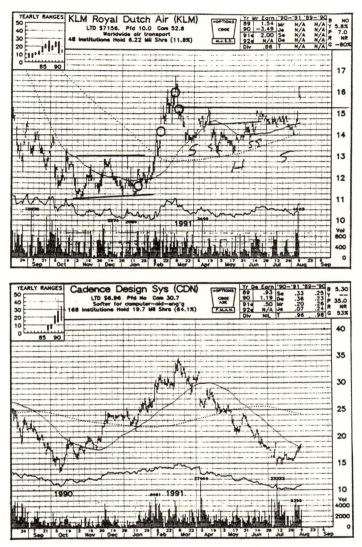

Source: Courtesy Standard & Poor's/Trendline.

and to sell high, and not the opposite. Most technicians suggest that a trader let the profits run, protecting capital with stop loss sell orders, while cutting losses short by setting stop loss sell orders beneath a nearby resistance level. Short traders should adopt the opposite strategy. Stock options and financial futures are sometimes used as hedges by stock portfolio managers.

Figure 5.12
Price Moves Often Lead a Fundamental Upturn

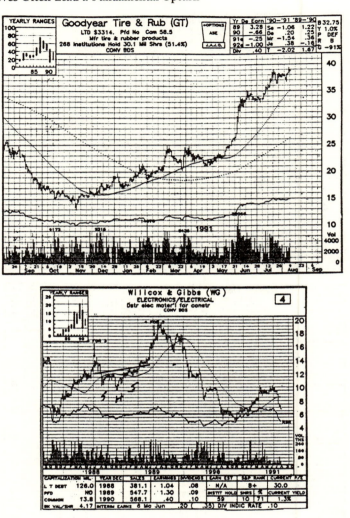

Source: Courtesy Standard & Poor's/Trendline.

In an orderly market (if we could ever have one), and when trading with the major tide (long in bull markets, short in bear markets), identifiable chart patterns appear to be trustworthy about 80–85% of the time. This certainly appears to be better odds than an outright guess. One should keep in mind, however, that large institutional traders often hold 50–90% of the outstanding shares for a given issue. Some of them manage vast amounts of mutual fund assets for the general public or for pension accounts. There is a certain follow-the-leader approach by the mutual fund managers, and once a stock comes under dumping pressure by large holders, it will fall faster and farther than one might have anticipated. An investor, however, should be alert, often buying thinly traded stocks on limited orders and selling them the same way (slightly below the anticipated price objective). Some profits should be protected by well-placed, stop-sell orders. In using charts, we have found that diligence and application of technical rules to trading will usually produce annual profits about two times that achieved on the popular S & P 500 stock average. In a bear market, an astute technician acclimated to long purchases is lucky to break even. The market is probably falling by 20–30%. You make the choice as to whether you want to become a fundamentalist, an efficient market defender, or a technician! But remember, more work and dedication to staying abreast of the market is required by a technician than by one of the other two adherents. A lazy technician usually loses her or his capital to more diligent ones.

SUMMARY

Charts can be used in several ways in developing strategies to manage the stock portion of a portfolio. The Dow Theory of a bull market and bear market dates to the 19th century and was one early attempt to detect major stock trends. Stock prices tend to change directions before shifts in their fundamental values become obvious.

Groups of stocks tend to move in the same direction, so group selection is important. In a given year, certain groups of stocks move much higher in price, most gain from 5 to 15%, and a few industry groups lose in value, even in a strong market. In a weak market, the reverse is true. Some investors attempt to locate leaders and laggards in groups of stocks.

Determining an appropriate selling price for a stock, and thus capturing most of the price advance, is more difficult than selecting an issue that will rise (or fall) in price. The methods of estimating a move that were described in Chapter 4 are further illustrated with graphs in this chapter. Still other stock portfolio managers hold stocks until bearish patterns are formed as a selling signal.

Some other useful tools to the technician include (1) support levels, (2) resistance levels, (3) relative strength index, and (4) moving averages. Charts illustrate these tools and how they should be properly used by the technician to good advantage.

Chapter 6

THE RATIONALE OF POINT AND FIGURE CHARTING

The asset allocation process involves decision making to determine the proper investments mix. Funds may be allocated, for example, among stocks, bonds, mutual funds, and cash. Asset allocation also includes reinvestment decisions after liquidations have taken place. In other words, the constant shifting of funds from one stock to another relates only to that part of asset allocation dealing with only one variable in the overall equation. In the next three chapters, much of the text concerns buying and selling individual equity issues within the framework of the total allocation decision. Later chapters explore asset allocation from the viewpoint of moving money from stocks into other assets and vice versa.

One's initial exposure to point and figure (P & F) charts seems unorthodox at best. However, further study indicates an harmonious evolution of configurations. P & F charts contain an orderly, logical flow in forming generally accepted patterns. The point and figure approach represents an established, time-tested evaluation of graphs as they apply to both individual stocks and the general market. As opposed to the vertical bar method, however, P & F charts consist of alternating columns of X's and O's.

When properly understood, P & F methods give analysts an advantage in timing decisions and in projecting future price movements. As a result, professionals utilize them in making decisions for both buying and selling transactions. Experienced market players maintain that knowing when to sell is the most difficult part of investing. A technique enabling investors to take profits in a timely manner provides a valuable investment tool.

THE THEORY BENEATH THE SURFACE

During the building of chart patterns, P & F graphs depict the interaction between supply and demand with alternating columns of X's and O's.[1] When lateral or sideways price movements take place, P & F charts indicate the stock (or other security) being plotted is fluctuating where supply and demand function in a state of equilibrium. Once prices move above former tops or below previous bottoms in the congestion area, a defined generally emerges. Price moves above or below base patterns dissolve the balance between supply and demand.

Dissolving this equilibrium condition between supply and demand during a lateral price movement warns of newly created imbalances where either supply or demand now dominates. When demand exceeds supply, bullish chart patterns occur and a strong price advance results. Conversely, bear chart patterns form from an excess of supply relative to demand and lead to price declines.

Buy signals are called upside breakouts, whereas sell signals are labeled downside breakouts. To reiterate, price moves above previous tops or below preceding bottoms furnish buy and sell signals, respectively. Chart patterns, buy and sell signals, trendlines, and related concepts make P & F charts an invaluable diagnostic tool and timing device.

Investors who emphasize market timing and the idea of "when to buy" are considered to be technicians. Conversely, those who place most of their emphasis on locating undervalued assets (i.e., value investing) on the basis of earnings, dividends, growth rates, book values, sales, competitive positions in the market, economic outlooks, and management quality, are called fundamentalists. Fundamental investors seem preoccupied with the idea of "whether or not the stock should be purchased" with little attention devoted to the timing of the decision.

Simply stated, technicians are short term in their investment horizons, whereas fundamentalists focus on the long term. Subscribing primarily to either of these two contrasting approaches does not preclude using them together for investment decisions. However, market volatility in the late 1980s and early 1990s suggests placing a premium on timing.

CONTRIBUTIONS FROM CHARLES DOW

Many investment pioneers consider Charles Dow as the founding father of technical analysis. Some of Dow's original works appeared around 1900 in the *Wall Street Journal* and provided the foundations for later ideas on investment analysis. Dow is perhaps best recognized for his research relating price movements of the industrial and transportation averages (formerly called the rails since they were the dominant form of transportation around 1900).

Dow believed that if the industrial average achieved a new high or low for a price move, the transportation average must confirm this price action with a similar new high or low. This principle of *confirmation* reinforced bullish or bearish investment forecasts. When the averages failed to confirm each other, a *divergence* warned investors that current market trends were in their final stages.

However, Dow's principal contribution to charting perhaps rests in his definition of bull and bear markets. Dow recognized that bull markets had a continuing pattern of higher tops and higher bottoms, whereas bear markets were identified by lower tops and lower bottoms. Chartists began to apply Dow's thesis of market trends to individual security charts. When stock prices rose above previous tops, a bullish signal with rising tops formed. Trends were bullish from the upside breakouts. Countervailing logic applied to bearish price trends, with downside breakouts giving lower bottoms and sell signals.

HOW TO KEEP YOUR OWN POINT AND FIGURE CHARTS

Technicians remain heavily focused on the interaction between supply and demand. Point and figure charts illustrate this interplay through the medium of alternating columns of X's and O's. Each column of X's indicates price advances, and a column of O's represents price declines. Generally, the more time occupied by the contest between supply and demand, the larger the number of alternating columns appearing in the lateral price action or base pattern.

More volatile stocks with higher beta factors usually form base patterns quicker and reach price targets faster. Slower-moving issues often require longer periods of time to complete the lateral price formations and to attain price forecasts. Less-volatile stocks may lead to sideways patterns with greater width. As a general rule, the wider the pattern, the greater the potential price move once a breakout occurs in either direction.

Point and figure charts use an arithmetic scale for plotting purposes. Charts priced below the $5 level should be maintained on a scale with unit values of $0.25 or ¼ point.[2] For stocks valued between $5 and $20, graph squares equal $0.50 or ½ point. Stocks selling between $20 and $100 are plotted with each square representing $1 or 1 point on the graph. High-priced securities trading for $100 or more should be graphed on the basis with each square worth $2 or 2 points.

This book uses the Chartcraft approach,[3] which emphasizes the three-square reversal method of point and figure charting. In other words, a price move of three squares in the opposite direction from the current trend constitutes a price reversal and establishes another column. All reproduced P & F charts in this book are courtesy of Chartcraft, Inc., of New Rochelle, New York.

Some traders demonstrate a preference for one-square reversal charts where a new column forms each time a single unit price change develops in the opposite direction. A problem with the one-square reversal approach centers on the evaluation difficulties from potentially large numbers of recordings. However, the largest problem relates to the number of false and misleading price moves and breakouts.

One-square charts often tend to be compressed and narrowly formed due to the many minor price reversals on the graph. Many price moves on one-square charts are meaningless and lead to interpretational errors. Price forecasts tend to be unwieldy and sometimes inconclusive when base patterns develop over a period of years.

Longer-term chartists extol the virtues of the five-square reversal method on the basis that charts have fewer recordings and offer simplicity and interpretation ease. However, many years of experience has lead us to employ the three-square approach with considerably better results. Whereas single-square reversal charts appear to be too sensitive, five-square reversal graphs are frequently too insensitive unless highly volatile securities are involved. Chartcraft's three-square reversal method represents a compromise approach combining the best of the different philosophies.

One criticism of point and figure techniques surrounds the view that buy and sell signals may occur too late. Delays nullify timing advantages offered by other methods, most notably vertical bar charts. However, strategies developed in the text enable readers to use the three-square P & F method for short-term trading as well as intermediate and long-term investing.

Applying the Information[4]

Let us review Table 6.1 for an understanding of actual chart construction. Hypothetical dates and prices appear in columns 1, 2, and 3. Notice that point and figure charts use daily highs and lows and disregard closing prices. Daily highs and lows are also employed for OTC stocks, but only the bid price is considered. However, ignoring closing price information can prove to be a mistake. We address this issue shortly.

Column 4 indicates the prevailing price trend in the stock. If the chart currently is in a column of X's, an uptrend exists. Charts in a column of O's mean a current downmove. A basic premise of point and figure charting is to assume a continuation of the existing price trend.[5] In other words, on the 4/18 market date in Table 6.1, we are in a column of X's with the price trending upward. Column 5 gives the price that chartists would read first when scanning daily prices. For example, we have a column of X's with a price of $36 recorded on 4/17. Chartists will check (or read) the daily high to see if another X can be recorded. Since the daily high (DH) on 4/18 reached 37 ⅜, an additional X can be added to the column at 37. Column 6 indicates that the price continuation can be justified.

Column 6 also lets us know whether another recording can be made in the present column. If another recording results, one need not check for a second reading in column 7. Note that on 4/18, column 7 reads "DL-No," indicating no need exists to check the daily low (DL) as the second reading. The first reading or price checked (DH) justified a continuation of the existing column. Since the trend continues, no reversal column originates in the opposite direction.

To reiterate, plotting intraday high and low prices presupposes a continuation of the prevailing trend. If the trend does not continue, check for a discontinuation

Table 6.1
Constructing a Point and Figure Chart

(1) DATE	(2) DAILY HIGH (DH)	(3) DAILY LOW (DL)	(4) PREVAILING TREND	(5) CHECK 1st READING	(6) CONTIN. JUSTIFIED ?	(7) CHECK 2nd READING	(8) REVERSAL OR DISCONT. JUSTIFIED ?	(9) POSTED CHART RECORDING
4/15	34 1/4	33 1/8	UP	DH	Yes	DL-No	No	X (34)
4/16	35 3/4	34	UP	DH	Yes	DL-No	No	X (35)
4/17	36 7/8	35 1/4	UP	DH	Yes	DL-No	No	X (36)
4/18	37 3/8	36 1/2	UP	DH	Yes	DL-No	No	X (37)
4/19	37 1/2	34 7/8	UP	DH	No	DL-Yes	No	------
4/22	35 5/8	33 3/4	UP	DH	No	DL-Yes	Yes	O (36)
								O (35)
								O (34)
4/23	34 1/4	32 7/8	DOWN	DL	Yes	DH-No	No	O (33)
4/24	33	32	DOWN	DL	Yes	DH-No	No	O (32)
4/25	33	31 1/8	DOWN	DL	No	DH-Yes	No	------
4/26	34 1/8	32 7/8	DOWN	DL	No	DH-Yes	No	------
4/29	33 5/8	32	DOWN	DL	No	DH-Yes	No	------
4/30	34	32 3/8	DOWN	DL	No	DH-Yes	No	------

Table 6.1 Continued

5/1	35 1/8	33 5/8	DOWN	DL	No	DH-Yes	Yes	X (33)
								X (34)
5/2	35 5/8	34	UP	DH	No	DL-Yes	No	X (35)
5/3	34 1/2	33	UP	DH	No	DL-Yes	No	------
5/6	34 1/8	33 3/4	UP	DH	No	DL-Yes	No	------
5/7	35	34 3/8	UP	DH	No	DL-Yes	No	------
5/8	35 1/8	34 5/8	UP	DH	No	DL-Yes	No	------
5/9	34 1/2	33	UP	DH	No	DL-Yes	No	------
5/10	35	33 1/2	UP	DH	No	DL-Yes	No	------
5/13	36 1/8	33 3/4	UP	DH	No	DL-No	No	X (36)
5/14	37 3/8	36	UP	DH	Yes	DL-No	No	X (37)
5/15	37 1/2	35	UP	DH	No	DL-Yes	No	------
5/16	37	35	UP	DH	No	DL-YEs	No	------
5/17	36 1/2	35 1/8	UP	DH	No	DL-Yes	No	------
5/20	37	35	UP	DH	No	DL-Yes	No	------
5/21	36 1/8	34	UP	DH	No	DL-Yes	Yes	O (36)
								O (35)
								O (34)
5/22	34 3/4	32 7/8	DOWN	DL	Yes	DH-No	No	O (33)
5/23	34	33 3/8	DOWN	DL	No	DH-Yes	No	------
5/24	35 1/8	33 7/8	DOWN	DL	No	DH-Yes	No	------

5/27	36	34 1/2	DOWN	DL	No	DH-Yes	Yes	X (34)
								X (35)
								X (36)
5/28	36 1/2	35 7/8	UP	DH	No	DL-No	No	------
5/29	36 3/4	36 1/8	UP	DH	No	DL-No	No	------
5/30	37 1/4	37	UP	DH	Yes	DL-No	No	X (37)
5/31	37 7/8	37 1/4	UP	DH	Yes	DL-No	No	------
6/1	38 3/8	37 1/2	UP	DH	Yes	DL-No	No	6 (38)
6/2	39 5/8	38	UP	DH	Yes	DL-No	No	X (39)

or price reversal. In a column of X's, one should look at the intraday high to see if an X can be added. If not, look at the intraday low to determine whether a reversal should be recorded. Movements of one, two, or three squares—whichever reversal rule is being followed—may constitute a price swing in the opposite direction. In a column of O's, look to see if one or more O's can be added. If not, check the intraday high to evaluate whether sufficient price change merits a reversal in trend (i.e., one, two, three, five squares, etc.).

Column 8 designates whether a price reversal ensues. To illustrate, let us review prices for 4/19. A daily high of 37 ½ does not justify another X at $38. Column 6 reveals that the uptrend does not move higher, so column 7 reads "DL-Yes." Since the first reading does not yield another recording, we must examine the daily low price or second reading option. The price did not decline the necessary three squares to 34 on an intraday low basis, so a reversal column likewise did not result. Therefore, no recording transpires.

However, let us assume the stock closed at the daily low price of 34 ⅞. For those who choose to ignore closing prices, a potential timing error may result. With the final price near a level that would yield a three-square downside reversal (at 34), the stock suggests near-term price weakness, which may extend into the next few sessions. Chartists who neglect the closing price still see the stock's price at 37. Continued selling pressure on the stock during the next few days will be observed late from failure to consider depressed closing prices from late-session selloffs. Subsequent transactions may therefore be undertaken too late and translate into diminished profits.[6]

Column 9 helps keep track of recordings posted in either continuing or reversing price trends. Notice that an X is posted on 4/18 at the 37 level and continues the price move to the upside. However, on 4/19, we could not justify another X to continue the uptrend nor another O for a price reversal and another column of O's. However, on 4/22, our suspicions from examining the closing price on 4/19 were confirmed. The daily high only reached 35 ⅝ and failed to continue the uptrend, but the daily low reached 33 ¾. Since the last recording was an X at 37, a daily low of 34 represents a three-square downside price reversal in a column of O's. Notice that column 9 has O's recorded in the 36, 35, and 34 price squares. Thus a new column is formed.[7]

Given their emphasis on price as opposed to volume and time, point and figure charts are often considered to be single dimensional by critics. However, time is recorded by many P & F chartists. A number 1 through 12 may be recorded in place of X's and O's to illustrate the first price recording in a particular month. For example, Table 6.1 has a 5 recorded in a column of X's at 35 and a 6 at 38 because they represent the first recordings in the months of May and June, respectively. If the first recording in a given month is a three-square reversal, the numerical entry appears in the third square. Some technicians use the numbers 1 through 9 for January through September and the letters A, B, and C to represent October, November, and December. Double digit entries (i.e., 10, 11, and 12) to

Exhibit 6.1
A One-Square Reversal P & F Chart

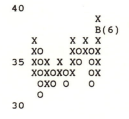

```
40
                        X
                       B(6)
          X       X X X
          XO      XOXOX
     35   XOX X   XO OX
          XOXOXOX  OX
           OXO O   O
            O
     30
```

record beginning monthly prices in the last quarter of the year are therefore avoided.

P & F Charts: The Final Product[8]

We are now ready to take the data from Table 6.1 and construct one-square and three-square reversal charts in Exhibits 6.1 and 6.2, respectively. To reiterate, the principal difference in the one-square chart stems from establishing another column any time the price of the stock changes by one square in the opposite direction. One-square reversal charts are more sensitive and occupy extra space because they require additional recordings. The three-square chart in Exhibit 6.2 is more compact. Another column is not formed unless a price reversal of at least three squares takes place. Only more meaningful price shifts appear on the chart.

A REVIEW OF PRICE SCALE BASICS

Sometimes chartists commit a common error by referring to these P & F graphs as "three-point reversal charts." Remember, three squares constitute a reversal, and there are four different price scales. Stocks priced between zero and five would be termed "three-quarter-point charts" because a reversal of three squares represents three-fourths of a point ($3 \times \frac{1}{4} = \frac{3}{4}$). Stocks selling between 5 and 20 are on a one-half-point scale, so a three-square reversal would require a price change of $1 \frac{1}{2}$ points. Thus chartists call charts on the 5 to 20 scale as "$1 \frac{1}{2}$ point charts" ($3 \times \frac{1}{2} = 1 \frac{1}{2}$). Only stocks priced between 20 and 100 would be correctly called "three-point charts" because each square value is one point. Stocks selling for 100 or more would be located on "six-point charts" ($3 \times 2 = 6$).

Fractions only appear on charts from zero to 20, and are ignored on prices of 20 or more. For example, a declining stock in a column of O's drops to $41 \frac{3}{8}$. The lowest O recorded would be in the forty-two square. An advancing stock in a column of X's reaches $64 \frac{7}{8}$. The highest X recording is placed in the 64 square because fractions are disregarded beyond 20.

Stocks charted on more than one scale are a special case and may benefit from

Exhibit 6.2
A Three-Square Reversal P & F Chart

```
40
                    X
                    B(6)
                X  X  X
                XOXOX
35  XO5OX
    4OXOX
    OXO
    O

30
```

an illustration. A stock reaches 22 in a column of X's and reverses downward. A reversal move to 19 ½ would be necessary for a three-square reversal (i.e., 21, 20, 19 ½) in a column of O's.

PSYCHOLOGY, CYCLES, AND P & F CHARTS

Before proceeding with chart patterns, some additional ideas underlying technical analysis should be introduced. Most investors are either directly or indirectly influenced by the thoughts and opinions of their peers. Their desire to conform stems from human nature, and people logically develop similar patterns of thought and action. Majority viewpoints tend to evolve and dominate mainstream thinking. However, financial success seems to be earmarked for the creative few, a minority of investors with distinctly unique mentalities and thought processes. The P & F charting system is designed to remove outside influences from the decision process. Proposed methods herein attempt to replace majority thought with individual reasoning. In other words, we substitute a systematic approach for emotional behavior.

Goethe once remarked "I find more and more that it is well to be on the side of the minority, since it is always the more intelligent." Gustave LeBon,[9] the brilliant French sociologist, argued that crowds were responsible for collective thinking that was devoid of caution, questions, and the critical spirit. He further asserted that crowds blindly accepted mass opinions with a religious fervor. LeBon maintained that a creed accepted by a collective group "is always adopted without discussion, and fervently venerated."[10]

Garfield Drew earned the respect of the Wall Street community as one of its keenest students of market psychology. Drew argued that "Every successful speculator and every student of psychology knows that the mass of people are less intelligent than the few."[11] Drew further asserted that "only 5 percent of the population think for themselves, 10 percent copy the 5 percent, and 85 percent believe what they read and hear and do what they are told."[12]

Humphrey B. Neill[13] expressed similar views when he developed the theory of contrary opinion. In his works, Neill sought to challenge opinions, popular viewpoints, and majority thinking. Neill did not contest facts. However, he did encourage the questioning of rumors, tips, gossip, and other insidious propaganda that lead people to incorrect judgments and hastily formed decisions. Neill felt that people relied too heavily on the thoughts of others and that such collectivism precluded individual success. LeBon assailed crowd conformity and collective thought by stating that "all that has gone to make the greatness of civilizations: sciences, arts, philosophies, religions, military power, etc., has been the work of individuals and not of aggregates."[14]

Themes from great writings of notable authorities in the investment arena and related fields send one resoundingly clear message—success originates from individual efforts and thoughts. The creative tend to be like Neill's "contrarians" in that they contest the popular view and challenge conventional wisdom from an often uninformed majority.

Examining a Complete Market Cycle

Psychology represents an integral part of successful investing. Cycles are another area of the utmost importance. Not surprisingly, the two are closely interrelated. Let us begin with the bottoming phase of the stock market after it has concluded a major move downward.

Near stock market bottoms, business news continues to worsen, the economy enters a recession, corporate earnings deteriorate, and the mass of investors grow increasingly pessimistic. Investment authorities refer to the bottom of the stock market cycle as the accumulation phase because professionals began to purchase shares. It is at this point we learn that the market has two underlying motivational factors—*greed* and *fear*. Greed may be depicted on charts near the highest X recordings, whereas fear is associated with the area of lowest O's. In other words, greed may be found at market tops and fear appears at bottoms. The uniformed majority seemingly does the wrong thing at key extremes in the market—they are inclined to buy at tops and sell at bottoms.

Investors accelerate their selling efforts as the economic outlook seems increasingly bleak. Large-scale liquidation of stocks by the majority of market players suggests acts of fear prompted by a high degree of pessimism. However, most investors fail to recognize that a recession offers the best opportunity to buy stocks at any time during the cycle. Interest rates are low so there are few if any attractive fixed-income alternatives for investable funds. In addition, corporate earnings generally undergo sizable declines and reach their lowest levels during economic turmoil and uncertainty.

Another consideration during the accumulation phase at market bottoms concerns the emphasis placed by the market on *expected future earnings*. Investors reap rewards by evaluating expected performance rather than current profit and loss information. A classic example is the case of Chrysler selling at $3 per share.

When investors paid $3 for Chrysler stock, they were not buying the fact that the company suffered enormous losses and mounting debt. Rather the focus of buying efforts centered on informed investor belief that Chrysler would recover and post profits in the future. Expected improvements in future earnings are greatest during a recession when profits are depressed.

Logically, rational investors should prefer to buy stocks with depressed earnings and great expectations as opposed to firms with record profits. Firms with peak performances discover that sustaining such levels is difficult at best. The path of least resistance frequently is downward, which means that unprecedented earnings are often followed by disappointment—a reinforcement of the old adage that "it is easier to follow failure than success." Or stated differently, we should "buy low and sell high."

As the stock market advances during the early phases of the bull market cycle, most investors greet the rise with skepticism. Initial reaction is one of disbelief and suspicion. As the advance continues, the bull market climbs "a wall of worry" as most investors cite economic difficulties and other fundamental measures as reasons why the rally will fail. Late in the upmove, the public recognizes the market's strength and decides to participate. Constant media attention directed toward the bull market induces public interest.

Meanwhile, the professional element watches public awareness build and begins to sell stocks into this new wave of market liquidity provided by the unsuspecting late buyers. As the market top continues to form, the economy has strengthened considerably. Economic news is positive, and fundamental research reports from investment firms are favorable. Most investors disregard the initial phases of the market decline because the obvious investment climate (earnings, dividends, sales growth, etc.) seems too positive.

Large numbers of investors doubt the market slide for most of the downmove because of strong developments in the economy. However, once fundamentals begin to deteriorate, the public majority recognizes the possibility of lower prices. Wholesale selling develops at and near market bottoms, whereas informed professionals recognize reversals in public sentiment and begin to accumulate shares.

The cycle starts over and repeats itself. Patrick Henry once commented: "I have but one lamp by which my feet are guided, and that is the lamp of experience. I know of no way of judging the future but by the past."[15] What we learn from investment psychology and cycles emphasizes the importance of technical analysis and a market timing system such as P & F charting. Given the multinational dimensions, institutional domination, and volatility of today's stock markets, timing approaches assume added importance from the standpoint of investment profits.

Investors must recognize the long-standing relationship between the stock market and the economy. Learned Wall Street traders refer to the stock market as a *barometer,* which means that movements in the stock market precede moves in the economy by several months. Lead times may vary from three or four months up to eight months or more. Late in the bull market when caution should prevail, fundamentals improve dramatically from a stronger economy and are usually misleading. Similarly, as major downmoves begin, fundamentals continue strong and often improve when selling would be prudent. Failure to devote attention to technical timing can be detrimental.

Charts provide a recurring, updated picture of investment psychology. For example, breakouts reflect an influx of buying or selling that may be tied to investor optimism or pessimism. At the end of long downmoves, downside breakouts may indicate excessive pessimism, which triggers panic liquidations. Conversely, buy signals occurring after lengthy price advances could portray speculative excesses and greed displayed by the investment majority.

The psychology of announcements also appears on P & F charts. Dividend cuts, earning disappointments, and management changes, to name a few, show up on graphs. Such negative pronouncements often cause heavy selling and "flush the stock out" by scaring investors. Panics often appear late in a cycle, and create more downside breakouts, signaling buying opportunities from deeply oversold stocks. Charts are also instrumental in reflecting changes in investment fundamentals and outlooks. As we progress into more advanced chart ideas, interrelationships between P & F charts, investment, psychology, and cycles become apparent. Readers will gradually note symptoms such as increasing numbers of false breakouts near the end of advancing cycles. Similarly, more false sell signals occur near bottoms after protracted declines.

We learn from technical analysis that price is determined from the relationships between supply and demand. However, the supply-demand concept is a given. What is responsible for changes in supply and demand? We can conclude that investment psychology and market cycles influence supply and demand. As a result, buy and sell signals form and lead to new trends.

GENERALLY ACCEPTED P & F CHART CONFIGURATIONS

Readers may wonder about the reasons for including the fundamentals of investment psychology in a book on asset allocation and market timing. Successful asset selection techniques, however, reflect underlying principles of investment psychology perhaps more than anything else. Further, most investment approaches focus their timing efforts on the asset trends within overall market and economic cycles. We can safely conclude that investment psychology and cyclical behavior heavily influence point and figure chart patterns.

We divide our coverage of point and figure chart formations into two basic categories—(1) the more conventional or generally accepted investment patterns and (2) the trading patterns which are heavily linked to investment psychology. Coverage of trading patterns follows in Chapter 8.

Four-Column Patterns

Figures 6.1 and 6.2 illustrate the *double top* and *double bottom* patterns, respectively. These patterns normally depict swift, volatile stocks or other securities in the midst of a reversal price swing.

Figure 6.1
Double Top Reversal Patterns

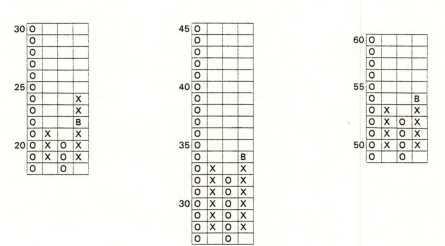

Figure 6.1(A) shows a stock with a rapid sell-off to 19 followed by a retest of the 19 area in the third column. The two bottoms suggest a support level at 19. Bottoms on P & F charts indicate areas of support, whereas previous tops reveal resistance levels. Breakouts or buy and sell signals result from price movements above previous resistance or below prior support levels. The fourth column in a double top pattern shows a buy signal and reversal in price trend with a move to 22.

When the advancing price reaches 22, it penetrates a previous top by one square and suggests the downtrend is over. We include a "B" in the illustrations to represent "buy" signals and an "S" for sell signals. A bullish trend emerges from the double top buy signal. Price action at bottoms is level with each downside move concluding at $19.

Similar buy signals occur at 34 and 55 in Figures 6.1(B) and 6.1(C). Double tops (and bottoms) are comprised of only four columns because they normally reflect the activity of volatile issues with high beta factors. Little time is required to form tops or bottoms as price reversals happen quickly. Notice the long column of O's on the left in the first column of the double top pattern. Lengthy, uninterrupted columns of O's indicate a steep decline in price and the potential for a bottom on the charts. Long declines are referred to as a "wall of O's" for future purposes.

Double bottoms are the downside counterpart to the double top. Throughout these illustrations, the bullish pattern is covered initially followed by its companion bearish formation. Double bottoms are a four-column pattern with an ex-

Figure 6.2
Double Bottom Reversal Patterns

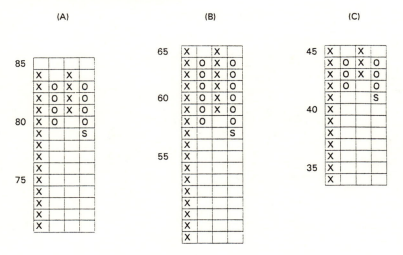

tended "wall of X's" (i.e., a lengthy, uninterrupted price advance) forming the first column. Sell signals result when a downside move penetrates the previous bottom by one square. Such downside breakouts occur at 79, 58, and 41 in Figures 6.2(A), 6.2(B), and 6.2(C), respectively.

Chartists may anticipate price reversals from double tops and bottoms because of the long, uninterrupted columns showing either sustained price declines or advances. Stocks have become oversold or overbought from emotional activity by uninformed investors. In investor psychology terms, *greed* and *fear* lead to extremes in investor sentiment and create turning points or junctures on the charts.

Bullish and bearish signal formations appear in Figure 6.3. The bullish signal formation almost replicates the double top with one exception. Bullish signal formations have rising or ascending bottoms in conjunction with a buy signal received from penetrating a previous top. Once a buy signal occurs, the combination of higher tops and higher bottoms develops, thus fitting Dow's classic definition of a bullish trend. Illustrations in Figure 6.3 differ only in the degree of ascent in the rising bottoms.

Bearish signal formations are illustrated in the bottom half of Figure 6.3 (parts D, E, and F). Sell signals evolve in the fourth columns in combination with lower tops. Dow's bear market description of lower tops and lower bottoms fits perfectly and gives the pattern its name. Implications are the same from all three examples, with only the degree of descent distinguishing the patterns.

TRIPLE TOPS AND BOTTOMS

Triple tops and bottoms represent the most basic and reliable of all P & F chart patterns. Figure 6.4 includes several examples of the six-column triple top reversal

Figure 6.3
Bullish and Bearish Signal Formations

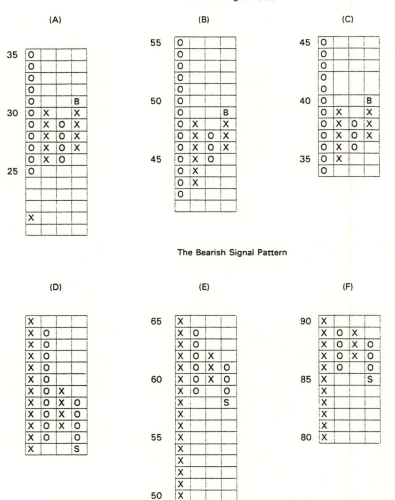

The Bullish Signal Pattern

The Bearish Signal Pattern

formation, which occurs after a sustained downside price move. A declining price is evidenced by the extended column of O's on the left-hand side of the pattern and indicates a possible juncture or turning point in the stock's price movement.

By definition, a triple top occurs after a third column of advances penetrates the two previous tops by one square. This upside breakout confirms a new bullish move. Figure 6.4 provides several variations of triple top reversal patterns, which are six-column formations. Triple-top reversals include the normal five columns

Figure 6.4
Triple Top Reversal Formations

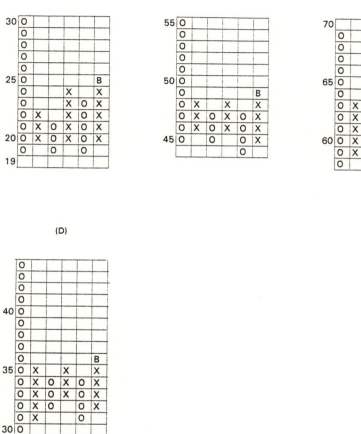

plus a "wall of O's" indicating a change in direction. Triple top reversal patterns complete junctures at pattern bottoms. Regardless of the form of triple top, one common denominator exists—we achieve a buy signal by moving one square above the two previous tops (denoted by the "B") in each illustration.

Triple tops may have level bottoms, as in Figures 6.4(A) and 6.4(C). However, more potent triple tops form in conjunction with rising or ascending bottoms [Figure 6.4(D)]. The combination of higher tops from the buy signal and ascending bottoms make for a stronger formation and subsequent upmove. Level-bottom triple tops follow in order of strength, with descending-bottom patterns [Figure 6.4(B)], usually resulting in the weakest of the triple top patterns. Volatile stocks typically build triple top configurations faster and offer the best price potential.

Figure 6.5
Triple Top Continuation Formations

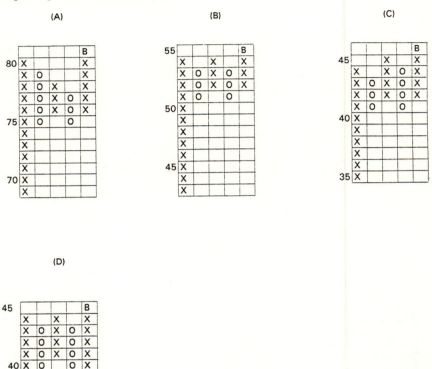

Gradual price movers require more time both to complete the patterns and price moves.

Figure 6.5 illustrates triple top continuation formations. These are five-column patterns, which also need a third rally (column of X's) to exceed two previous tops by one square for a buy signal. Bottoms may similarly be level, ascending, or descending. In contrast to the six-column triple top reversal patterns, which constitute a change in the direction of the move, triple top continuations reaffirm the uptrend. These continuations occur while the advance is in progress and merely provide an extension of the prevailing bullish trend. However, the same interpretation rules apply to both cases.

Triple bottom reversal formations mark the end of an upmove and signal the beginning of a downtrend. As seen in Figure 6.6, such patterns contain six col-

Figure 6.6
Triple Bottom Reversal Formations

(A)

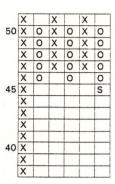

(B)

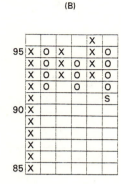

(C)

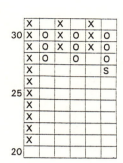

(D)

X		X		X	
X	O	X	O	X	O
X	O	X	O	X	O
60 X	O	X	O		O
X	O	X			O
X	O				O
X					S
X					
55 X					
X					
X					

umns with the "wall of X's" in the first column and the sell signal occurring in the last. Sell signals develop from a decline that penetrates the two previous bottoms by one square. Tops may be level, ascending, or descending. The most powerful triple bottom patterns generally associate with declining tops. Once sell signals take place, Dow's classic bearish definition of lower tops and lower bottoms materializes. Swift downside action normally transpires.

Figure 6.7 furnishes a look at the *triple bottom continuation pattern,* which reinforces an existing downtrend. The triple bottom continuation reflects a pause or interruption in a stock's decline before a move to lower levels. These patterns consist of five vertical columns rather than six and generate sell signals (indicated by an "S" in the illustrations) when a column of O's penetrates two previous bottoms by one or more squares.

Figure 6.7
Triple Bottom Continuation Patterns

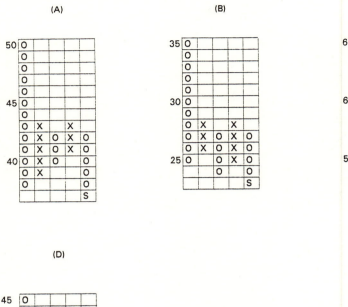

(A) (B) (C)

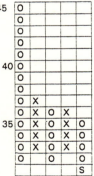

(D)

SOME MODIFIED TRIPLE TOP FORMATIONS

The *bullish catapult formation* in Figure 6.8 (parts A, B, and C) begins with the basic triple top as a nucleus. The column with the initial buy signal normally does not contain more than seven recordings. Once the bullish signal develops, a price pullback occurs almost immediately. However, these price dips are moderate and do not result in a sell signal.[16]

The trend reversal from the buy signal appears to lack conviction and doubts are fueled by a quick pullback. A marginal move above previous tops by only one or two squares precedes a swift decline back to the breakout area. The old resis-

Figure 6.8
Bullish and Bearish Catapult Patterns

(A)   (B)   (C)

```
                 B                              B                              B
           B   X                          X   X                           B   X
   X   X   X O X                          B O X                   X   X    X O X
40 X O X O X O X        50 X     X     X O X          60 X O X O X O X
   X O X O X O             X O X O X O                   X O X O X O
   X O X O X              X O X O X                      X O   O
   X O X O X              X O   O                        X
35 X O   O            45 X                           55
```

The Bearish Catapult Formation

(D)   (E)

```
   O                              X   X   X
   O                              X O X O X O X
   O                           80 X O X O X O X O
90 O X     X                      X O   O   O X O
   O X O X O X                    X       S   O
   O X O X O X O                  X           S
   O   O   O X O                  X
       S   O                   75
85       S
```

tance area is eliminated by the buy signal, and the resulting correction moves back to what is now called new support. Old resistance becoming new support on the chart illustrates the importance of not allowing doubts to alter judgments formed from reliable strategies.

Bearish catapult formations in Figure 6.8 (parts D, E, and F) are diametrically opposite to the bullish companion pattern. Timid sell signals from modest downside breakouts form with not more than seven O's in the sell-signal column. "Reflex-action" pullbacks emerge prior to the resumption of the newly created downtrend. Bearish catapult patterns illustrate the concept of old support becoming new resistance. Previous bottoms represented support levels that were eliminated by the sell signal. Prior support levels now mean newly formed resistance areas or overhead supply.

Bullish and bearish symmetrical triangles appearing in Figure 6.9 are uncertainty patterns that combine ascending bottoms with descending tops. The direction of the breakout is disguised while the formation merges toward a common point.

Figure 6.9
Bullish and Bearish Symmetrical Triangles

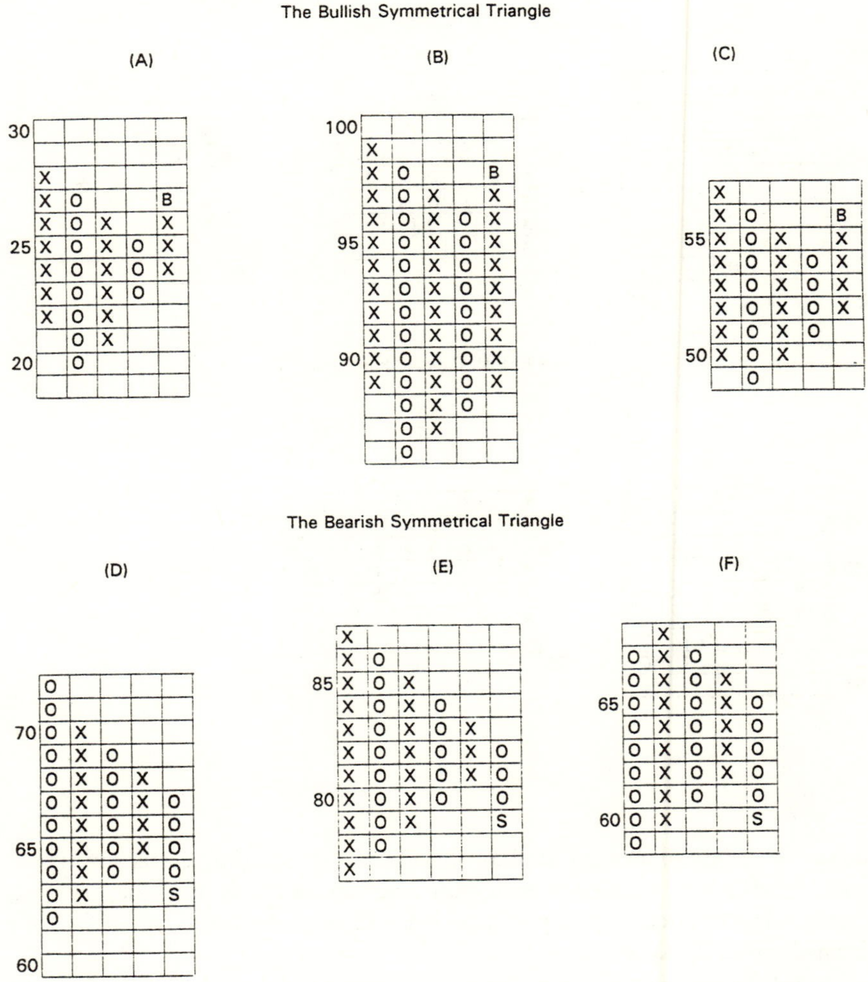

The Bullish Symmetrical Triangle

(A)

```
30
    X
    X  O              B
    X  O  X           X
25  X  O  X  O  X
    X  O  X  O  X
    X  O  X  O
    X  O  X
       O  X
20     O
```

(B)

```
100
     X
     X  O              B
     X  O  X           X
     X  O  X  O  X
95   X  O  X  O  X
     X  O  X  O  X
     X  O  X  O  X
     X  O  X  O  X
     X  O  X  O  X
90   X  O  X  O  X
     X  O  X  O  X
        O  X  O
        O  X
        O
```

(C)

```
     X
     X  O              B
55   X  O  X           X
     X  O  X  O  X
     X  O  X  O  X
     X  O  X  O  X
     X  O  X  O
50   X  O  X
        O
```

The Bearish Symmetrical Triangle

(D)

```
     O
     O
70   O  X
     O  X  O
     O  X  O  X
     O  X  O  X  O
     O  X  O  X  O
65   O  X  O  X  O
     O  X  O     O
     O  X        S
     O
60
```

(E)

```
     X
     X  O
85   X  O  X
     X  O  X  O
     X  O  X  O  X
     X  O  X  O  X  O
     X  O  X  O  X  O
80   X  O  X  O     O
     X  O  X        S
     X  O
     X
```

(F)

```
        X
     O  X  O
     O  X  O  X
65   O  X  O  X  O
     O  X  O  X  O
     O  X  O  X  O
     O  X  O  X  O
     O  X  O     O
60   O  X        S
     O
```

In the bullish triangle, a buy signal evolves from a price advance that moves above the top of the most recent column of X's. All previous tops do not have to be penetrated.

The bearish triangle culminates when a sell signal results from a downmove exceeding the bottom of the previous column of O's. Only one bottom has to be breached for a valid downside breakout. Triangle patterns generally signal a continuation of the previous price move and represent an interruption or consolidation in the overall trend.

Figure 6.10
Triple Top Patterns in Conjunction with Higher Bottoms

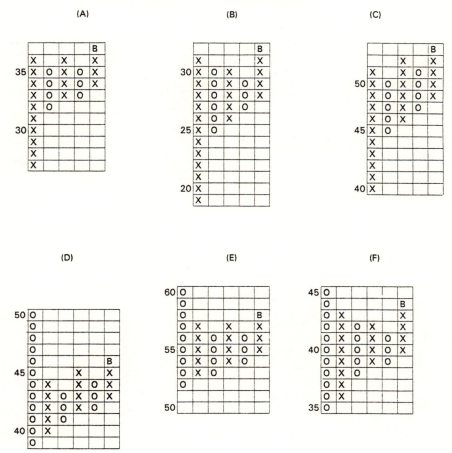

Combination triple top and bottom patterns are illustrated in Figures 6.10 and 6.11. Figure 6.10 includes both triple top continuation and reversal formations that contain ascending bottoms. The rising bottoms form in conjunction with the buy signal. Combination triple top patterns generally provide potent price moves.

Figure 6.11 reveals different types of triple bottom patterns with lower tops with a downside breakout (sell signal) yielding lower bottoms. Market players should be aware of the potential volatility associated with combination triple bottom patterns. Action must be taken quickly on short sales and long put positions because prices decline faster than they rise. Long positions should be liquidated as soon as these downside combinations are identified.

Figure 6.11
Triple Bottom Patterns in Conjunction with Lower Tops

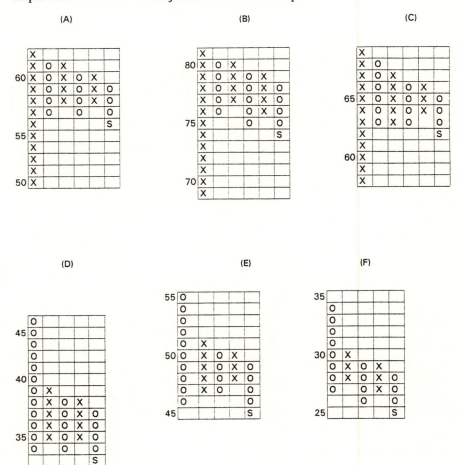

THE BEST OF THE REST

To complete our introduction of generally accepted P & F chart patterns, several key formations remain. We can easily make the argument that these are also derivatives of the basic triple top and bottom configurations. Triple tops and bottoms remain central to the discipline of chart analysis because they parallel lateral price moves or bases. Such areas denote situations where uncertainty dominates and the forces of supply and demand engage in a battle for ultimate supremacy.

Remaining chart configurations of note include broadening formations, spread triple tops and bottoms, wide bases with price breakouts in either direction, bullish and bearish signal reversed patterns, and triple tops and bottoms with pullbacks.

Broadening Formations

All versions of the bullish broadening formation display five distinct points—(1) a top, (2) a bottom, (3) a higher top, (4) a lower bottom, and (5) another top, which gives a buy signal by exceeding both of the previous tops. Bearish broadening patterns are similar in that they have a bottom, a top, a lower bottom, a higher top, and another bottom, which penetrates both earlier bottoms to generate a sell signal.

The top half of Figure 6.12 illustrates bullish broadening formations, while the bottom half includes the bearish version. Each of the five points are labeled in both sets of formations along with sell signals (S) and buy signals (B). The steeper-than-usual vertical columns advise that broadening formations demonstrate volatility.

Broadening patterns often develop during the midst of a well-defined trend and presage unusually strong price action in either direction. Such patterns also project uncertainty because chartists cannot determine the direction of the price move until the breakout occurs at the conclusion of the pattern. More often than not, however, broadening formations represent continuation patterns, which extend the life of the prevailing trend.

Figure 6.13 illustrates wider base-broadening formations. Although these expansive patterns are more complex and harder to identify, they contain the same basic characteristics as all broadening formations. The basic difference is that five points do not occur successively but over a longer period of time. Although the wide base-broadening formations consume more time and space on the charts, they possess the potential for protracted price movements in both directions.

Spread Triple Tops and Bottoms

Spread triple top and bottom patterns are an obvious derivative of basic triple tops and bottoms. The principal differences lie in the width of the patterns and the manner in which buy and sell signals are received. A buy signal originates when a column of X's exceeds two previous level tops that are not successive. In other words, the three tops must all be located at the same price level. These patterns may require from several months to several years to form.

As we see from Figure 6.14, the buy signal develops when two previous level tops are penetrated by a third price advance. Conversely, spread triple bottom sell signals evolve when a downmove penetrates two previous level bottoms that are not successive. As with spread triple tops, the length of time required for completion may vary considerably. In either case, we can formulate one fundamental rule of thumb that applies to all base formations. Volatile stocks (usually those with higher beta factors) tend to form and complete patterns more quickly.

Figure 6.12
Broadening Formations

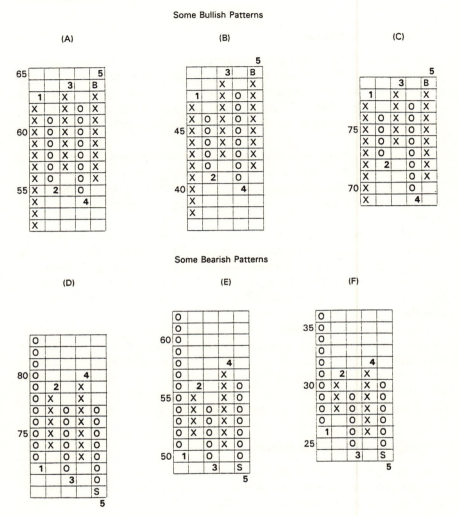

Some Bullish Patterns

(A)   (B)   (C)

Some Bearish Patterns

(D)   (E)   (F)

Less volatile issues with lower beta factors typically require more time before a breakout occurs.

Base Formations

Figure 6.15 illustrates a pair of bullish base formations consummated by upside breakouts. In Figure 6.15(A), the last rally moves above all other tops in the base at 16. Since all near-term tops have been eliminated, there is no resistance to

Figure 6.13
Wide Base-Broadening Formations

Bullish Example

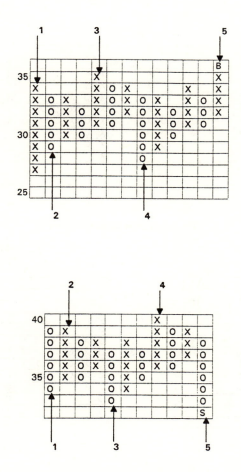

contend with in the immediate future. Upside breakouts are important because they "take out" or remove anticipated selling (overhead supply or resistance). Similarly, sell signals result from downside breakouts because expected buying or support is removed. Any price pullbacks generally return to the previous area of resistance (now called new support) or to the former area of support (now called new resistance).

Figure 6.15(B) discloses another interesting facet of breakouts. Notice that the first buy signal at 35 (B1) exceeds all adjacent tops on a near-term basis. However, a final top remains at 37 from earlier price activity. Another buy signal (B2) at 38 removes all previous tops recorded in the recent past and clears the way for a

Figure 6.14
Spread Triple Top and Bottom Formations

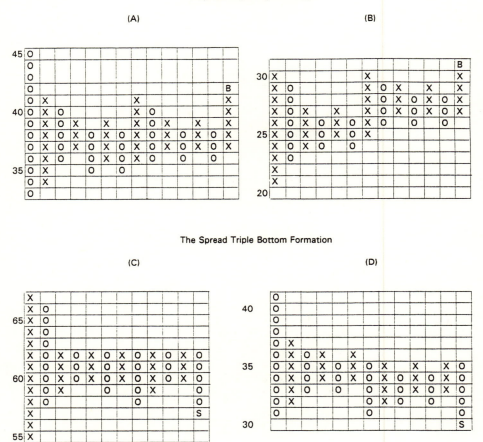

The Spread Triple Top Formation

move without visible resistance. A key point for illustration purposes focuses on the idea that wide base areas often require the penetration of more than one top to eliminate overhead supply affecting immediate price moves.

The same concepts and logic apply to downside breakouts from bearish base formations. Figure 6.16(B) gives an interesting insight for traders who wish to anticipate the sell signal and go short or buy puts earlier. Notice the pattern displays persistently lower tops prior to the sell signal. Descending tops over time warn of bearish tendencies or technical weakness in the security and frequently signal distribution. Similarly, sustainable periods of ascending bottoms suggest accumulation and advise chartists that strength is building in the stock.

Figure 6.15
Bullish Base Formations

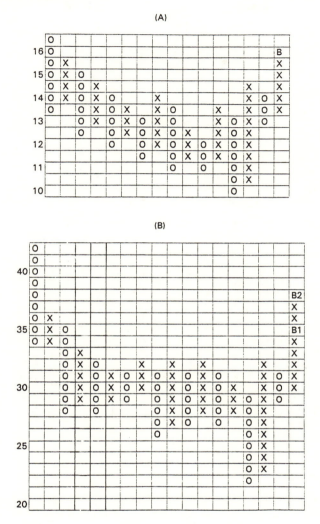

Bearish and Bullish Signal Reversed Patterns

Figures 6.17 and 6.18 serve as examples of rather unusual configurations, known as bearish and bullish signal reversed patterns, respectively. The bearish signal reversed patterns show the first six columns with descending tops and bottoms. However, the seventh column turns upward sharply and registers a buy signal by penetrating the previous top by one square. This single breakout reverses the previous pattern of lower tops and bottoms and establishes a new uptrend.

Figure 6.16
Bearish Base Formations

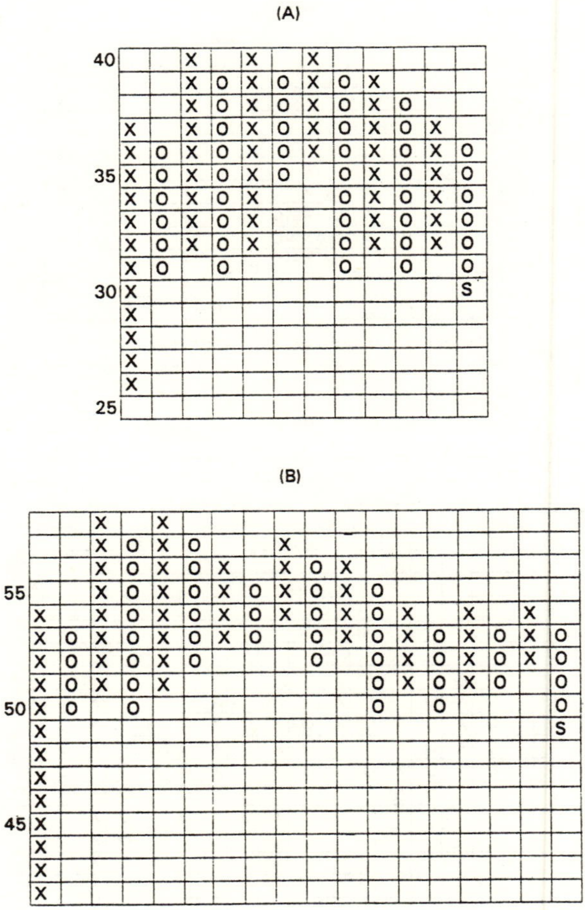

(A)

	1	2	3	4	5	6	7	8	9	10	11	12
40		X		X		X						
		X	O	X	O	X	O	X				
		X	O	X	O	X	O	X	O			
	X	X	O	X	O	X	O	X	O	X		
	X	O	X	O	X	O	X	O	X	O	X	O
35	X	O	X	O	X	O		O	X	O	X	O
	X	O	X	O	X			O	X	O	X	O
	X	O	X	O	X			O	X	O	X	O
	X	O	X	O	X			O	X	O	X	O
	X	O		O				O		O		O
30	X										S	
	X											
	X											
	X											
	X											
25												

(B)

	1	2	3	4	5	6	7	8	9	10	11	12	13	14	15	16
		X		X												
		X	O	X	O		X									
		X	O	X	O	X		X	O	X						
55		X	O	X	O	X	O	X	O	X	O					
	X	X	O	X	O	X	O	X	O	X	O	X		X		X
	X	O	X	O	X	O	X	O		O	X	O	X	O	X	O
	X	O	X	O	X	O		O		O	X	O	X	O	X	O
	X	O	X	O	X			O		O	X	O	X	O		O
50	X	O		O						O		O				O
	X															S
	X															
	X															
	X															
45	X															
	X															
	X															
	X															

Only the immediately preceding top must be penetrated for a buy signal. The trend reversal occurs swiftly with little warning and no base building.

The bullish signal reversed patterns contain six columns with steadily rising tops and bottoms. However, the seventh column declines sharply and without warning. A sell signal results as the falling price moves below the previous bottom by one square. The classic bullish expectation of higher tops and bottoms concludes quickly by the unexpected downside price reversal, and a new downtrend forms.

Triple Tops and Bottoms with Pullbacks

Triple top and bottom patterns with pullbacks are a final derivative pattern. Figure 6.19 includes both triple top reversal and continuation formations with

Figure 6.17
Bearish Signal Reversed Patterns

(B)

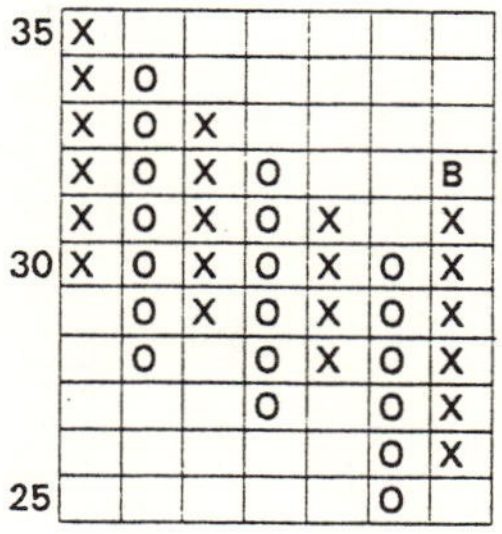

```
35 | X |   |   |   |   |   |   |   |
   | X | O |   |   |   |   |   |   |
   | X | O | X |   |   |   |   |   |
   | X | O | X | O |   |   |   | B |
   | X | O | X | O | X |   |   | X |
30 | X | O | X | O | X | O | X |
   |   | O | X | O | X | O | X |
   |   | O |   | O | X | O | X |
   |   |   |   | O |   | O | X |
   |   |   |   |   |   | O | X |
25 |   |   |   |   |   | O |
```

(B)

```
50 |   |   |   |   |   |   |   |
   | X |   |   |   |   |   |   |
   | X | O | X |   |   |   | B |
   | X | O | X | O | X |   | X |
   | X | O | X | O | X | O | X |
45 | X | O | X | O | X | O | X |
   | X | O | X | O | X | O | X |
   |   | O |   | O | X | O | X |
   |   |   |   | O |   | O | X |
   |   |   |   |   |   | O |
40 |   |   |   |   |   |   |
```

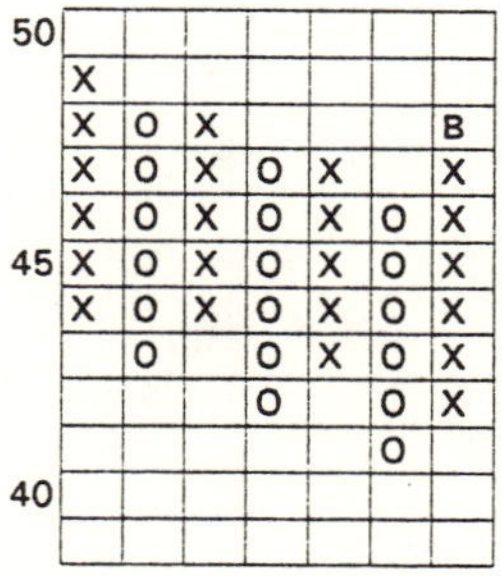

initial buy signals (B1) followed by pullbacks to the old resistance area. A second advance follows the price decline and resumes the uptrend. Some chartists refer to B2 as a second successive buy signal when it exceeds the highest point of the initial breakout column by one square.

Pullbacks simply represent a temporary interruption in trend and in no way alter your bullish or bearish interpretation from recent buy or sell signals. Whether you choose to think of these patterns as two consecutive buy (or sell) signals or as a pause in the overall trend, the message remains the same. A definitive uptrend is now in place and will continue unless a disruption in the move occurs from a sell signal. More on trend reversals follows in Chapter 7.

Figure 6.20 illustrates a pause in the downtrend with a pullback to previous support areas. The breakdown in the chart pattern develops from the initial sell signal (S1) and is reaffirmed by another downmove (S2) exceeding the low point of the column containing S1. Pullbacks in triple bottoms illustrate old support becoming new resistance when the stock tries to advance in price. Further, pullbacks offer short sellers and put buyers another opportunity to enter the stock or option if they missed their chance earlier. Whether you elect to regard triple bottoms with pullbacks as two successive sell signals or as a disruption in the

Figure 6.18
Bullish Signal Reversed Patterns

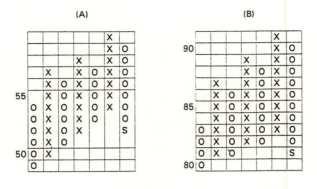

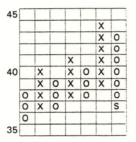

decline from the first downside breakout, your interpretation remains undaunted. The stock now functions in a bearish mode.

SUMMARY

This chapter introduced the discipline of point and figure charting along with its underlying rationale. Few investors realize that the foundation for the P & F investment approach is linked to Charles Dow. Further, point and figure charts illustrate accumulation, distribution, cycles, and investment psychology in both individual stocks and the market as a whole.

Buy signals develop when one or more previous tops are penetrated by at least one square. Similarly, sell signals evolve when one or more bottoms are breached by at least one square. Buy and sell signals are therefore received in much the same way regardless of configuration.

Many patterns are derivatives of the basic triple top and bottom formations. This chapter also places a heavy emphasis on traditional investment-oriented pat-

Figure 6.19
Triple Top Patterns with Pullbacks

(A)

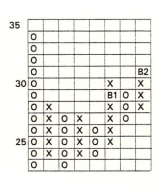

(B)

50	O								
	O								
	O								B2
	O				X		X		
	O				X	O	X		
	O				B1	O	X		
45	O		X		X	O	X		
	O	X		X	O	X	O		
	O	X	O	X	O	X			
	O	X	O	X	O				
40	O		O						

(C)

30	O								
	O								
	O								
	O								B2
	O						X		X
	O						B1	O	X
	O	X		X			X	O	X
25	O	X	O	X	O	X	O	X	
	O	X	O	X	O	X	O		
	O		O		O				
20									

(D)

55						B2
				B1		X
	X			X	O	X
	X	O	X	X	O	X
55	X	O	X	O	X	O
	X	O	X	O	X	
	X	O		O	X	
	X			O		
	X					
50	X					
	X					
	X					

(E)

40					X		B2
					X	O	X
					B1	O	X
	X		X		X	O	
	X	O	X	O	X		
35	X	O	X	O	X		
	X	O	X	O	X		
	X	O	X	O	X		
	X	O	X	O			
	X	O					
30	X						
	X						
	X						
	X						
	X						
	X						
	X						

Figure 6.20
Triple Bottom Patterns with Pullbacks

(A)

	X		X				
	X	O	X	O	X		
90	X	O	X	O	X	O	
	X	O	X	O	X	O	
	X	O	X	O	X	O	
	X	O	X	O		O	X
	X	O			S1	X	O
75	X				O	X	O
	X				O		O
	X						S2
	X						
	X						
	X						
70	X						
	X						

(B)

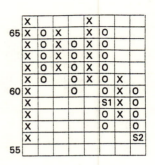

(C)

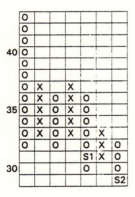

(D)

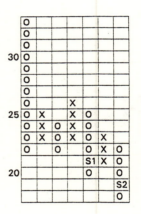

terns as opposed to trading formations stressed in Chapter 8. Chapter 7 introduces trendlines, trading techniques, price objectives, and related ideas.

NOTES

1. A. W. Cohen, *How to Use the Three-Point Reversal Method of Point and Figure Stock Market Trading,* 9th ed. (New Rochelle, N.Y.: Chartcraft, Inc., 1987).

2. Michael L. Burke, *The All New Guide to the Three-Point Reversal Method of Point and Figure Construction and Formations* (New Rochelle, N.Y.: Chartcraft, Inc., 1990).

3. Earl Blumenthal, *Chart for Profit Point and Figure Trading* (Larchmont, N.Y.: Investors Intelligence, 1975).

4. This section is adapted from other works by the authors. See Carroll D. Aby, Jr., *The Complete Guide to Point and Figure Charting* (Birmingham, Ala.: Colonial Press, 1992), 9–15.

5. Earl Blumenthal, *Chart for Profit Point and Figure Trading* (Larchmont, N.Y.,: Investors Intelligence, 1975), 9–19.

6. As we see shortly, experienced chartists learn early the importance of checking everything, particularly daily highs and lows and closing prices. Exceptions can prove costly.

7. Had we ignored the closing price in this example, we would have overlooked a near-term price reversal of several points. Such price swings often have value to traders.

8. Adapted from Aby, *The Complete Guide to Point and Figure Charting,* 13–14.

9. Gustave LeBon, *The Psychology of Socialism* (Wells, Vt.: Fraser Publishing Company, 1965).

10. LeBon, *The Psychology of Socialism,* 86.

11. Garfield A. Drew, *New Methods for Profit in the Stock Market* (Wells, Vt.: Fraser Publishing Company, 1966), 169.

12. Ibid., 170.

13. Humphrey B. Neill, *The Art of Contrary Thinking* (Caldwell, Idaho: The Caxton Printers Ltd., 1963).

14. LeBon, *The Psychology of Socialism,* 25.

15. From Patrick Henry's speech given in the Virginia House of Delegates, March 23, 1775.

16. Cohen, *How to Use the Three-Point Reversal Method of Point and Figure Stock Market Trading,* 38.

Chapter 7

INITIAL TRADING TECHNIQUES FOR ASSET ALLOCATION STRATEGIES

Thus far we have explored generally accepted chart formations in point and figure charting. Unknown to most budding chartists, however, is a common misconception—chart patterns alone are inadequate for portfolio decisions.

One of the complaints frequently directed toward P & F charts focuses on the misleading price movements and false breakouts that occur. Ideas in this chapter include trendlines, trendline revision, forecasting price objectives, zones of greed and fear, and relative strength. These approaches improve portfolio decisions and eliminate mistakes. Interpretation errors are greatly reduced by techniques introduced in this chapter and Chapter 8.

We begin with trendline construction and analysis. Remember, our approach views generally accepted chart patterns as a beginning, not an end. This and Chapter 8 contain numerous strategies that improve the reliability of charts and enhance your understanding of both P & F charts and technical analysis.

THE MAJOR UPTREND LINE

For rising stocks, the major uptrend line is known as the *bullish support* line. Trendline theory embraces the view that stocks (or other securities) tend to move along an imaginary straight line in a particular direction for long periods of time. This straight line remains intact throughout the trend (up, down, or sideways). If security prices penetrate this trendline, we have a price reversal. A directional shift in the price move occurs, and a new trend forms.

Let us examine the AlliedSignal chart in Figure 7.1. A buy signal forms in June 1991 from a bullish signal formation and turns the trend upward. Once a buy

Figure 7.1
The Bullish Support Line

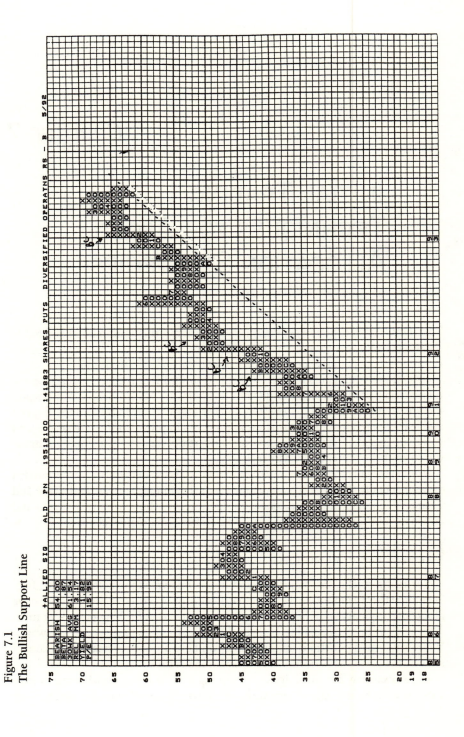

138

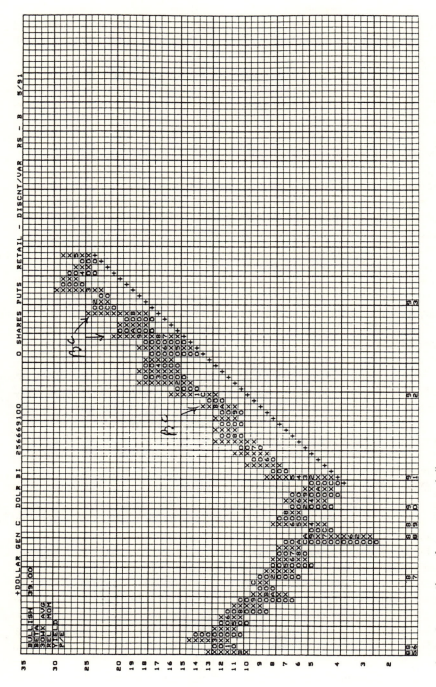

Source: Courtesy Chartcraft, Inc., New Rochelle, N.Y.

139

signal occurs, we draw the bullish support line by dropping one square below the lowest O in the base or bottom. Draw a 45-degree line connecting successively higher corners on the graph. This bullish support line may not be constructed until a buy signal develops, thus indicating a reversal in the stock's price trend. Otherwise, the prevailing downtrend line continues for the stock.

Both examples in Figure 7.1 illustrate the tendency of security prices to follow established trendlines. Several key points of understanding may be found in the AlliedSignal and Dollar General charts. First, look for additional buying opportunities when stock prices fall to the trendline and then resume their advance. Bullish support lines provide price support and serve as buying opportunities for late investors who missed earlier chances.[1]

Second, both AlliedSignal and Dollar General reveal sell signals slightly above the bullish support line. As long as the stock price remains above the major uptrend line, the primary trend is considered bullish. Sell signals immediately above the bullish support line generally prove to be false and misleading. Investors should disregard such sell signals unless a break is recorded in the bullish support line (this is covered shortly).

Third, traditional theorists contend that the long-term bullish support line should remain in its original form throughout the life of the uptrend. In other words, there should be no revision or modification of the established line. We disagree with this contention and discuss it shortly. However, the major problem with original bullish support lines deals with volatile stocks that undergo rapid price advances and become too far removed from the trendline. Investors become out of touch with current developments in the stock as a result of dated trendlines.

Fourth, selling short or buying puts on stocks with sell signals well above the bullish support line may be considered. However, such activity should be reserved for those who recognize the inherent risks in going against the grain of an advancing stock. You should note that in each of our examples on the bullish support line, any short positions assumed from sell signals above the trendline would have reversed quickly. In addition to little or no profits, you would have been "stopped out" of most positions.

Only stocks considerably above the bullish support line should be evaluated for trading or "scalping" on the short side of the market. Longer-term profit horizons are discouraged unless the bullish support line is broken, thus signaling a reversal in trend.

Finally, bullish support lines must often be drawn on charts with multiple bottoms, all of which are at or near the low point or lowest O. Such is the case with the Dollar General chart. Where multiple bottoms are involved, drop one square below the most recent O and draw a 45-degree line intersecting successively higher corners of the graph. Sometimes the most recent O does not represent precisely the low point in the formation. However, selection of the square below the latest "low O" is more functional and the trendline will not be drawn through the middle of the recordings that form the bottom.

Figure 7.2 contains a chart of Compaq Computer, which provides a textbook

Figure 7.2
Bullish Support Line with Multiple Bottoms

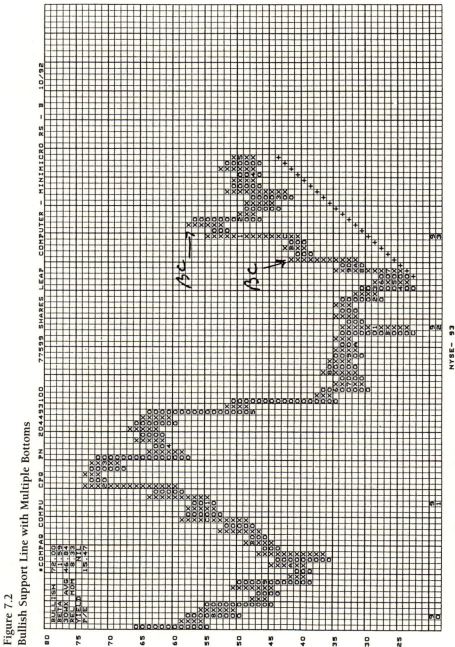

Source: Courtesy Chartcraft, Inc., New Rochelle, N.Y.

illustration of drawing a bullish support line with multiple bottoms. Although two previous bottoms appear at 23 (the lowest O), we draw the uptrend from one square below the most recent O at 24.

Compaq's chart shows breakouts above previous tops from 35 to 38 in October 1992. The advance develops swiftly and carries the price well above the trendline. True to form, however, a retracement begins in January and February of 1993 to correct speculative excesses and return the stock toward the trendline. Although critics of technical analysis try to refute fundamental charting principles, stocks repeatedly fluctuate along a path approximating a straight line.

Trend Reversals

Trendlines do not remain intact forever, however. Figure 7.3 furnishes two examples of trendline penetrations that lead to price reversals. In the case of Pacificorp, a January 1985 buy signal at 13 sets the advance in motion. Given a situation involving multiple bottoms, the trendline is drawn from one square below the most recent O at 8. The bull market trend continues until 1993 with the bullish support line solidly intact.

Let us examine several relevant aspects of the Pacificorp chart. An October 1987 sell signal leads to a correction ending on the bullish support line as the penetration fails to take place. Another sell signal surfaced in July 1990, but concluded immediately above the uptrend line. However, the stock begins to lose momentum, and another downward thrust in November 1992, almost breaks the trendline. In February 1993, a sell signal at 18 penetrates the bullish support line and inaugurates a downtrend for the stock.

When major uptrend lines are broken with a sell signal accompanying the downmove, the penetration of the bullish support line is valid. The combination of a downside breakout (i.e., sell signal) and breach of the uptrend line results in a trend reversal. All long positions should be closed out. Speculators should give some thought to short sales or puts. Once the sell signal and valid trendline break are complete, a downside trendline should be constructed (to be covered shortly).

Federal Paper Board ends a downmove in October 1990. The stock then receives a buy signal at 16 and allows the establishment of a new uptrend line. However, a January 1993 sell signal at 23 breaks the bullish support line and a new downtrend line is formed. Chart illustrations in Figure 7.3 indicate reversals of uptrends now entering new downmoves.

Both examples also should make aspiring chartists aware of sizable, lateral price moves. Wide base patterns that culminate in upside breakouts ordinarily confirm the process of accumulation. Similarly, lengthy lateral price action completed by downside breakouts often signify distribution. Pacificorp and Federal Paper Board reveal distributional activity as the informed elements sell their positions after pronounced upmoves. Beware of long base patterns after sizable advances because the downside risk increases. On the other hand, take a hard look at extensive bases after long declines. Buy signals confirm the latter phases of accumulation.

Figure 7.3
Valid Penetration of the Bullish Support Line

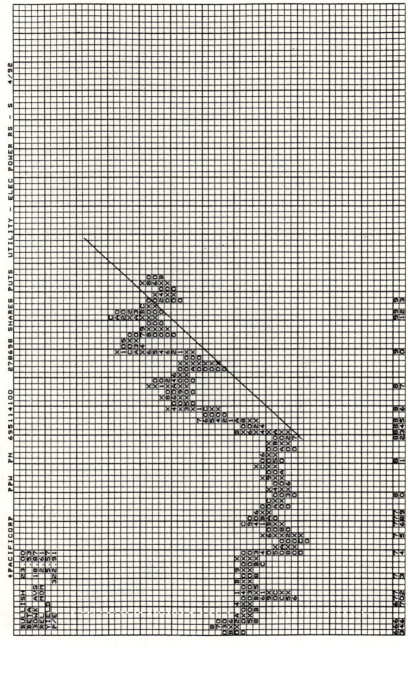
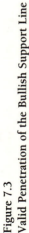

Figure 7.3 Continued

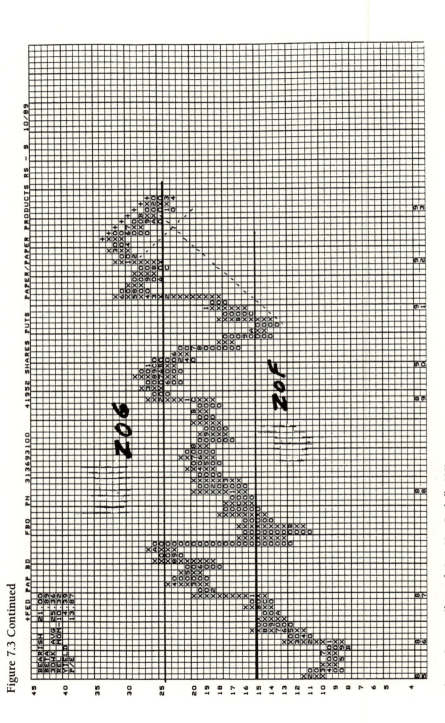

Source: Courtesy Chartcraft, Inc., New Rochelle, N.Y.

Good upside potential and a favorable risk-reward ratio combine for attractive investment potential.

False Trendline Penetrations

To distinguish between valid and false penetrations of the bullish support line, let us examine the Interpublic chart in Figure 7.4. The long-term bullish support line is breached in both 1988 and 1990. In both cases, however, no sell signal emerges. At the time of each downside penetration, a buy signal remains intact. The uptrend should continue without a reversal unless a sell signal occurs.

We regard the two penetrations as false[2] or ostensible because no downmove exceeded a previous bottom in either case. By definition, stock prices tend to move *approximately* along an imaginary straight line for long periods of time. Such "minor" violations do not alter our judgment or chart interpretation.

To finalize the distinction between valid and false breaks in the bullish support line, we can proceed further on the Interpublic chart. In February 1993, a downmove to 28 occurs on the strength of a sell signal and marks a valid break of the uptrend.

Immediately following this valid penetration, we should observe that a "pullback" took place. Since stocks tend to follow trendlines for long periods, a natural reaction is for the stock to undergo a "reflex" action by moving back to the trendline. This pullback or "knee-jerk rally" attempt does not alter your interpretation of the chart, nor does it change the fact that a new downtrend now dominates. Pullbacks are commonplace and must be understood to avoid interpretational errors.

In the Allergan chart, a bullish support line formed in 1990. By early 1992, a basing action takes place on the chart and violates the uptrend line. As chartists, however, we would remain cautiously bullish on Allergan because no sell signal develops. Since no downmove drops below a previous bottom, the breach of the bullish support line at this point must be regarded as ostensible.

THE BEARISH RESISTANCE LINE

The *bearish resistance line* represents the major downtrend line in point and figure charting. Interpretation and construction of the bearish resistance line are precisely opposite to that relating to the bullish support line. Figure 7.5 provides two interesting illustrations of how the trendline remains in effect for long periods of time.

The T2 (T Squared) Medical example constitutes a classic bearish resistance line. The stock tops out at 67, so we move one square above the highest X in the topping process and draw a 45-degree line connecting successively lower corners on the graph. As with many other medical stocks, the decline has been precipitous. T2 Medical drops well below the trendline but rallies back toward it in late 1992 in the 25–27 area. The stocks's rally attempt bounces off the bearish resis-

Figure 7.4
Valid versus False Penetration of Uptrends

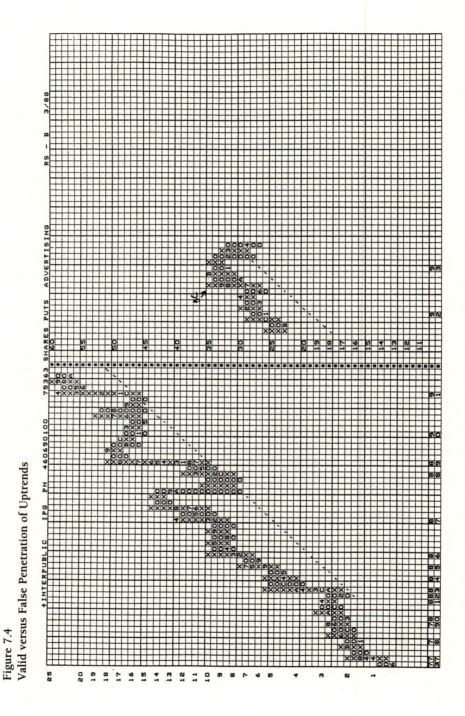

Figure 7.4 Continued

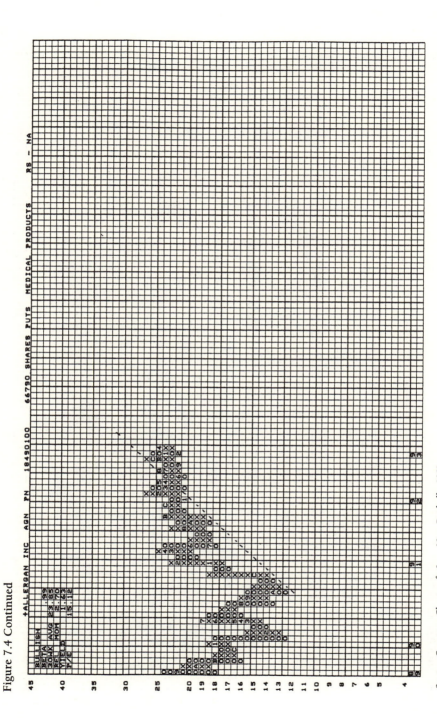

Source: Courtesy Chartcraft, Inc., New Rochelle, N.Y.

Figure 7.5
The Bearish Resistance Line

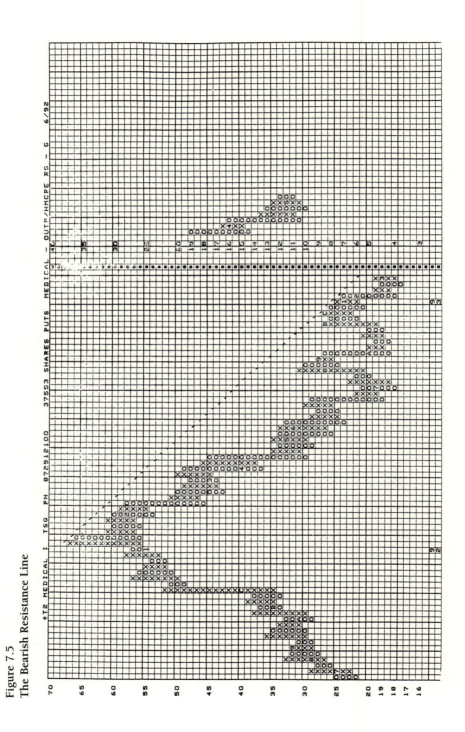

148

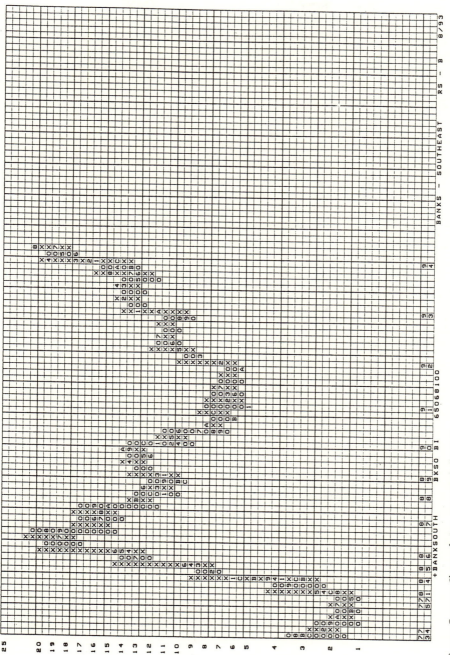

tance line and resumes its descent. Later in 1993, T2 reached the $6 area and continued its difficulties.

Banksouth is very similar to T2 Medical in terms of constructing the trendline. During the downtrend, however, Banksouth attempts to rally on the strength of a buy signal in April 1989. The rally fails and the stock continues its downmove. A valid reversal does occur in February 1992 at 9 when Banksouth breaks out above the base in conjunction with a penetration of the bearish resistance line.

Some Key Principles

Several points require mention. When stocks "bounce off" the bearish resistance line following a rally attempt, an additional opportunity to sell short or liquidate long positions presents itself. All points along the downtrend line indicate potential resistance where the stock should encounter further difficulty.

Buy signals that occur close to the bearish resistance line are suspect and should be disregarded. Decisions to acknowledge buy signals well below the bearish resistance line should be reserved for short-term traders seeking a few points. Inordinate amounts of risk exist when buying stocks below long-term downtrend lines because such purchases are going against the flow of the stock.

Finally, penetrations of bearish resistance lines should be recognized as valid only when accompanied by a buy signal to confirm an actual reversal of trend. Major downtrend line breaks not supported with buy signals are false and prove to be misleading to chartists trying to identify directional shifts.

Valid Versus Ostensible Penetrations

The Tenneco chart in Figure 7.6 enables us to recognize both valid and false penetrations of the bearish resistance line. In September 1991 (indicated by the number "9"), Tenneco rallies to the trendline and then retreats. However, a second attempt to advance occurs in October 1991 when the stock price reaches 42.

The bearish resistance line is violated by one square without the strength of an existing buy signal. Failure to move above the trendline with a buy signal in force means the penetration must be regarded as false or ostensible. A valid penetration develops in February 1992 in conjunction with an upside breakout at 38.

As an added insight, let us refer to both the Tenneco and Inland Steel charts to establish the bearish resistance line. In each case, multiple tops form during the topping out process. We move one square above the most recent "highest X" and draw a line intersecting successively lower corners on the graph. Although the most recent X may not mark precisely the highest point in the top, it serves as the most appropriate place from which to originate the trendline. In this way, we avoid the problem of trendlines through the middle of the chart pattern.

Two key trading ideas for chartists develop from the penetrations on the Tenneco chart. Once the advance failed following the false penetration, the stock price continued its downside movement with a precipitous drop. Also, once Ten-

Figure 7.6
Valid and Ostensible Penetration of the Bearish Resistance Line

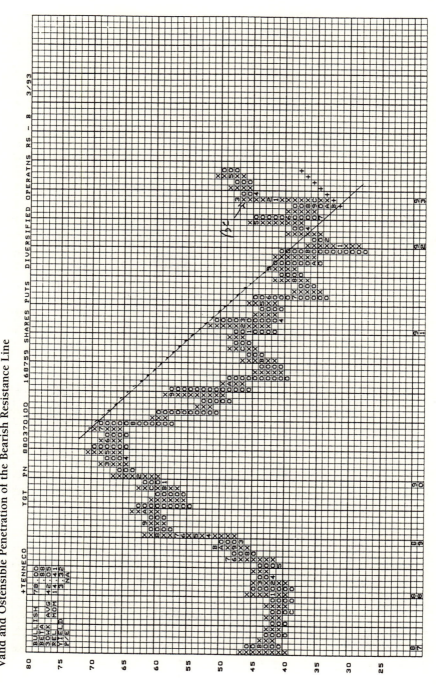

Figure 7.6 Continued

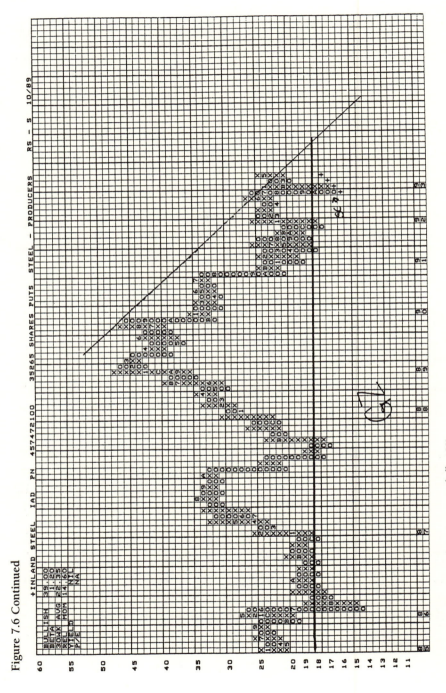

Source: Courtesy Chartcraft, Inc., New Rochelle, N.Y.

neco entered its bullish movement following the valid penetration, the stock retraced or corrected with the price falling back to the previously established bearish resistance line. Such pullbacks are commonplace and stem from the tendency of stocks to cling to a straight line (trend line) during a particular path of movement. Tenneco found support during its retracement from the old resistance line.

Something to Think About

One interesting point should be noted on the Inland Steel chart. The stock moves above the bearish resistance line in June 1992 with a newly formed buy signal. However, this new breakout breaches the downtrend line by only one square. The stock then declines abruptly and moves to new lows. Why did such a failure occur?

Many veteran chartists argue that legitimate penetrations should exceed established trendlines by more than one square to ensure validity. Such an argument contains considerable merit in a large number of cases. If the trendline must be penetrated by two squares in either direction to ensure legitimacy, no problem is created. Remember, the stock is only beginning a new trend at this point. What difference does one recording make in timing transactions? Better safe than sorry.

REVISING THE BULLISH SUPPORT LINE

A potential indictment of P & F charting relates to the traditionalist view that major trendlines should remain in their initial form until broken. In effect, a trend reversal cannot develop until the original line is violated. The major problem that may arise focuses on volatile stocks that distance themselves from established trendlines rather easily. We do not subscribe to the traditional view, so we are offering what we believe to be a substantial improvement.[3] To illustrate, let us refer to Figure 7.7.

In the Sbarro chart, the original bullish support line (BSL) forms in the regular manner. However, the stock began a steep, almost vertical price move and becomes too far removed from the BSL. In effect, the trendline ceases to be sensitive and current enough to be useful. When trendlines are relegated to a point of being out of touch, they can no longer be effective for interpretation and reallocation decisions.

Our initial uptrend line (BSL 1) begins from a bottom in the 6 ½ to 7 area. However, the stock rapidly advances to 34. The original BSL 1 quickly becomes out of touch with current developments surrounding the stock. In September 1990, Sbarro receives a sell signal well above BSL 1 and undergoes a minor correction. We disregard sell signals above the BSL because they are contrary to the primary trend of the stock and generally of little use. However, we believe that such sell signals offer an excellent opportunity to revise the original BSL.

These new bullish support lines commence from one square below the lowest O in the sell signal column. The end result is to keep this major uptrend line

Figure 7.7
The Bullish Support Line Revised

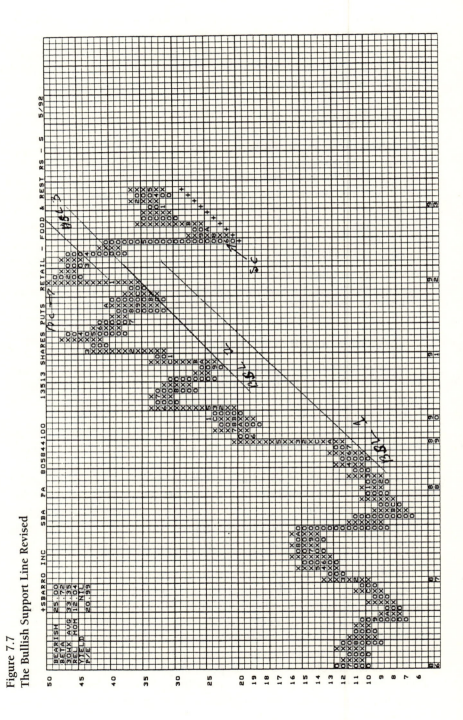

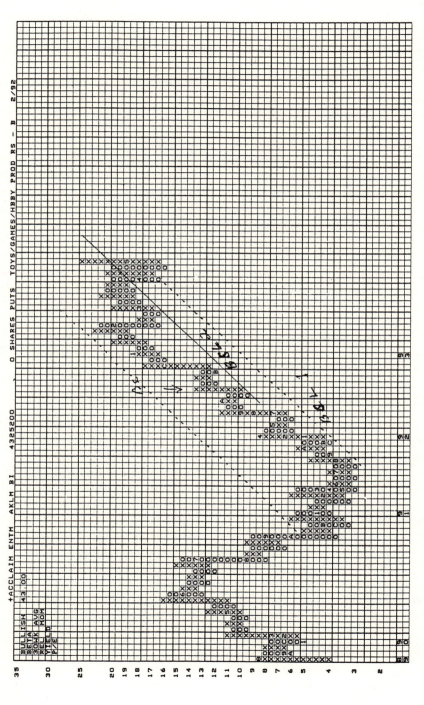

Source: Courtesy Chartcraft, Inc., New Rochelle, N.Y.

more responsive to current market conditions. To illustrate, let us refer to the September 1990 sell signal on the Sbarro chart in Figure 7.7. We draw the line from one square below the lowest O in the sell signal column with a straight edge. Ideally, all trendlines should be drawn so they extend across the entire graph because of their value as future support (or resistance) levels.

In November 1991, we can observe a false or ostensible penetration of BSL 2 during a corrective phase of Sbarro's bullish trend. However, in March 1992, we receive another sell signal and establish BSL 3. A valid penetration of BSL 3 materializes one month later (April 1992) at 44 because the sell signal remains intact. Another sell signal at 43 confirms the earlier break.

What is the principal advantage of trendline revision? Not only have we made the trendline more responsive, but we have received a much earlier warning about the forthcoming reversal in trend that Sbarro is about to experience. We liquidate our long position in the stock in the 43–44 area as opposed to some ten points lower when the decline breaches the initial BSL. Those chartists who fail to update BSLs often receive little or no warning until later in the downtrend. Updating the BSL can result in huge profit differentials.

All revised trendlines are subject to the same review and interpretation. Trendline revisions do not alter the rules or guidelines already discussed. However, the updating offers a significant timing advantage in most cases because decisions can be made much more quickly or earlier. This method for revising trendlines is vital to asset allocation because the technique applies to both stocks and the general market. Major turning points in the broad market can be identified much sooner by using similar approaches.

REVISING THE BEARISH RESISTANCE LINE

Revising the bearish resistance line (BRL) takes place each time a buy signal occurs below the original downtrend line. Similar timing benefits and profit advantages accrue from the updating. To illustrate, let us refer to Figure 7.8.

The BMC Software chart shows that the stock reaches a peak at 84 and then begans a rather precipitous descent. The decline accelerates and becomes greatly distanced from BRL 1 currently in place. However, two buy signals in March 1993 enable us to establish BRL 2 and BRL 3. We move one square above the highest X in each of the buy signal columns and draw 45-degree lines intersecting successively lower corners on the graph. We receive a valid upside penetration of BRL 3 at 51 and an early signal to buy the stock. Timing and profit advantages emanate from keeping the BRL more current. Similar activity and results appear on the Rochester Savings Bank chart where two revisions BRL 2 and BRL 3 update BRL 1 and furnish early warnings of a trend reversal.

MINOR TRENDLINES

Minor trendlines provide another means of keeping BSLs and BRLs more current. Intermediate- and short-term uptrend and downtrend lines lack the signif-

Figure 7.8
Revising the Bearish Resistance Line

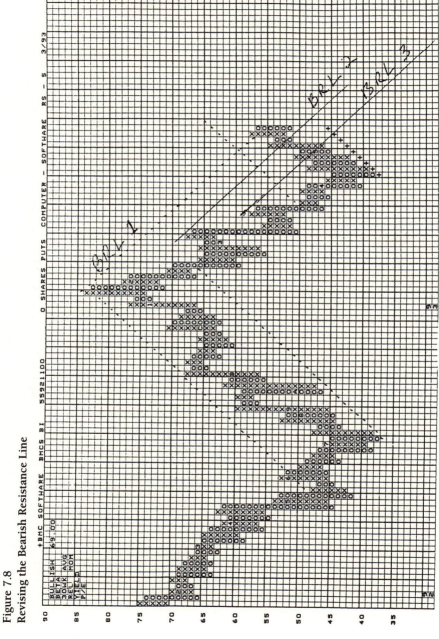

Figure 7.8 Continued

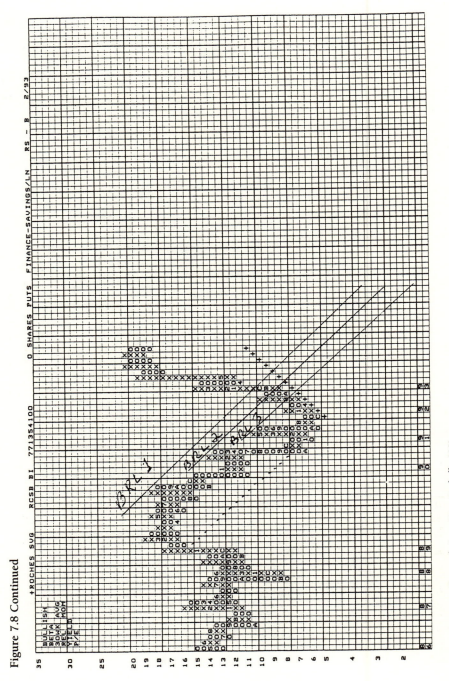

Source: Courtesy Chartcraft, Inc., New Rochelle, N.Y.

icance and permanence of the major lines, but their interpretation remains the same. Valid breaks of so-called minor trendlines often warn of reversals well in advance of major trendline strategies. Let us examine them briefly.[4]

Intermediate Trend Lines

Figure 7.9 reveals several illustrations of the *intermediate uptrend line* (IUTL). In contrast to major trendline revisions (BSLs and BRLs), IUTLs serve the same purpose but contain no sell signal. The example at the top of Figure 7.9 shows that four rising or ascending points in succession (O, X, O, X or 1, 2, 3, 4) in a 45-degree straight line form an IUTL.

Intermediate trendlines (ITLs) form during the course of a trend and contain neither a buy or sell signal. Four successive points in ascending (IUTL) or descending order (intermediate downtrend lines or IDTLs) constitute intermediate trends. From Figure 7.9, both the Johnston Industries and Centex Corporation charts have IUTLs that show valid penetrations and indicate technical damage in the charts. Early warning signals encourage prudent chartists to assume near-term bearish postures until more evidence appears on the charts. Centex demonstrates the "pullback effect" after the IUTL is violated. However, you should regard the stock cautiously during the short term.

Although IUTLs are not as permanent or significant as the major trendlines, nonetheless a breach of intermediate trendlines suggests the stock has incurred problems and will require time before resuming any trend. Longer-term investors may choose to ignore intermediate-term trend reversals so long as the major trendline remains intact. However, valid penetrations of ITLs often require longer-than-usual periods of consolidation to recover from the technical damage.

Figure 7.9 also includes two other interesting examples of IUTLs. The First American Bank and the First Bank System both have IUTLs that contain six points. What does an IUTL with more than four points mean? These illustrations say two things. Four points are a minimum for ITLs, but more than four happen fairly often. Also, ITLs with more than four points in succession may be better formed, stronger, and longer in duration. Penetrating ITLs with larger numbers of successive points could be very meaningful and imply more serious technical damage if the line is broken.

Figure 7.10 gives examples of the intermediate downtrend line. Again, no sell signals are needed for ITLs. Four successive descending points (X, O, X, O or 1, 2, 3, 4) in a 45-degree straight line furnish an IDTL.

Charts with IDTLs in Figure 7.10 depict the general advantages of updating major trendlines with minor ones, particularly earlier warning signals and greater profits. However, both Browning Ferris and the First Union Realty charts confirm that interpretation remains the same for all trendlines with the same prevailing risks and rewards. These two charts show marginal buy signals (a move above the previous top by only one square) and penetrate the IDTLs by a single square. Both stocks immediately reverted back downward in a display of weakness.

Figure 7.9
The Intermediate Uptrend Line (IUTL)

O							X	
O						X	X	
O						X	O	X	(IUTL)
O						X	O	X
O				X		X	O	X
O				X	O	X	O
O				B	O	X	(4)
O	X		X	X	O	(3)
O	X	O	X	O	X	(2)
O	X	O	X	O	X	(1)	(O, X, O, X)
O	X	O	X	O
O	X	O
O	X
O	

Intermediate Uptrend Lines (IUTLs)
are a means of updating bullish
support or major uptrend lines--
they form with no sell signal. IUTLs
require four points to establish--
1, 2, 3, 4 or OXOX in successively
higher order

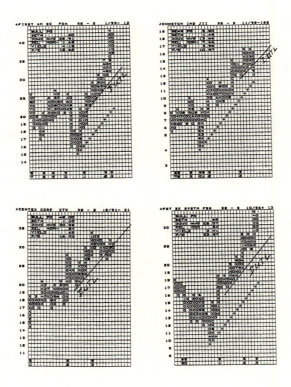

Source: Courtesy Chartcraft, Inc., New Rochelle, N.Y.

Figure 7.10
The Intermediate Downtrend Line (IDTL)

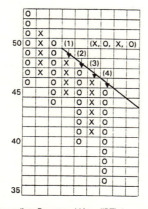

Intermediate Downtrend Lines (IDTLs) serve to
update bearish resistance lines and make trend
lines more sensitive--IDTLs form without a buy
signal and require four points to establish--
1, 2, 3, 4 or XOXO in successively descending
order.

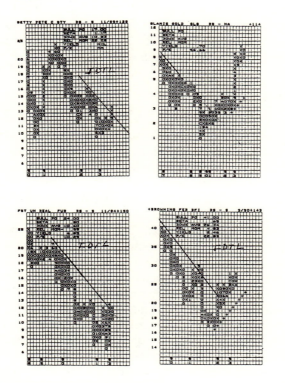

Source: Courtesy Chartcraft, Inc., New Rochelle, N.Y.

Short-Term Trendlines

Short-term trendlines (STTLs) are shown in Figures 7.11 and 7.12. Figure 7.11 includes examples of the short-term uptrend line (STUL), which forms without a sell signal. In contrast to IUTLs, STULs require only two successive ascending points (O, X or 1, 2) at a 45-degree straight line.

STTLs provide valuable updates of major trendlines and are more plentiful than ITLs or revised major lines. In addition, short-term trendlines provide early warning signals and timing advantages that yield profits to the disciplined chartists.[5] In the Capital Cities Broadcasting stock, we have four STULs to update and support the major BSL. A valid penetration of STUL 4 is about to transpire, which would turn the stock negative on a short-term basis. Penetration of STLs does not carry the same weight or have the strong implications that a break in an intermediate or major trendline does. However, Capital Cities stock would need some time to recover from the technical damage incurred from a short-term reversal in the stock. In the case of Caesars World, a break in STUL 2 was brief and required little time for recovery.

Figure 7.12 shows the basis for establishing short-term downtrend lines (STDLs) with only two successive descending points required (X, O or 1, 2). No buy signal emerges in the formation of the trendline. For illustration purposes, let us refer to the Keystone chart. In this case, a valid penetration of the STDL provides a buy signal well in advance of a movement above more permanent trendlines. Timing advantages and profits resulted.

USING CHANNEL LINES

Another type of trendline includes the *bullish resistance* and *bearish support* lines, companion supplements to the bullish support and bearish resistance lines, respectively. Some chartists refer to them as minor trendlines, but perhaps a more appropriate description is the term channel lines. These channel lines parallel the major or long-term trendlines and define a path or pattern of movement that generally contain the stock price. Chartcraft often refers to these lines as corollary trendlines.

The Arrow Electric chart in Figure 7.13 shows a bottom formed from 1989 to 1991, with a buy signal developing in January 1991. Once the buy signal reverses the downtrend, a bullish support line can be established. To construct the bullish resistance line, we locate the first wall of O's, which must protrude above the adjacent column of X's by at least two squares.

We then move one square above the highest X in the adjoining X or right-hand column and draw a 45-degree line intersecting succesively higher corners of the graph and precisely parallel to the bullish support line. Once both lines are constructed, we have a channel or prescribed path in which the stock price fluctuates.

The Adaptec chart of Figure 7.13 provides another illustration of the bullish resistance line. Most bullish resistance lines do not remain intact for as long as

Figure 7.11
The Short-Term Uptrend Line (STUL)

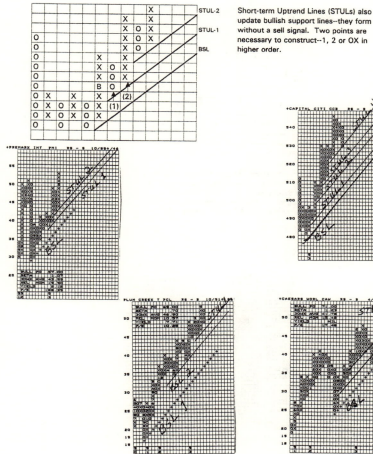

Short-term Uptrend Lines (STULs) also update bullish support lines--they form without a sell signal. Two points are necessary to construct--1, 2 or OX in higher order.

Source: Courtesy Chartcraft, Inc., New Rochelle, N.Y.

Figure 7.12
The Short-Term Downtrend Line (STDL)

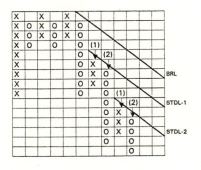

Short-term Downtrend Lines (STDLs) keep the
bearish resistance line attuned to current
price developments--they are drawn with no
buy signal. Two points are necessary to
draw them--1, 2 or XO in descending order.

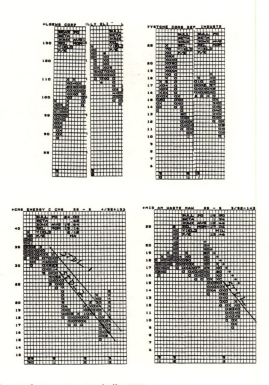

Source: Courtesy Chartcraft, Inc., New Rochelle, N.Y.

Figure 7.13
The Bullish Resistance Line

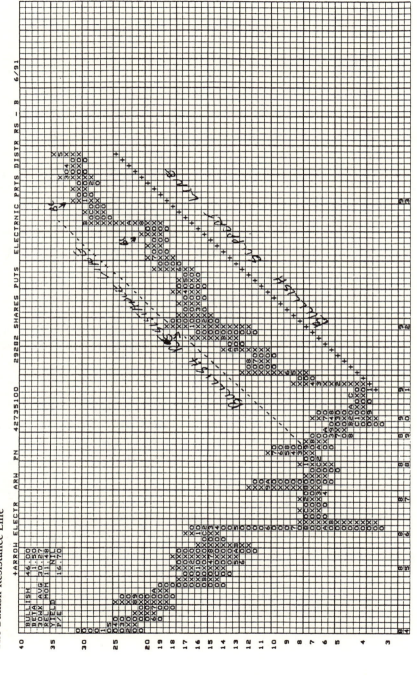

Figure 7.13 Continued

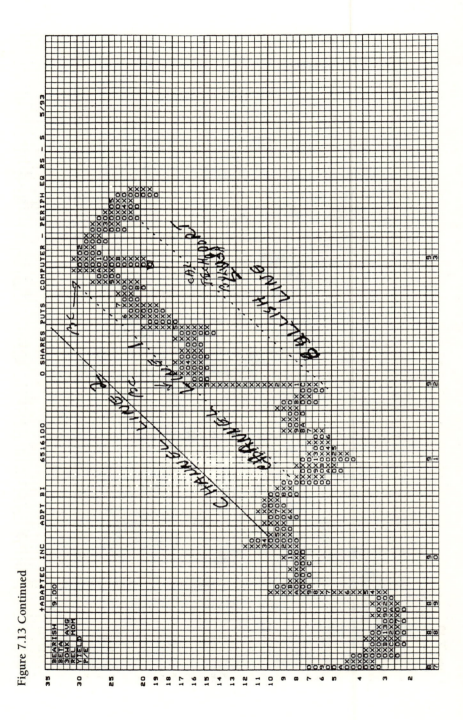

166

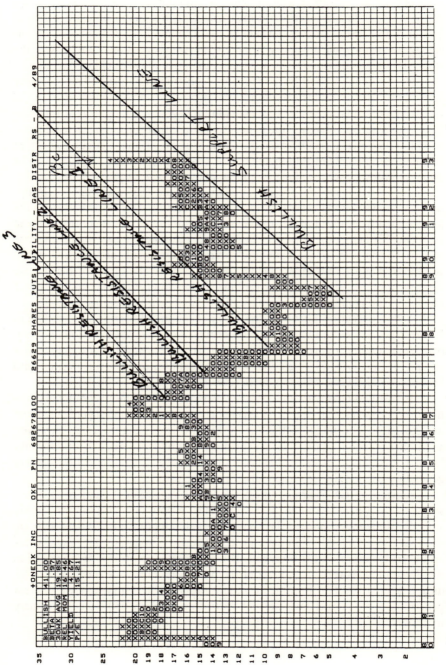

Source: Courtesy Chartcraft, Inc., New Rochelle, N.Y.

167

bullish support lines; in fact, channel lines are rather easily penetrated. Penetrations of channel lines are less meaningful than trendlines. A general rule of thumb pertaining to bullish resistance line breaks suggests the establishment of a second line once the first is broken. Generally, two channel lines contain a large percentage of major price advances. If more than two channel lines are broken, the stock should be entering the final stages of the price move in either direction.

From the Adaptec chart we learn how to construct multiple bullish resistance lines. Once the first bullish resistance line is broken, we locate the next wall of O's, which extends above the adjacent column of X's on the right by at least two O's. Once a second channel line is penetrated in either direction, increased vulnerability becomes a factor and either long or short positions should be closed out. For purposes of illustration, the Oneok chart in Figure 7.13 shows how three different bullish resistance lines would be drawn if necessary.

Figure 7.14 contains the second corollary trendline known as the bearish support line. We draw the bearish support line by locating the first wall of X's to the left. To qualify as a wall of X's, this lengthy column of advances must include at least two X's below the lowest O in the next column. We can then move one column to the right to the adjoining column of O's. Find the lowest O in the column and move one square below that O to mark the origin of the bearish support line. We may then draw a 45-degree line intersecting succesively lower corners of the graph and precisely parallel to the bearish resistance line.

ICN Pharmaceutical illustrates the break of the initial bearish support line in Figure 7.14. Once the first penetration occurs, we locate the next long column of X's and establish another corollary line. To reiterate, when prices exceed a second channel line, the stock reaches an oversold (or overbought) position and becomes highly susceptible to a price reversal.

Most volatile stocks with high beta factors require one or more additional channel lines. However, one channel line generally encompasses more gradually moving stocks as illustrated in the Arrow Electric chart, Figure 7.13. However, additional bearish support lines may be more critical than extra bullish resistance lines because stock prices decline faster than they rise. Therefore, more volatility generally exists on the downside rather than the upside.

In contrast to ICN Pharmaceutical, the Policy Management chart gives an example of an oversold extreme on the downside. A bottom begins to form shortly after the downmove violates the second bearish support line. Traders who are "bottom fishing" could begin partial accumulations of long positions once a second bearish support line is breached. Three bearish support lines are included in the illustration. Surprisingly, none of them held the downside move, which indicates a rapid decline from acute selling pressure. Remember, however, that penetrations of channel lines are not viewed as seriously as breaks in primary trendlines.

ZONES OF GREED, ZONES OF FEAR

Some earlier remarks focused on *greed* and *fear* serving as underlying factors in gauging technical weakness and strength in the stock market. We spend more time in Chapter 8 on identifying well-defined extremes of greed and fear as they relate to the aggregate stock market. However, identifying overbought and oversold areas in individual stocks is of equal importance. In order to evaluate properly overbought and oversold issues, we use *zones of greed* and *zones of fear*, respectively. When an individual stock's price reaches one of these areas, strategies must be changed.

Zones of greed (ZOGs) indicate an area on the chart where we expect selling, whereas zones of fear denote chart areas for buying. ZOGs may be identified as areas where previous tops have formed; in other words, past upmoves have concluded in this range. Similarly, zones of fear (ZOFs) represent areas where earlier bottoms have formed. Downmoves typically terminate in a ZOF. From a slightly different perspective, we expect resistance or overhead supply in a ZOG and buying or support in a ZOF. Investor sentiment becomes too optimistic (greedy) in ZOGs and too pessimistic in ZOFs. Go contrary to the sentiment extremes.

To illustrate, let us refer to Figure 7.15. In the Mentor Corporation chart, previous bottoms form in the general area of $10. Thus we can designate a ZOF. Both traders and long-term investors can start accumulating the stock on downmoves approaching 10. Similarly, major tops with sharp reversals usually develop in the 19–20 area. So, we designate this as a ZOF.

The Oshkosh chart indicates the formation of major bottoms in the 15–19 area. We label it as a ZOF. The 40–43 area indicates the building of past top areas of distribution, so we mark this a ZOG. Buy signals in a ZOG or sell signals in a ZOF are likely to be false and highly misleading, often resulting in sizable losses. Conversely, buy signals in a ZOF or sell signals in a ZOG (liquidation of long positions or establishing short positions) ordinarily prove to be timely and afford handsome returns.

PREDICTING INTERMEDIATE-TERM PRICE MOVES

Point and figure charts help chartists estimate the extent of future price movements. The ability to forecast price targets (or price objectives) allows technicians to obtain good ideas on when to sell in addition to the timing of purchases. Of course, chartists must develop predictions in conjunction with previous support and resistance areas, ZOFs and ZOGs, and trendlines.

The Horizontal Count

The horizontal count provides an intermediate-term estimate of a security's price move. To implement the horizontal count on a rising stock, we must first locate the base pattern or sideways price movement. We then evaluate whether

Figure 7.14
The Bearish Support Line

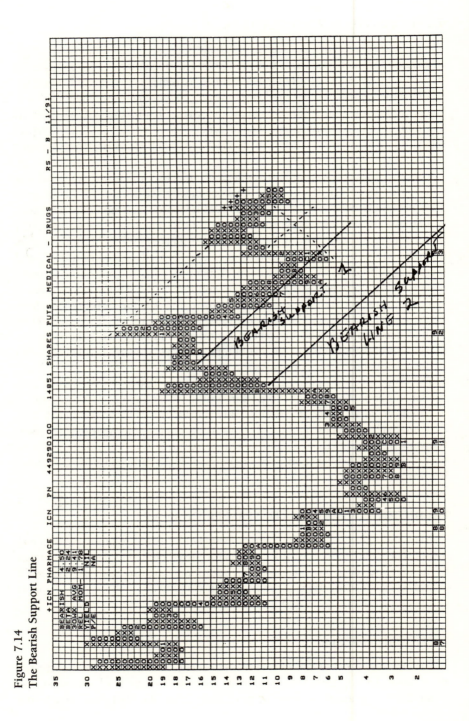

170

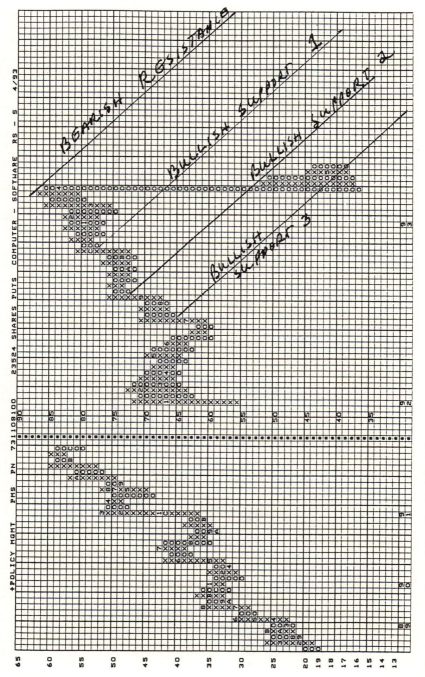

Source: Courtesy Chartcraft, Inc., New Rochelle, N.Y.

171

Figure 7.15
Zone of Greed, Zone of Fear

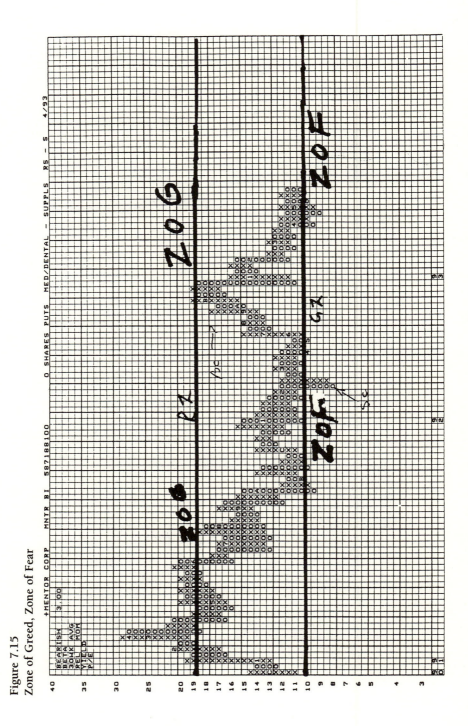

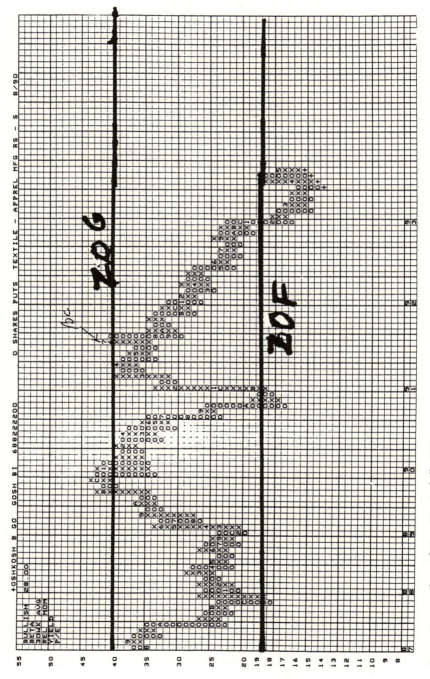

Source: Courtesy Chartcraft, Inc., New Rochelle, N.Y.

the base pattern indicates a reversal of trend or a continuation of a previous price move. A wall of O's on the left-hand side followed by a buy signal suggests a reversal of the previous downtrend. A wall of X's on the extreme left of the base followed by a buy signal indicates a continuation pattern.

We determine the width of the base by beginning our count from left to right starting with either the wall of O's or X's. Using the line with the most recordings (or the least number of unoccupied squares), count the number of squares in the base from the wall to the buy signal. Although more than one line may contain the same number of recordings, either is acceptable.

Once the width of the base has been determined, we multiply by the reversal rule on the particular chart in question. In Figure 7.16(A), we count twelve squares across the base from the wall to the buy signal. Since this stock is priced between $5 and $20, we are on a 1 1/2 point chart where each square equals 1/2 of a point (i.e., three squares form a reversal, which requires 1 1/2 points). By multiplying twelve times the chart reversal rule of 1 1/2 points, our product equals 18. We then add the product of 18 to the lowest O recording (13) in the base. Our intermediate-term price forecast or objective is $31.

In Figure 7.16(B) we have a continuation pattern nine squares wide. Since the stock is priced between 20 and 100, each three-square reversal equals three points, which is our reversal rule. We add a product of 27 to the lowest O (32) to arrive at a price objective of 59 [(9 × 3 = 27) + 32 = 59].

Figure 7.17 includes examples of low-priced stocks under $5 where the reversal rule is three-fourths and of high-priced issues of 100 or more, which require a six-point swing for a reversal. In every instance, the product from multiplying the width of the base times the reversal rule must be added to the lowest O recording in the base.

Downside Horizontal Counts

The value of forecasted price targets cannot be given enough emphasis. However, we must be careful not to abuse this technique. Rather, we arrive at price objectives in a careful, *conservative* manner. To illustrate conservatism in forecasting techniques, let us review Figure 7.18.

In Figures 7.18(A) and 7.18(B), we project full downside moves. Then Figure 7.18(C) helps demonstrate the more conservative approach to horizontal counts on the downside. In Figure 7.18(A), we have a ten-square-wide base multiplied by the chart reversal rule of 3. We then subtract our product from the highest X in the base or top area of distribution. We arrive at a downside target of 51 [(10 × 3 = 30), 81 − 30 = 51]. In Figure 7.18(B) a seven-square-wide base on a 1 1/2 point chart gives us 10 1/2 to be subtracted from the highest X (19 1/2) to equal a downside target of 9.

Downside counts pose a problem for chartists for several reasons. First, there is a long-term, upward bias to the stock market. In other words, price advances tend to be larger than price declines. Therefore, full target projections or forecasts

Figure 7.16
Price Objectives: The Horizontal Count

(A)

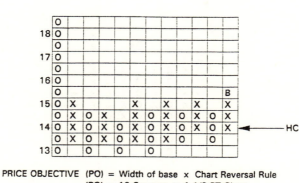

PRICE OBJECTIVE (PO) = Width of base x Chart Reversal Rule
                (PO) = 12 Squares x 1 1/2 PT Chart
                (PO) = 18 + 13 (lowest "O")
                (PO) = 31

(B)

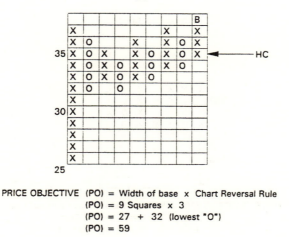

PRICE OBJECTIVE (PO) = Width of base x Chart Reversal Rule
                (PO) = 9 Squares x 3
                (PO) = 27 + 32 (lowest "O")
                (PO) = 59

(i.e., multiplying by the whole reversal rule) tend to be more accurate for bullish moves than they do for bearish moves. And second, many downside moves often result in corrections rather than bear markets. Therefore, many downside price forecasts are ultimately overstated because we use the same counting technique that we use on upside moves. To forecast the move for a downside correction, a modified (or conservative) target should be sought out first.

Let us illustrate by reviewing Figure 7.18(C). The base is nine squares wide and appears to have formed as a part of continuation pattern. The full reversal

Figure 7.17
More Horizontal Counts with Different Chart Reversal Rules

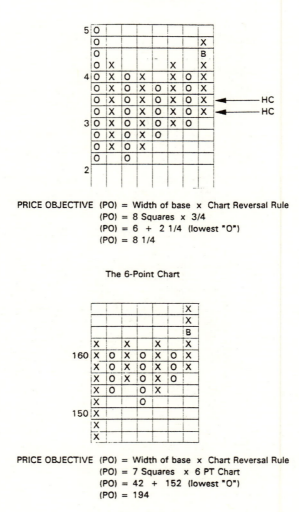

The 3/4-Point Chart

PRICE OBJECTIVE (PO) = Width of base x Chart Reversal Rule
                 (PO) = 8 Squares x 3/4
                 (PO) = 6 + 2 1/4 (lowest "O")
                 (PO) = 8 1/4

The 6-Point Chart

PRICE OBJECTIVE (PO) = Width of base x Chart Reversal Rule
                 (PO) = 7 Squares   x 6 PT Chart
                 (PO) = 42 + 152 (lowest "O")
                 (PO) = 194

rule is 3 since we are located on a three-point chart. We recommend that a reversal rule of two-thirds the normal amount be used first to project a conservative target.

In this case, $\frac{2}{3} \times 3$ equals 2. Thus our product initially is 18, and our first target is 36 [$(9 \times 2 = 18)$, $54 - 18 = 36$]. If the decline carries the price below 36, then we implement the full three-point reversal rule (since we are on the three-point chart) and reach an objective of 27 [$(9 \times 3 = 27)$, then $54 - 27 = 27$]. The initial objective of 36 essentially represents a shorter-term target, whereas

Figure 7.18
Forecasting Price Declines with the Horizontal Count

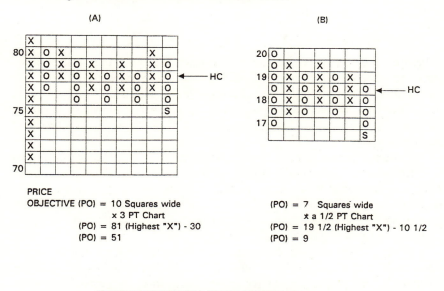

PRICE
OBJECTIVE (PO) = 10 Squares wide
                 x 3 PT Chart
           (PO) = 81 (Highest "X") - 30
           (PO) = 51

(PO) = 7   Squares wide
        x a 1/2 PT Chart
(PO) = 19 1/2 (Highest "X") - 10 1/2
(PO) = 9

USING THE HORIZONTAL COUNT CONSERVATIVELY

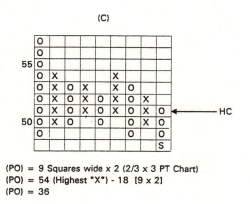

(PO) = 9 Squares wide x 2 (2/3 x 3 PT Chart)
(PO) = 54 (Highest "X") - 18 [9 x 2]
(PO) = 36

the longer-term projection of 27 provides the complete intermediate-term estimate.

DEVELOPING LONG-TERM PRICE FORECASTS

Traders rely heavily on horizontal counts for short-term and intermediate-term
price objectives. Since these speculators do not plan to hold investments for the
long haul, they adopt more of a "love 'em and leave 'em" philosophy. Holding

periods are traditionally short. However, those chartists who are in need of final or ultimate price targets need an alternative method of forecasting.

Vertical Counts

Vertical counts provide technicians with a means of arriving at ultimate or long-term price objectives. Vertical counts may be taken in one of two ways. First, take the number of X recordings in the initial upmove following the lowest O recorded in the previous decline. Or second, count the number of X recordings in the breakout leg following the bottom which contains the lowest O (or O's). Note that the first upmove and the breakout leg can be the same column.

To illustrate the first rule, let us refer to Figure 7.19(A). The stock hits bottom at 9, followed by an extended upmove in the next column. The advance of ten squares is multiplied by the chart reversal rule on the scale where the X's are recorded. Multiplying $10 \times 1\frac{1}{2}$ (since all X recordings are between 5 and 20) gives a product of 15, which must be added to the lowest O. Our ultimate price objective becomes 24 ($10 \times 1\frac{1}{2} = 15 + 9 = 24$).

In Figure 7.19(B), a double top formation develops in what would be a volatile stock used to illustrate rule two. Measure the number of X recordings in the breakout leg and multiply by the reversal rule depending on the scale where the X's may be found. All recordings are on the three-point chart, so we multiply the thirteen squares in the breakout leg times 3 ($13 \times 3 = 39 + 29 = 68$) and add the product of 39 to 29, the lowest O.

A unique aspect of the vertical count appears in Figure 7.20. Whether using the first upmove or the breakout leg, recordings will sometimes occur on two different price scales. In this case, part of the breakout leg is on the $1\frac{1}{2}$-point chart (between $5 and $20), whereas the remainder appears on the three-point chart (between $20 and $100).

To reach a final or long-term objective, count the number of recordings below 20 and multiply by the appropriate reversal rule ($5 \times 1\frac{1}{2} = 7\frac{1}{2}$), then do the same for the number of advancing squares at 20 and above ($10 \times 3 = 30$). Take the total of the two products ($30 + 7\frac{1}{2} = 37\frac{1}{2}$) and add it to the lowest O (17) to reach a target of $54\frac{1}{2}$ ($37\frac{1}{2} + 17 = 54\frac{1}{2}$). We can accommodate recordings on two different scales by simply treating recordings on each scale separately.

Downside Vertical Counts

We previously discussed intermediate-term, downside price forecasts using the horizontal count conservatively. Similar conservatism can be applied to the vertical count in estimating complete moves to lower price levels. Let us examine Figure 7.21 for proper use of the vertical count in forecasting downside price objectives.

Since we are unsure as to whether the sell signal provided by the move below 70 signals a correction or a more permanent move, apply a two-thirds reversal

Figure 7.19
Price Forcecasts Using the Vertical Count

(A)

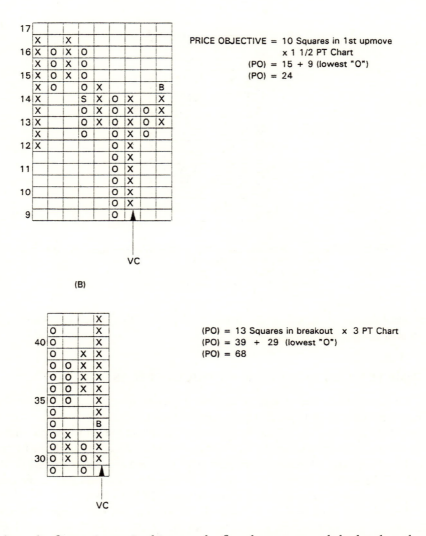

PRICE OBJECTIVE = 10 Squares in 1st upmove
x 1 1/2 PT Chart
(PO) = 15 + 9 (lowest "O")
(PO) = 24

(B)

(PO) = 13 Squares in breakout   x 3 PT Chart
(PO) = 39 + 29 (lowest "O")
(PO) = 68

rule to the first estimate. In this case, the first downmove and the breakout leg
are one and the same. Multiply the twelve recordings in this column by 2 ($\frac{2}{3}$ ×
3 = 2) and subtract the product (24) from the highest X (12 × 2 = 24, then,
81 − 24 = 57). Our first projection on this downside move is 57, which furnishes
a reasonably good target if the move turns out to be a correction. What happens
if the decline goes below the initial estimate of 57? Assuming a worst-case scenario
of a full-fledged downmove often associated with bear markets, we use the full

Figure 7.20
Using the Vertical Count on Two Different Scales

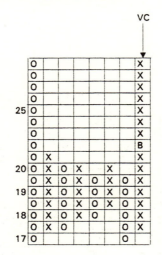

```
PRICE OBJECTIVE (PO) = # Squares below 20 x 1 1/2 + # Squares above 20 x 3 PT Chart
              (PO) = (5 x 1 1/2) + (10 x 3)
              (PO) = 7 1/2 + 30
              (PO) = 37 1/2 + 17 (Lowest "O")
              (PO) = 54 1/2
```

reversal rule of 3 (12 × 3 = 36, then 81 − 36 = 45) to forecast a decline to the 45 area.

SOME FINAL ILLUSTRATIONS OF PRICE FORECASTS

Let us conclude our treatment of price forecasts by evaluating some recent long-term charts. To illustrate the horizontal count, let us refer to the Houston Industries chart in Figure 7.22. From the wall of O's on the left to the buy signal on the right, there are twenty-four columns of recordings. By multiplying the width of the base (24) times the reversal rule (1 ½), we arrive at a product of 36. (24 × 1 ½ = 36 + 16 ½ = 52 ½ to 53). Adding 36 to the lowest O in the base (16 ½), we can forecast an expected move to the 52 ½ to 53 area.

Another key point evolves in Figure 7.22. Some of the recordings are below 20 on the 1 ½-point chart, while others are above 20 on the three-point chart. Since we use charts conservatively, first use the smaller reversal rule to establish initial targets. If the stock proves to be an exceptional mover and surpasses the earlier objective, then run another count with the larger reversal rule. However, in this case, using the larger reversal rule is unlikely because of the large width of the base pattern.

Figure 7.23 furnishes two illustrations of the vertical count. Let us look at the Solectron chart first. The first upmove (marked "VC 1") consists of nine squares,

Figure 7.21

Forecasting Downside Price Objectives with the Vertical Count

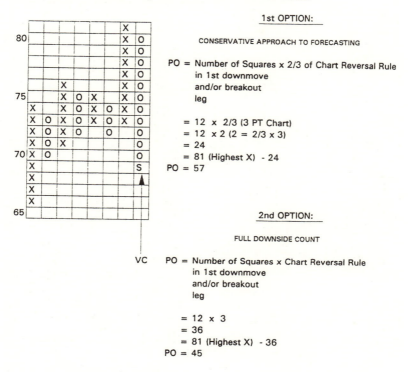

1st OPTION:

CONSERVATIVE APPROACH TO FORECASTING

PO = Number of Squares x 2/3 of Chart Reversal Rule
     in 1st downmove
     and/or breakout
     leg

= 12 x 2/3 (3 PT Chart)
= 12 x 2 (2 = 2/3 x 3)
= 24
= 81 (Highest X) - 24
PO = 57

2nd OPTION:

FULL DOWNSIDE COUNT

PO = Number of Squares x Chart Reversal Rule
     in 1st downmove
     and/or breakout
     leg

= 12 x 3
= 36
= 81 (Highest X) - 36
PO = 45

which enables us to project a move $(9 \times 1\frac{1}{2} = 13\frac{1}{2} + 11 = 24\frac{1}{2}$ to 25) to the 24–25 area. The stock moves to 26, then declines sharly to 17 ½. We gain attractive profits and liquidate our positions in a timely fashion. Now, we must pose the question "What about the possibility of reentering the stock?"

Another technique can be applied to the vertical count during the course of a trend in either direction. Up to now, we have dealt with the vertical count primarily at the beginning of an upmove or downmove. However, the vertical count may also be reestablished in an uptrend each time a sell signal results or in a downtrend each time a buy signal unfolds.

To illustrate, Solectron undergoes a sell signal in April 1992 above the bullish support line. We may run another vertical count in the usual way. The first upmove after the bottom from the sell signal includes two different scales. To calculate the vertical count, we have four squares below 20 and four above. Our new price objective is 35 ½ to 36 [$(4 \times 1\frac{1}{2} = 6) + (4 \times 3 = 12)$], then [$(6 + 12 = 18 + 17\frac{1}{2} = 35\frac{1}{2})$]. Rather than deal in ½-point projections, some chartists prefer to round off to the nearest whole number in either direction.

Solectron furnishes the opportunity for a third vertical count (VC 3), which furnishes a price forecast of 44 $(8 \times 3 = 24 + 20 = 44)$. We can use either the

Figure 7.22
The Horizontal Count Illustrated

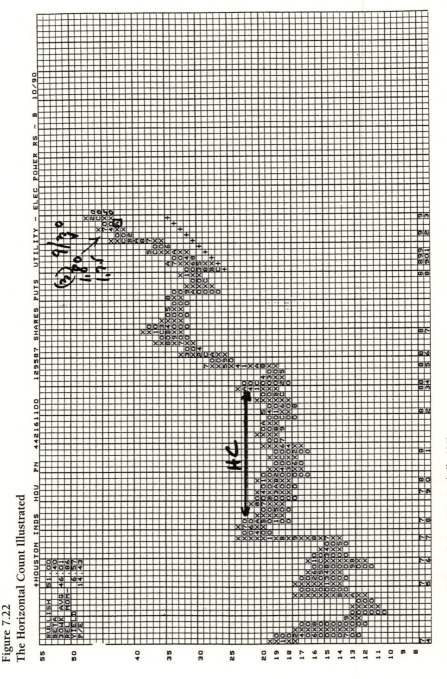

Source: Courtesy Chartcraft, Inc., New Rochelle, N.Y.

182

Figure 7.23
An Example of the Vertical Count

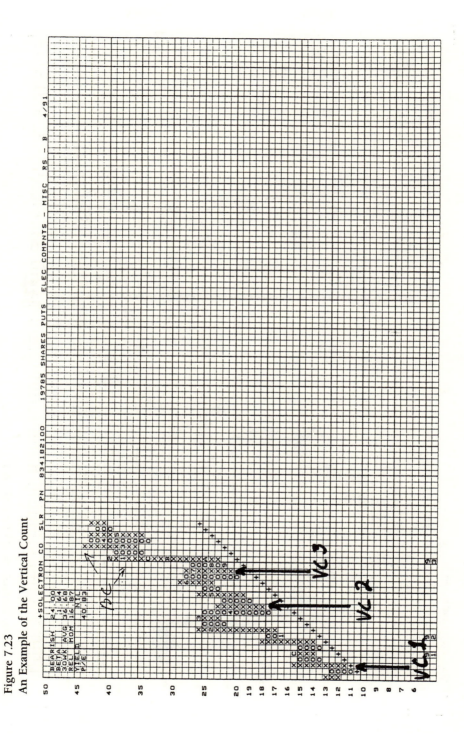

Figure 7.23 Continued

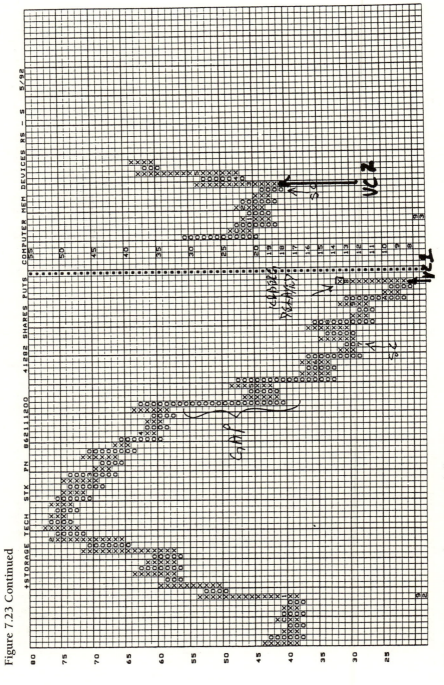

Source: Courtesy Chartcraft, Inc., New Rochelle, N.Y.

first upmove from the lowest O following the most recent sell signal, or we may measure the breakout leg in the event a base forms after the sell signal. Notice the stock advances to 44, then sells off sharply to 34. Although price forecasts are not necessarily precise, they are an excellent tool for chartists.

In reestablishing vertical counts, however, always use them cautiously. If more weight has to be assigned to one of the counts, always refer back to the initial estimate taken at the bottom of the decline. Revised vertical counts often confirm the initial estimate. One fundamental rule should always come to the forefront in using both horizontal and vertical counts. Revised projections made after a trend has been underway for some time may be liberal and overstate the prediction. Always use counts conservatively. Never lose sight of estimates from original vertical counts or horizontal counts taken from unusually wide bases (see Figure 7.22).

Storage Technology appears to reach bottom at 21 in October 1992. We establish our first vertical count with a price objective of 54 ($11 \times 3 = 33 + 21 = 54$). However, we encounter another sell signal and calculate a second vertical count from the column marked (VC 2). We have three squares below 20 and 10 above 20, so our price forecast is 52 ½ to 53 [($3 \times 1 \frac{1}{2} = 4 \frac{1}{2}$) + ($10 \times 3 = 30$), then $34 \frac{1}{2} + 18 = 52 \frac{1}{2}$ to 53]. In essence, the second vertical count reaffirms the first, so long-term investors should look to take profits in the low 50s.

THE CONCEPT OF RELATIVE STRENGTH

Our entire focus in this chapter centers around updating, improving, and revising the discipline of P & F charting. A principal thrust has been to eliminate mistakes and to identify false and misleading moves. In the asset allocation process, it becomes prohibitively expensive to continually reallocate on the basis of systems and strategies filled with timing errors. Perhaps the most critical idea in eliminating mistakes is the concept of relative strength.

Relative strength reveals how an individual stock is performing relative to the aggregate stock market. Figure 7.24 reveals the classic Chartcraft illustration of relative strength calculation.[6] Their approach takes an individual stock and divides its Friday closing price by the last price of the Dow-Jones Industrial Average (DJIA) each week. Although some technicians prefer the use of another market proxy such as the S & P 500 or the New York Composite, the DJIA provides essentially the same results.

Note from reading Figure 7.24 that the resulting relative strength ratio can be converted from fractions to whole numbers by simply moving the decimal point the required number of places to the right to get a whole number and treating it like a regular stock price. The Chartcraft approach allows us to construct P & F charts of a stock's relative strength with the whole number conversion process described in Figure 7.24. Once the P & F chart is plotted, our interpretation of

Figure 7.24
The Chartcraft Approach to Relative Strength

EXPLANTION OF RELATIVE STRENGTH

AS AN IMPORTANT FEATURE IN THIS BOOK WE PUT THE P & F RELATIVE STRENGTH SIGNALS ON THE UPPER RIGHT CORNER OF EACH STOCK CHART. (THIS SIGNAL IS BEFORE THE INVESTORS DAILY INDUSTRY GROUP .) WE KEEP RELATIVE STRENGTH CHARTS ON ALL NYSE & ASE ISSUES + ABOUT 2000 OTC STOCKS.

THE USEFULNESS OF RELATIVE STRENGTH CHARTS AS AN AID TO STOCK SELECTION CANNOT BE UNDERESTIMATED. AS A REFRESHER WE'LL REVIEW THIS USE.

SUPPOSE A STOCK IS $80 AND THE DJIA IS 2000. IF WE DIVIDE $80 BY 2000 (AND MOVE THE DECIMAL OVER 3 PLACES) WE GET A RESULT OF 40.0. LET US SUPPOSE THE DJIA DROPS TO 1600 WHILE THIS STOCK FALLS TO $72. NOW IF WE DIVIDE THE STOCK PRICE ($72) BY THE DJIA (1600) WE GET A RESULT OF 45.0, AFTER MOVING THE DECIMAL.

WHAT DOES THIS TELL US? FIRST, A CHART OF THE PRICE OF THE STOCK WOULD SHOW A COLUMN OF "O'S FROM $80 TO $72. SECOND, A CHART OF THE RELATIVE STRENGTH WOULD SHOW A COLUMN OF "X'S" FROM 40.0 TO 45.0.

THE MARKET ITSELF INFLUENCES INDIVIDUAL STOCKS VERY MUCH IN THAT IF IT RISES IT CARRIES LOTS OF STOCKS WITH IT WHILE IF IT DECLINES MOST STOCKS ALSO DROP. WHAT RELATIVE STRENGTH ATTEMPTS TO DO IS ELIMINATE THE MARKET AS A FACTOR IN THE ACTION OF A STOCK. IN THE EXAMPLE SHOWN ABOVE WE SURMISE THAT THE ONLY REASON THE PRICE OF THE STOCK IS DROPPING IS THE DECLINING MARKET. IF THE MARKET WERE TO MOVE SIDEWAYS OR RISE THIS STOCK WOULD LIKELY BE A LEADER ON THE UPSIDE. STOCKS LIKE THIS ALSO TEND TO BOTTOM OUT LONG BEFORE THE DJIA IN BEAR MARKETS.

WE USE SIMPLE POINT & FIGURE BUY AND SELL SIGNALS ON RELATIVE STRENGTH CHARTS TO TRY TO FIND THE STOCKS THAT WILL LEAD THE WAY UP IN BULL MARKETS OR LEAD THE MARKET ON THE DOWNSIDE IN BEAR MARKETS.

SOME STOCKS HAVE R.S. SIGNALS THAT LAST FOR YEARS. GENERAL MOTORS, FOR INSTANCE, HAS GIVEN FOUR RELATIVE STRENGTH SIGNALS IN THE PAST 11 YEARS. "GM" RS GAVE A BUY IN JUNE '82, BEFORE THE GREAT BULL MARKET LIFT OFF, WITH THE STOCK ABOUT $23. THE RS REMAINED BULLISH UNITL MAY '85 WHEN A SELL WAS GIVEN WITH THE STOCK AT $35. SINCE THEN THE RS HAS REMAINED NEGATIVE, EXCEPT FOR THE BRIEF NOV '88- MAY '89 PERIOD, AND GM IS STILL TRADING ABOUT THE $35 LEVEL. ON THE OTHER HAND THE DOW JONES INDUSTRIAL AVERAGE HAS RISEN FROM 1300 IN MAY '85 TO OVER 3200.

INVESTORS USING RELATIVE STRENGTH WOULD HAVE SIMPLY NOT CONSIDERED "GM" FOR LONG TERM PURCHASE DURING MOST OF THIS PERIOD OF TIME. IF THEY FOLLOWED THE R.S. SIGNALS THEY WOULD HAVE SEEN EARLY GAINS AS AUTO'S RECOVERED FROM 1982 LOWS BUT WOULD AVOIDED YEARS OF SIDEWAYS ACTION IN "GM" WHILE THE MARKETS EXPLODED.

Example of the Presentation of Relative Strength Signals

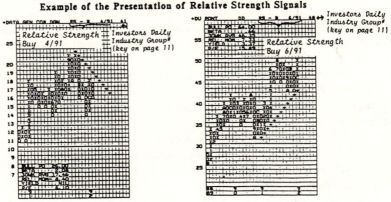

Source: Courtesy Chartcraft, Inc., New Rochelle, N.Y.

relative strength is simplified because we evaluate buy and sell signals just as we do on any other chart.

A buy signal means that the relative strength has turned bullish and the stock should outperform the general stock market. A sell signal indicates the relative strength has turned bearish, and we would expect the stock to underperform the market in the period ahead. Outperforming the market does not prevent the stock from going down, however, but it should decline less than the market as a whole. Similarly, underperforming the market does not keep the stock from enjoying an increase in price, but the advance will not be as strong as that of the general market.

How do we use relative strength (RS) in developing market strategies? Perhaps the most critical aspect of relative strength interpretation deals with the duration of buy and sell signals. Once buy or sell signals are received on RS charts, they generally remain intact for long periods of times. It is not uncommon for RS buy and sell signals to continue for periods of several years.

Furthermore, buy signals with positive RS signals are much more reliable than those with negative RS charts. Sell signals with negative RS signals ordinarily result in much larger downmoves than do those with a positive RS. Downmoves with a bullish RS more often than not end with a correction as opposed to a bear market type of downmove. Sell signals with a bearish RS typically produce protracted downmoves. Conversely, chartists should beware of long positions in stocks experiencing price declines with a bearish RS because the drop may be worse than expected. Similarly, short sellers should approach stocks with bullish RS with extreme caution because price declines usually do not meet expectations in terms of the magnitude of the decrease.

Stated succinctly, investment decisions regarding the allocation of funds toward specific common stocks should include a fundamental view espoused of the authors. Take long positions primarily in stocks with a bullish RS. When the RS turns bearish, liquidate positions and take profits. Assume short positions primarily in stocks with a bearish RS. If the RS turns bullish, take profits and close out shorts and puts. Since RS signals tend to endure for periods up to several years, let the RS trend serve as your guide. Do not go counter to the dictates of RS on a recurring basis.

To summarize the significance of RS, let us examine Figure 7.25. Norwest and SPX corporations have RS signals in the upper right-hand corner of their respective charts. Notice that the Norwest RS turned bullish in July 1988, whereas the SPX RS gave a sell signal in August 1988. The general stock market was in the midst of a strong advance coming on the heels of the October 1987 debacle.

With its bullish RS, Norwest has advanced from 10½ to 56 thus far. Meanwhile, SPX with its bearish RS underwent a decline from 44 to 11. These two divergent moves occurred at the same time period during a strong market advance. Figure 7.25 also reinforces the enduring nature of RS buy and sell signals. In each case, current RS signals have been in force for five years. We repeatedly hear such adages as "go with the flow (of the market)" and "the trend (of the market) is

Figure 7.25
Illustrating the Importance of Relative Strength

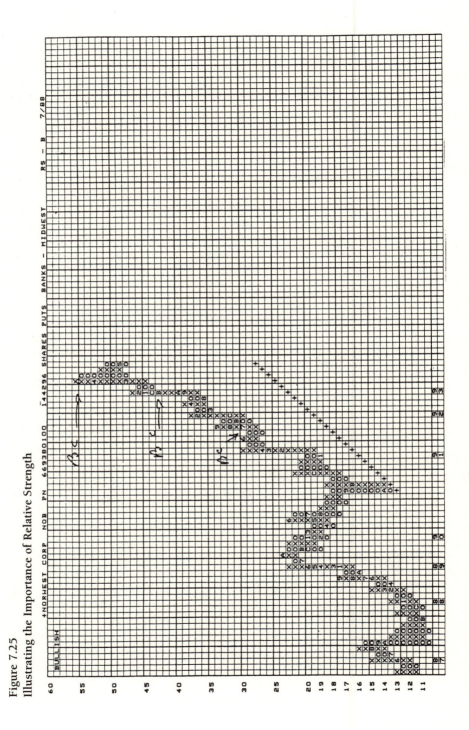

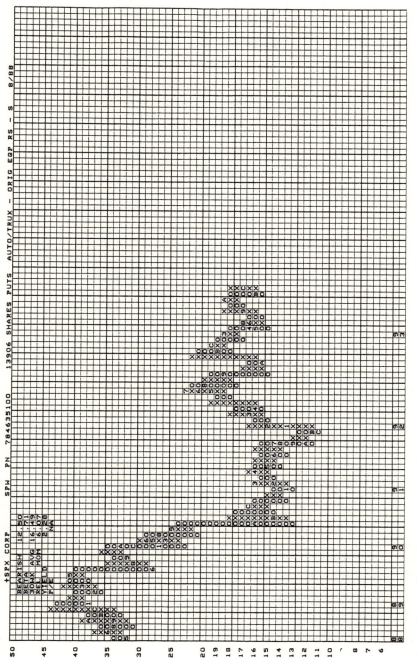

Source: Courtesy Chartcraft, Inc., New Rochelle, N.Y.

189

your friend." Despite a strong bull market, the potential from investing in SPX stock was limited. Norwest simultaneously provided generous returns. One cannot ignore the RS concept in portfolio strategies and allocation decisions.

SUMMARY

This chapter features numerous improvements in the P & F disciplines, including trendlines, trendline revisions and updates, major and minor trends, and corollary or channel lines. We also look at price objectives, reestablishing price forecasts, zones of greed and zones of fear, and relative strength, to name a few.

This chapter continues to provide avenues for eliminating mistakes and interpretation errors. If the asset allocation process is to be effective, we must develop as close to an "error-free" approach as possible. We have also presented many thoughts on price forecasting. The ability to ascertain price objectives and make timely decisions on closing out positions remains at the forefront of investment analysis.

Chapter 8 features some additional P & F patterns, many of which are predicated on investment psychology. Further, we explore additional strategies such as price estimates for the general market, technical indicators to anticipate market junctures, and special emphasis on investor sentiment approaches to detect market junctures.

NOTES

1. A. W. Cohen, *How to Use the Three-Point Reversal Method of Point and Figure Stock Market Trading,* 9th ed. (New Rochelle, N.Y.: Chartcraft, Inc., 1987), 43–54.

2. Michael L. Burke, *The All New Guide to the Three-Point Reversal Method of Point & Figure Construction and Formations* (New Rochelle, N.Y.: Chartcraft, Inc., 1990), 23–47.

3. This emphasis on distinguishing between valid and false or ostensible penetrations originates from Chartcraft, Inc., and can primarily be attributed to A. W. Cohen and Michael L. Burke.

4. Some preliminary work on trendline revision was performed by Earl Blumenthal a number of years ago. Much of his early work centered on commodities, their volatility, and the need for more current approaches. See Earl Blumenthal, *Chart for Profit Point and Figure Trading* (Larchmont, N.Y.: Investors Intelligence, 1975), 49–64.

5. Carroll D. Aby, Jr., *The Complete Guide to Point and Figure Charting* (Birmingham, Ala.: Colonial Press, 1992), 146–165.

6. The authors wish to acknowledge the overall contributions of Michael Burke, John Gray, and the entire Chartcraft staff to this manuscript. All reproduced P & F charts were furnished by Chartcraft, and their total support of this manuscript facilitated the completion of the book. Our friendship with this organization and these individuals spans many years. However, it is difficult to express our appreciation for their unflagging commitment and dedicated efforts.

Chapter 8

THE FINISHING TOUCHES TO ASSET ALLOCATION WITH STOCKS

The two preceding chapters focus on using P & F charts in the allocation of funds between individual common stocks. This chapter not only completes the process, but it emphasizes aggregate market timing where funds shift into or out of stocks completely. The aggregate market view is more commonly associated with asset allocation. Investment returns can be significantly improved by using technical analysis to trade the proper markets, the best groups, and leading individual issues.

This chapter contains a treatment of group analysis. By chapter's end, you will learn the importance of buying a strong stock in a good group in a rising market. You will also gain understanding as to the role of the general market in the asset allocation process.

We begin with the last of our chart patterns. Note that many of these patterns are psychology based with a trading orientation.[1] The psychology background acquired in Chapter 6 can be used in trading techniques to shift between individual stock selections.

TRADING PATTERNS AND INVESTMENT PSYCHOLOGY

Bull and bear traps evolve from vertical bar charting techniques where stocks make a marginal new high or low for the move. A bull trap develops when a stock's advance exceeds two or more previous tops by a single square (sometimes two squares). Once the upside breakout occurs, unsuspecting chartists make purchase commitments in anticipation of a strong rally. Abruptly the stock undergoes a sharp sell-off and the P & F chart yields a sell signal in the next column.

Figure 8.1
The Bull Trap Formation

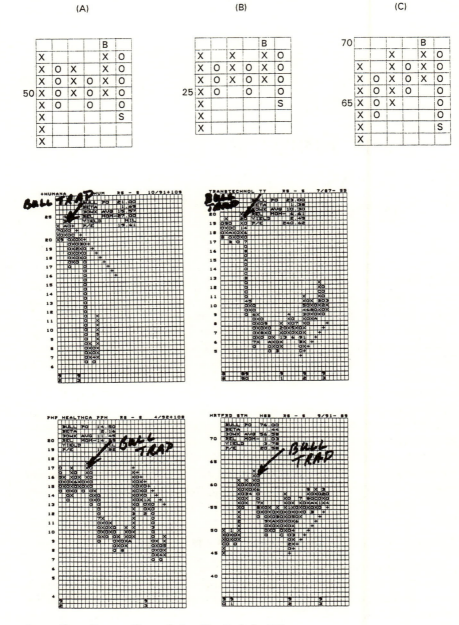

Source: Charts Courtesy Chartcraft, Inc., New Rochelle, N.Y.

This combination of a new high for the move followed by a sell signal can be termed a *key reversal*, which suggests that the stock will experience either a correction or major downmove in the near term. Bull traps often materialize in a ZOG (zone of greed) where previous tops have formed at or near all-time highs. Figure 8.1 illustrates the bull trap formation.

Let us look at the Transtechnology chart in Figure 8.1 as a supporting illustration. Notice the stock reaches a new high for the advance, but a swift decline yields a sell signal in the following column of O's. The slide begins at 24 and does not reach bottom until the 6 ½ area.

Bear trap patterns contain a downside move that exceeds two or more previous bottoms by a single square (sometimes two). Bear traps form with a combination of a new low for the move followed by a rally that generates a buy signal in the succeeding column of X's. This key reversal is made possible by the sell signal, which induces more sellers and exhausts selling pressure. With a dominance of buyers versus remaining sellers, the stock undergoes a rapid advance and reverses the trend of the stock. Bear traps often form in a ZOF (zone of fear) where previous bottoms occur near recent or all-time low prices.

Let us look at the Pepsico chart in Figure 8.2. The stock experiences a sell signal, which ends a downside correction. The following upmove penetrates a previous top, with the buy signal setting the stage for a continuation of the uptrend. Similarly, Hudson Foods deludes investors with a downside breakout at 7 in March 1992. Notice the 6 ½ to 7 area constitutes a ZOF where another upturn was launched.

Once the additional selling pressure is absorbed, buyers are versus sellers and the rally is underway. When sell signals correspond with heavy selling, some Wall Street technicians like to say the stock is "washed out" (or "cleaned out"), which amounts to the stock being prepared for an advance. Sellers are removed from the picture.

Triple bottom and top failure patterns represent slight deviations from bear and bull tops. In a triple bottom failure pattern, two previous bottoms are exceeded by one square followed by a reversal to the upside of at least three squares. Although a buy signal does not result, the quick reversal upward casts doubts regarding the strength and validity of the decline. Figure 8.3 contains several examples of triple bottom failures (TBFs).

Notice the Dupont chart in Figure 8.3. The correction concludes with a sell signal followed by an immediate reversal upward. Although no buy signal results, the reversal is sufficient to negate the thinking from the sell signal. Questions are also raised concerning the downmove.

In the C. R. Bard chart, a similar situation results. Although a full-blown bull market may not develop for some time given the downtrend line, the TBF indicates that the worst of the slide is over. Once again, some evidence of the investment psychology surrounds the market. The psychology of investing appears in the P & F charts, particularly in these trading patterns.

Triple top failures (TTFs) are illustrated in Figure 8.4. The TTF is similar to

Figure 8.2
The Bear Trap Pattern

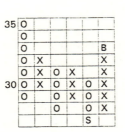

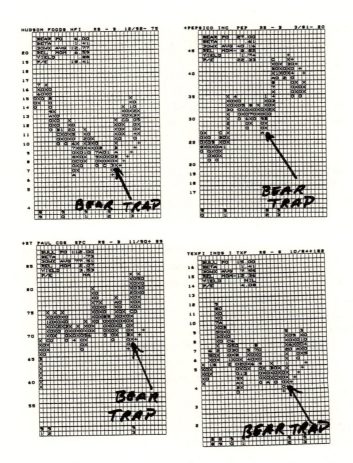

Source: Charts Courtesy Chartcraft, Inc., New Rochelle, N.Y.

Figure 8.3
The Triple Bottom Failure

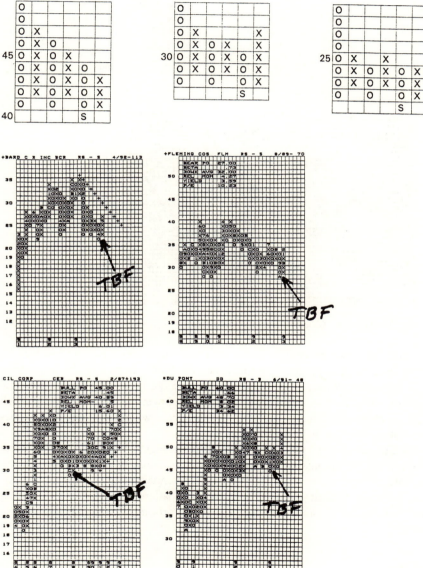

Source: Charts Courtesy Chartcraft, Inc., New Rochelle, N.Y.

Figure 8.4
The Triple Top Failure

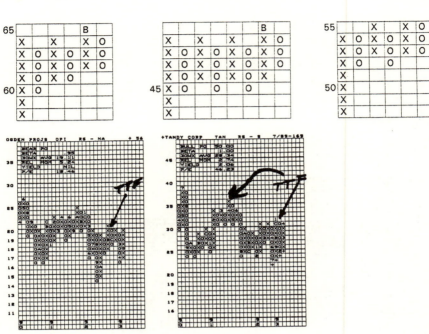

Source: Charts Courtesy Chartcraft, Inc., New Rochelle, N.Y.

the bull trap. Two previous tops are penetrated by a single square, followed by an immediate three-square reversal, which offsets the impact of the buy signal. TTF patterns cast suspicions on the validity of the breakout and the potential upmove. Once the buy signal occurs, a number of potential buyers enter the stock with the expectation that an upmove of consequence will result. Demand becomes exhausted, and supply is large relative to demand.

To illustrate, let us look at the Tandy Chart in Figure 8.4. The April 1991 and January 1993 breakouts indicate the potential for strong advances. However, immediate downside moves reduce the upside potential and give concern to chartists. Technical weakness evolves with the TTF pattern. As in the case with bear and bull traps, TBFs and TTFs frequently will form in ZOFs and ZOGs, respectively.

High and Low Poles

Two rather cryptic formations with significant implications for price changes include the *high pole* and *low pole patterns*. Earl Blumenthal originally discovered

Figure 8.5
High Pole Formation

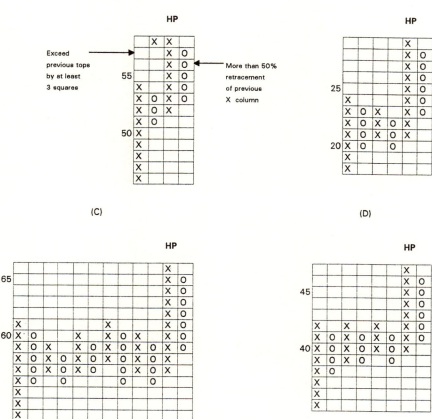

the high pole formation in his earlier works on technical analysis.[2] According to Blumenthal, a high pole may be defined as an upside breakout exceeding one or more previous tops by at least three squares followed by a retracement of more than 50% of the previous column of X's. The column containing the advance essentially stands alone like a "high pole" since it exceeds previous tops by at least three squares and is then followed by a sizable downmove. The peak of the advance stands in virtual isolation.

Sample illustrations of high pole formations appear in Figure 8.5. Figure 8.6 contains some actual examples of high poles, which reveal several key concepts. First, the high pole often signals a price run-up, which gets ahead of itself. In other words, the advance may be fueled by speculative excesses. The price moves up too quickly and requires a correction to ensure the health of the advance over

Figure 8.6
Some Examples of High Poles

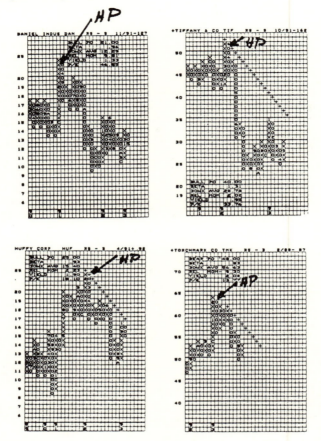

Source: Courtesy Chartcraft, Inc., New Rochelle, N.Y.

time. Second, the 50% retracement feature is distributional in nature and warns of some type of decline. Third, high poles that occur during bullish stock markets often result in a correction. However, high poles that form during bearish markets often lead to major price reversals in the stock. Fourth, high poles must be used in conjunction with relative strength.

Stocks with high pole formations and a negative RS (relative strength) often suffer major downmoves. The sell signal on the RS chart warns that the stock will underperform the market until the RS turns bullish with a buy signal. Remember, the RS signal appears in the upper right-hand corner of the P & F chart and describes the activity of the stock relative to the market without your having to make the calculation. Stocks with high pole formations and a positive RS usually experience downmoves in the form of a correction. In other words, weaker performing stocks are more apt to incur larger downmoves, whereas stronger performers generally experience minor retracements.

Let us examine the Tiffany (notice RS–S, 10/91) and Daniel Industries (RS–S, 11/91) charts in Figure 8.6. In both cases, a high pole forms and the RS charts for each stock are bearish (RS–S, 10/91, and RS–S, 11/91, respectively). Each issue lost more than 50% of its value. In the same figure, Torchmark (RS–B, 2/88) experienced a much milder downmove as a result of the buy signal on its RS chart (RS–B, 2/88). The Huffy chart illustrates another principle, however. Some corrections can still be quite severe and seem similar to a bear market. Despite retaining its positive RS, Huffy did undergo a larger-than-expected decline in a bullish stock market. However, the Huffy chart conveys the importance of a fifth rule critical to interpreting high pole patterns. High poles that occur following a protracted upside price move are more inclined to suffer a sharper downmove. High poles that follow smaller price advances tend to display smaller declines.

Michael Burke developed the low pole formation, which represents the bullish counterpart to the high pole.[3] A low pole forms when a price decline exceeds one or more previous bottoms by at least three squares, followed by an advancing column that retraces more than 50% of the previous column of O's. The retracement feature signals early signs of accumulation and strength in the stock. Low poles indicate speculative excesses and deeply oversold stocks due for a rally. The decline has been steep enough to exceed previous bottoms by a sufficient margin so the column seems in isolation as if it were an elongated pole.

Similar rules for interpreting high poles apply in reverse to low pole formations. Low poles that follow extended price declines tend to have stronger rallies than do low poles following brief declines. Low poles with a bullish RS tend to experience major price moves, whereas similar formations with a bearish RS usually show limited potential for advancement. A low pole formation in a bullish stock market may be considered bullish as it often marks the end of a corrective phase. However, a low pole in a bearish market normally signals a brief correction followed by a resumption of the downtrend. And finally, remember the 50% or more retracement signals strength and some accumulation in the stock.

Figure 8.7 provides some hypothetical examples of low pole patterns. Figure 8.8 contains several illustrations of actual chart situations. Notice that the Berry Petroleum chart forms a low pole with a negative RS signal intact (RS–S, 7/91). Although the stock appears to have bottomed, its rise does not compare with the Computer Associates chart displaying a bullish RS. Although the Athlone chart shows a reasonable bounce with a negative RS, remember the stock has undergone a pronounced decline in losing almost two thirds of its value. Remember that low poles following severe declines usually demonstrate stronger rallies, even if they have a bearish RS.

Shakeout Patterns

Earl Blumenthal always maintained that one should disregard the initial sell signal in a bull market.[4] Michael Burke later refined much of Blumenthal's re-

Figure 8.7
The Low Pole Formation

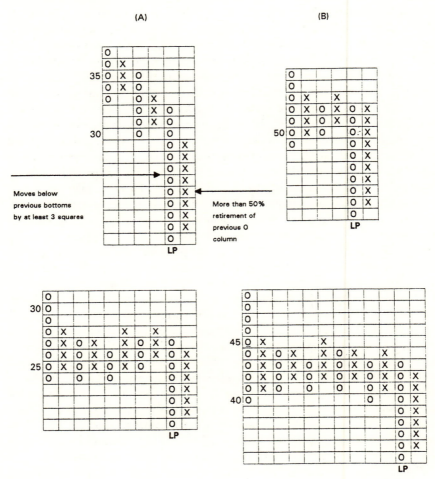

search and termed this first sell signal in a newly formed uptrend a *shakeout pattern*.[5] Aby believes most initial sell signals ended their slide back in the newly formed support area (now old resistance) or on the established bullish support line.[6]

The significance of this shakeout may be traced to investment psychology. Remember our earlier comments that bull markets originate in pessimism and disbelief. The first sell signal merely reinforces the view that this rally can not be a new uptrend because the fundamental evidence does not support higher prices. The fact remains that the shakeout pattern provides an additional place for purchasing the stock.

Figure 8.8
Low Pole Examples

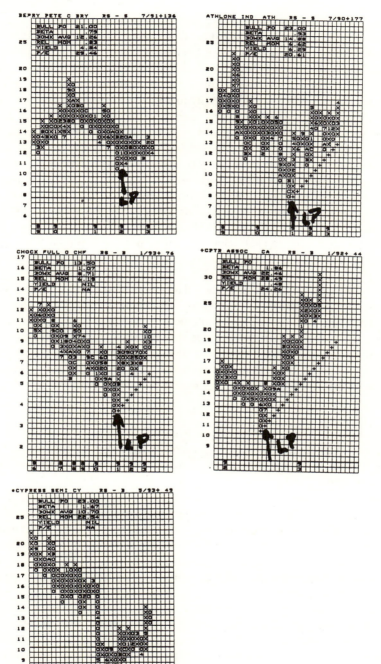

Source: Courtesy Chartcraft, Inc., New Rochelle, N.Y.

Figure 8.9 illustrates the shakeout pattern, and Figure 8.10 includes some actual examples. The shakeout deludes many investors into thinking a correction has ended and the downtrend will resume. Once again, however, the RS is a key to successful interpretation. Stocks with a bullish RS often experience rapid advances and minimal downside moves with the sell signal as in the case with J. P. Morgan. Stocks with a bearish RS usually demonstrate slower, gradual price advances and more volatile downside activity to accompany the sell signal.

Saucer patterns are more commonly referred to as "rounded bottoms" and "rounded tops," as displayed in Figure 8.11. To understand the significance of rounded bottoms and tops, we need to refer to Dow's idea that bull markets have higher tops and bottoms, whereas bear markets show lower tops and bottoms. By looking at the May Department Store chart in Figure 8.11, we note a rising trend with higher tops and bottoms. When the top "rounds off," the pattern of persistently higher tops comes to a close. This disruption in the sequence of rising tops warns of a topping process that will ultimately lead to weakness in the stock price. Lower tops and bottoms develop after the peak point in March 1993. The rounding concludes the bullishness and eventually results in lower tops and lower bottoms.

In an opposite case, let us refer to the Atlantic Southeast chart. The stock has undergone a long downmove with lower tops and bottoms as an obvious feature of the chart. The rounded bottom discontinues the pattern of lower bottoms and begins a series of higher bottoms and tops. The rounding begins before the low point of 12 in August 1990, when we gradually start forming higher bottoms and higher tops. Rounding patterns usually warn of an impending juncture or major reversal in a stock. Investment strategies should be reviewed accordingly.

SOME FINAL PATTERNS

When well-defined investor extremes emerge in individual stocks from either long and/or short positions, the need exists to take profits and allocate the funds elsewhere. Patterns that help identify overbought and oversold stocks are *upside* and *downside spikes*. Spikes are a long, uninterrupted move in either direction. Our rule calls for asset management strategists to be on guard any time a stock advances or declines in price from fifteen to twenty-five consecutive squares without a three-square reversal move. The first appearance or hint of a three-square reversal should cause concern and dictate that portfolio managers liquidate or cover existing positions. Spikes can produce sizable corrections and make it profitable to reenter positions later at favorable price levels.

The Boston Technology chart in Figure 8.12 shows a twenty-three-square advance without interruption before a correction begins. Similarly, the Dataflex Corporation chart reveals a twenty-five-square decline which reaches bottom at 4. From an investment psychology standpoint, long, unbroken price declines have bullish implications because the stock is deeply oversold. Buy the first three-square reversal to the upside for no less than a trading move.

Figure 8.9
The Shakeout Pattern

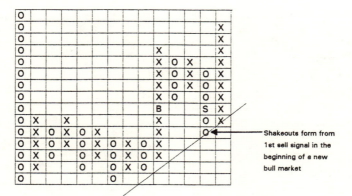

Shakeouts form from
1st sell signal in the
beginning of a new
bull market

Longer-term investors may also enter on the initial three-square reversal, although the base-building process may require a considerable period of time. In a similar vein, long, unbroken price advances contain bearish implications. Traders may consider taking profits and/or selling short at the first sign of a three-square reversal.

Weekly Key Reversal Tops and Bottoms

A key reversal top (KRT) can be defined as a new high for the near-term price movement followed by a loss for the week. Although somewhat similar to trap formations, key reversals do not necessarily result in sell or buy signals. A key reversal bottom (KRB) reflects a combination of a new low for the current move followed by a gain in price for the week. Key reversals point out temporary technical weakness (key reversal tops) or strength (key reversal bottoms). Chartcraft refers to KRTs as buying climaxes (BC) and to KRBs as selling climaxes (SC). Although these formations lack a particular identity on charts, you can get an idea in Figure 8.13. The easiest way to note KRTs and KRBs is to pursue a weekly summary of the financial pages from *Barron's* or a major newspaper.

Convergence and Divergence

One way to identify particularly strong stocks is to compare their price trends with trends of the general market. Figure 8.14 shows the market as measured by the Dow Jones Industrial Average (DJIA) with a pattern of consistently lower tops. However, charts of Smucker, Chiquita, and Pfizer simultaneously demonstrate rising tops and bottoms. In effect, the rising trend of these individual issues converges on a falling aggregate market trend.

The concepts of *convergence* and *divergence* help facilitate a comparison between

Figure 8.10
Some Shakeout Examples

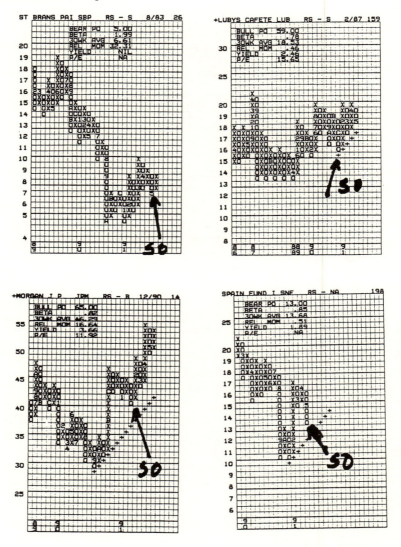

Source: Courtesy Chartcraft, Inc., New Rochelle, N.Y.

individual stock performances and general market activity. In this case of convergence, one would expect to buy Smucker, Chiquita, and Pfizer either now or when the market turns upward. These three stocks should certainly provide leadership for the market once its trend becomes bullish, as they are outperforming the market.

Figure 8.11
Saucer Patterns

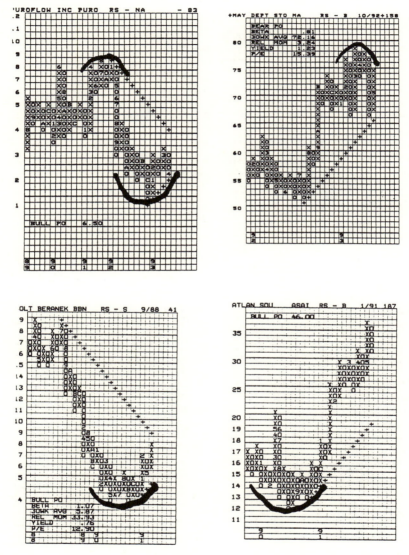

Source: Courtesy Chartcraft, Inc., New Rochelle, N.Y.

Figure 8.12
Upside and Downside Spikes

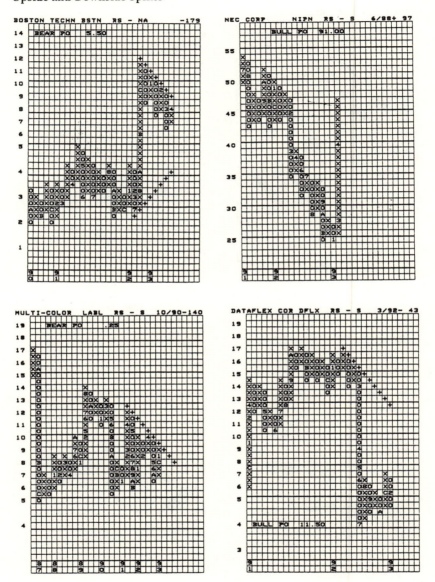

Source: Courtesy Chartcraft, Inc., New Rochelle, N.Y.

Figure 8.13
Key Reversals—Tops and Bottoms

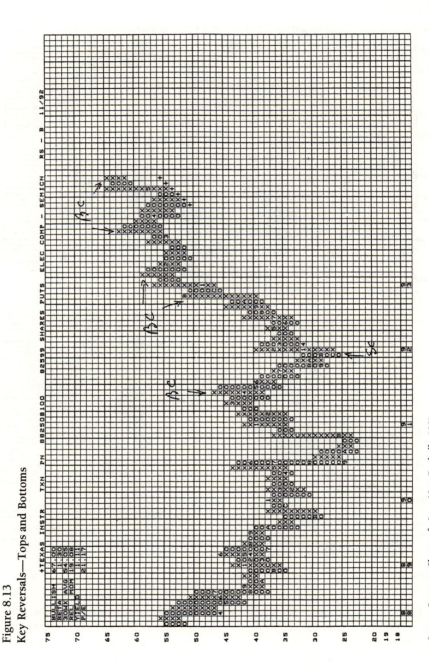

Source: Courtesy Chartcraft, Inc., New Rochelle, N.Y.

Figure 8.14
Illustrating Convergence

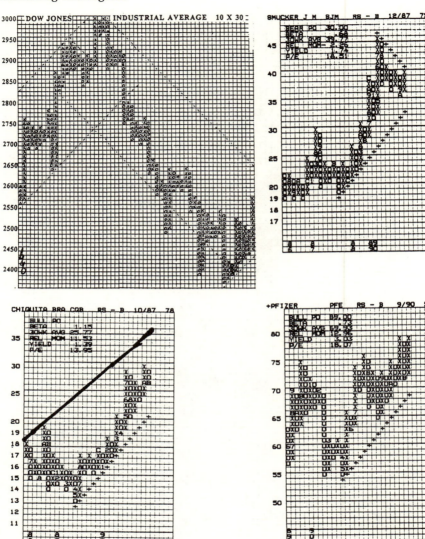

Source: Courtesy Chartcraft, Inc., New Rochelle, N.Y.

Figure 8.15 demonstrates a bullish general market with rising tops and bottoms. Meanwhile, Ionics, Newell, and Policy Management illustrate divergence by entering bearish phases with declining tops and bottoms. These three issues are underperforming the market by diverging from its primary uptrend. Thus

Figure 8.15
Illustrating Divergence

(Dow Jones Industrial Average 10 x 30)

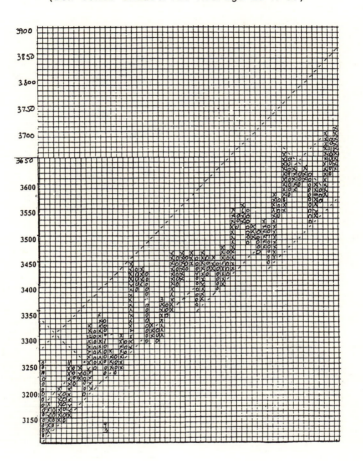

continues

convergence and divergence help select stocks on the basis of relative performance. Converging issues in a declining aggregate market should be considered for
long positions, both during the decline and when the market reverses upward.
Diverging issues in a rising general market help spot potential short sale candidates. Profits should be taken in long positions when stocks diverge from a bullish
market.

Figure 8.15 Continued

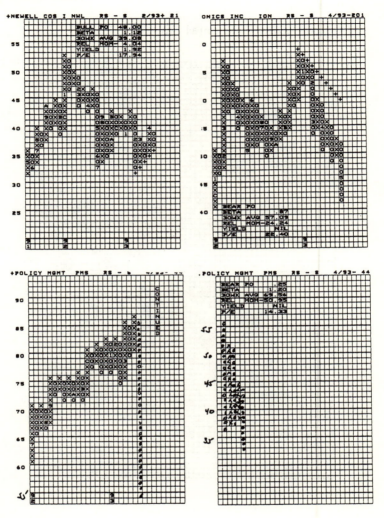

Source: Courtesy Chartcraft, Inc., New Rochelle, N.Y.

High Pole At the Bearish Resistance Line

Blumenthal argued that a high pole formation developing at the bearish resistance line was among the most bearish of all chart patterns.[7] Figure 8.16 illustrates the high pole at the bearish resistance line (BRL). Notice that an upside breakout exceeds the downtrend line (the BRL) and is immediately followed by a retracement of more than 50%. Not only does the large retracement suggest distribution, but it also nullifies the attempted reversal with the trendline penetration. Asset

Figure 8.16
High Pole at the Bearish Resistance Line

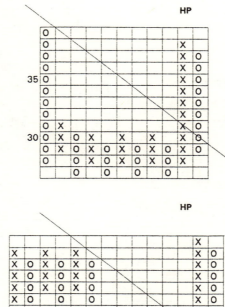

managers must be on guard for the high pole occurring at the downtrend line. Something that appears as a new-found positive suddenly becomes a negative in what may be a new selection to the portfolio.

Asset allocation between individual stocks involves an extensive commitment of time. However, most of the complexities have been covered. It is now appropriate to focus our attention on market timing—when funds should be placed in or taken out of the stock market as a whole. Although the list of measures attempting to identify money flowing in and out of the market is lengthy, let us take a look at a few proven technical indicators.

TECHNICAL INDICATORS FOR THE AGGREGATE MARKET

The most widely followed market measures always include the Dow Jones Industrial Average as a gauge of the general market. Figure 8.17 furnishes three different charts of the market's most popular Index. In the 20 × 60 chart, each square represents a twenty-point move, whereas sixty points are needed to estab-

Figure 8.17
Some Charts of the Dow Jones Industrial Average

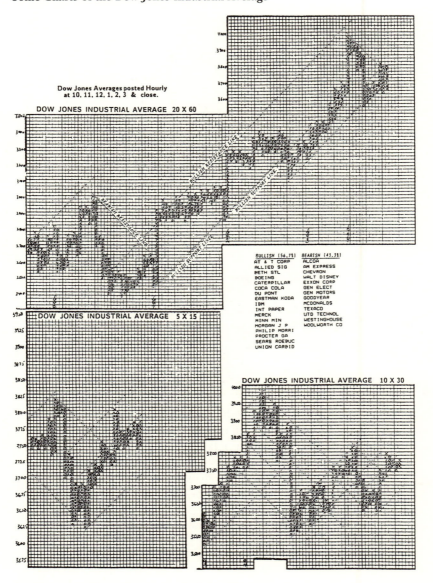

Source: Courtesy Chartcraft, Inc., New Rochelle, N.Y.

Figure 8.18
Some Other Market Measures

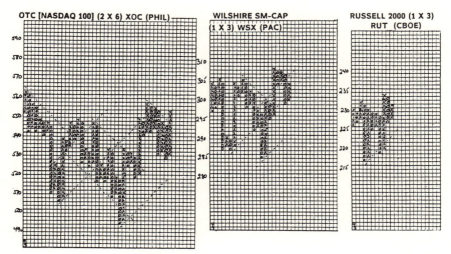

Source: Courtesy Chartcraft, Inc., New Rochelle, N.Y.

lish a reversal column. The principal advantages of the 20 × 60 chart are fewer recordings, more defined trends, and a better long-term view of the blue chip segment in the market. An obvious disadvantage lies in the insensitivity of this chart relative to the more trading oriented graphs such as the 5 × 15.

The 5 × 15 chart values each square at five points, whereas fifteen points are required for a reversal column. Similarly, the 10 × 30 chart means a value of ten points per square and thirty points for a reversal swing in price. Since the 5 × 15 is more sensitive, traders usually demonstrate a preference for it, whereas the 10 × 30 seems suited for intermediate goals for investors between the two extremes.

Although the DJIA should be used because of its following and coverage, do not regard it as a leading indicator of the overall stock market. At almost every broad-based market top, the DJIA shows a buy signal. Conversely, it gives a sell signal at major bottoms. The DJIA contains thirty blue chip stocks, which reflect activity in gilt-edge issues. Blue chips are the last to rise in a bull market and the last to fall in a bear market, so regard the DJIA as a lagging indicator of the general stock market.

Figure 8.18 reveals some other popular measures of the market, each of which offer option trading for speculators who wish to take a chance of predicting the market. The OTC (NASDAQ) measures the speculative presence in the market by gauging trading in unlisted securities. The Wilshire Small Cap Index also looks at speculative activity in terms of smaller capitalization issues. The Russell 2000 represents a broad-based measure of the market with emphasis on small caps, other domestics, and international stocks.

Figure 8.19 includes some other market indexes with options availability. Although the S & P 100 and 500 are relatively well known, the NYSE Composite consists of all issues traded on the New York Stock Exchange. The Value Line Index is comprised of 1,700 stocks with a cross-sectional appeal to a variety of individual investors. The Major Market Index consists of twenty blue chip stocks and resembles the DJIA in composition. All of these indexes are useful in measuring different aspects of the market.

SOME OTHER MARKET MEASURES

Figure 8.20 depicts the *American Market Value Index,* which represents the American Stock Exchange (ASE). Like the NASDAQ, the ASE reflects speculative activity. When both the NASDAQ and the ASE advance sharply on heavier trading volume, speculative activity increases. Some speculation is helpful to the market, but excesses indicate the market will soon undergo a downmove to correct the viewpoint of the majority.

All of these indexes, which are helpful in the evaluation of market trends, should be analyzed like common stocks. Trendlines, price objectives, buy and sell signals, and support and resistance enter into the analysis of different market segments.

However, a critical issue surfaces at this point. We always hear commentators and investors refer to "the market." What is "the market?" The term "market" applies to where your investments are at a given time. Although the media almost universally use the DJIA as a proxy for the market, the inclusive thirty blue chip stocks do not represent the aggregate stock market. If you are in OTC stocks, the NASDAQ represents the market that you must follow. Stocks listed on the ASE are followed by observing the American Market Value Index, whereas NYSE stocks are on the "big board" market. If your assets are committed to antique cars, the antique car market is the one of concern. Real estate investors should follow the real estate market, and the beat goes on.

Utilities and Transportation

The Dow Jones Utility Average (DJUA) appears in Figure 8.21. The significance of the DJUA lies in its sensitivity to interest rates (see Chapter 11). Utility stocks, along with fixed-income securities, compete for conservative investment dollars. When interest rates rise, bond prices fall and yields increase. Utility stocks show a corresponding increase in yield (and drop in price) as rates rise. Utility stocks are close companions to bonds and show similar patterns of price activity.

To carry the logic a step farther, the stock market is highly interest rate sensitive. When rates fall, bond and stock prices advance as fixed-income alternatives become less attractive while investors aggressively seek better returns. Rising interest

Figure 8.19
Some Market Indexes with Options Available

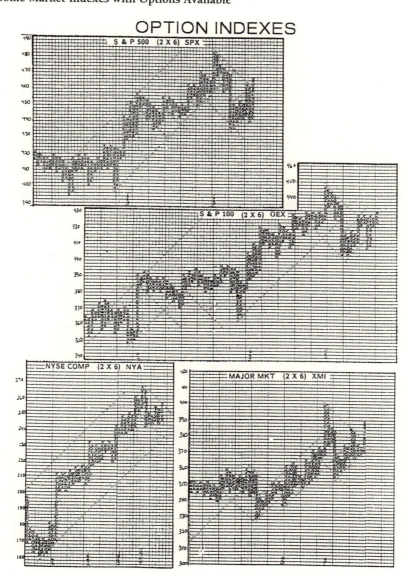

Figure 8.19 Continued

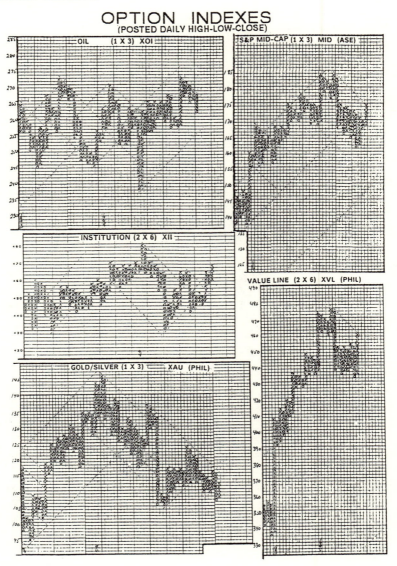

Source: Courtesy Chartcraft, Inc., New Rochelle, N.Y.

Figure 8.20
The American Market Value Index

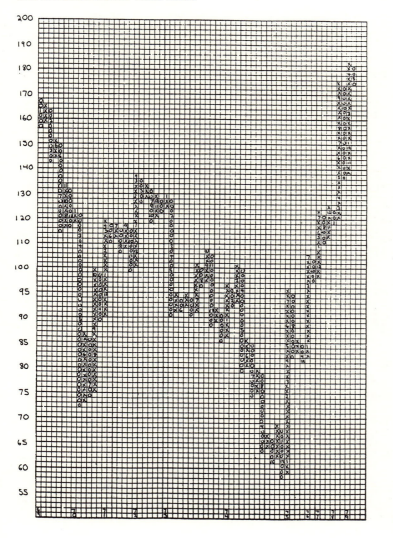

continues

rates are a disincentive to stocks because investors are risk averse. Demand shifts to more conservative investments with guaranteed returns.

Like bond prices, utility stocks turn up or down before common stocks. The real value of utility issues can be traced to their reliability as leading indicators of the general stock market. Directional shifts or trend changes in the DJUA have preceded similar reversals in the DJIA by at least one month at almost every major top or bottom. Portfolio managers who are involved with market timing will find

Figure 8.20 Continued

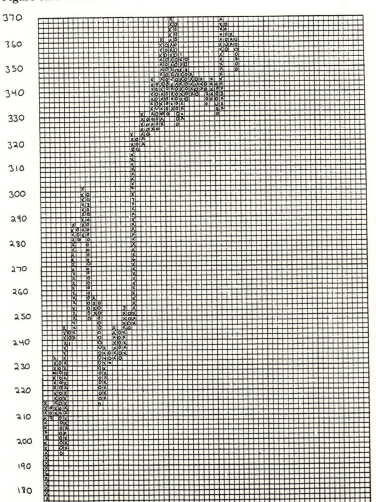

the DJUA to be an invaluable technical indicator with an outstanding predictive record for the overall market.

Although not graphically portrayed, the Dow Jones Transportation Average (DJTA) similarly possesses merit as a technical tool. One reason the DJTA commands attention from analysts stems from its role in the Dow theory. Another factor concerns the highly leveraged nature of the transportation industry.

Heavy use of debt among transportation issues suggests two key considerations. First, the DJTA is highly interest rate sensitive because of the heavy reliance on

Figure 8.20 Continued

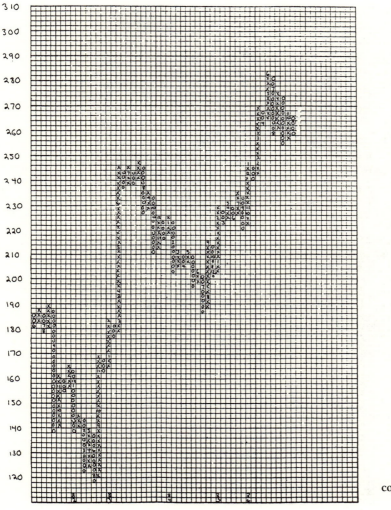

continues

debt by component stocks. Second, heavily leveraged transportation stocks are more speculative in nature because of the volatile shifts in earnings patterns. Relatively heavy or light trading indicates growing or reduced amounts of speculation in the stock market.

Interestingly enough, many of the trading-oriented chart patterns introduced earlier in this chapter work well in forecasting the DJUA and the DJTA. Low poles and high poles, among others, help make these technical tools more functional and predictive.

Figure 8.20 Continued

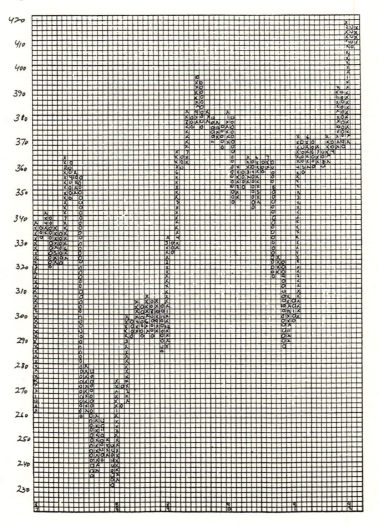

The Dow Jones 20 Bond Average

From the preceding section, we learn that bond prices are critical to the performance of common stocks (covered in detail in Chapter 11). Bond prices parallel stock price movements most of the time. However, bonds become even more significant in the asset allocation process at major junctures in the market because of their status as a leading indicator of stock prices.

P & F analysis can be used to evaluate bond prices and trends. For example,

Figure 8.20 Continued

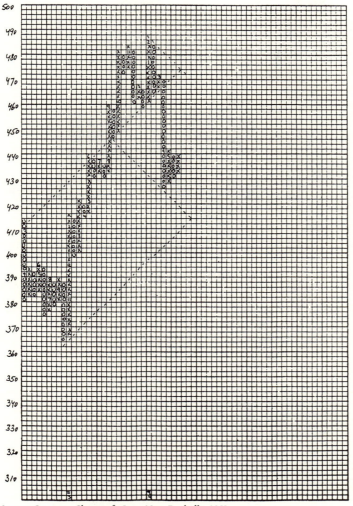

Source: Courtesy Chartcraft, Inc., New Rochelle, N.Y.

let us take a cursory look at Figure 8.22. Notice the effectiveness of the trading patterns such as high poles, low poles, and high poles at downtrend lines. Other trading techniques such as channel lines can also be helpful.

Through proper analysis of bond prices, we have an excellent technical indicator of forthcoming common stock trends. Bond prices are also heavily interrelated with other markets. As we see in Chapter 11, bond prices depend on commodity prices, precious metals markets, the dollar, energy prices, and foreign currency trends, among others. At this point, however, the key aspect of our

Figure 8.21
The Dow Jones Utility Average

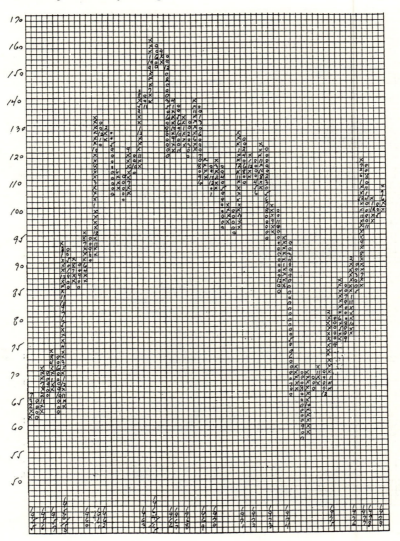

analysis focuses on applying trading techniques to anticipate discernible swings in bond prices. The importance of bond analysis as a leading technical tool cannot be emphasized enough.

THE NYSE BULLISH PERCENTAGE

The remainder of the technical indicator list includes the most effective tools we have found available to the stock market. Developed by Chartcraft, Inc., *the*

Figure 8.21 Continued

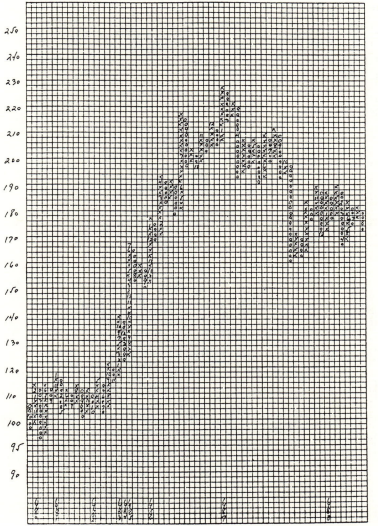

continues

NYSE bullish percentage ranks among the most reliable indicators ever used as a forecasting technique for stock prices.[8] The idea underlying the bullish percentage is to identify well-defined overbought and oversold extremes. By detecting periods of excesses, the indicator enables us to anticipate major turning points and assume long or short positions in advance. The bullish percentage leads directional shifts in the market. Its status as a *leading indicator* makes the bullish percentage vital to asset managers looking for an edge in market timing. Never underestimate the importance of the NYSE bullish percentage![9]

Figure 8.21 Continued

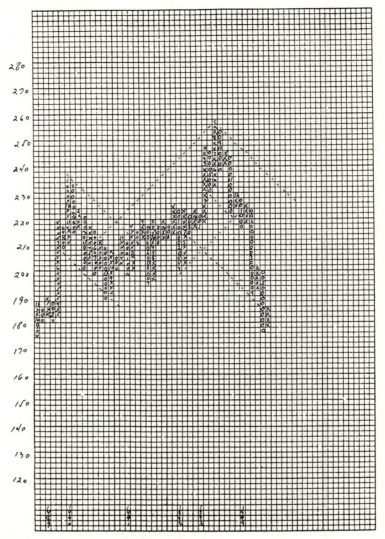

Source: Courtesy Chartcraft, Inc., New Rochelle, N.Y.

The bullish percentage concept applies to both aggregate market analysis and to group evaluation and thus assumes a paramount role for the remainder of the book. By definition, Chartcraft, Inc., determines the percentage of all NYSE stocks with buy signals on their P & F charts. The number of bullish stocks is then divided by all stocks (bullish + bearish) on the NYSE.

Figure 8.23 indicates that only forty-two columns of recordings transpired from 1981 to early 1993. Since the bullish percentage indicator is not volatile, its

Figure 8.22
The Dow Jones Twenty–Bond Average

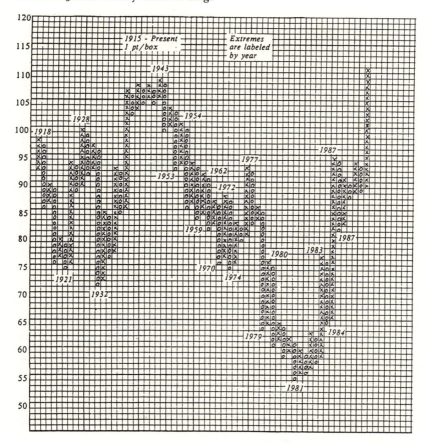

Figure 8.22 Continued

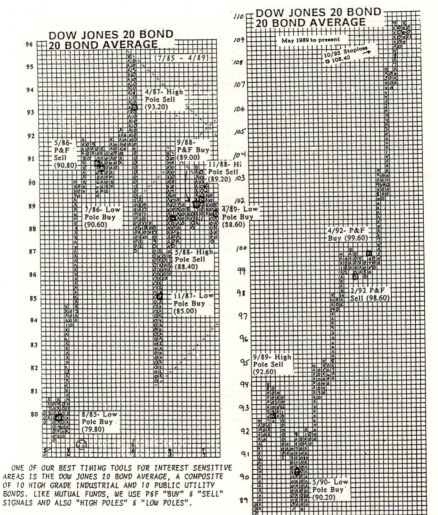

ONE OF OUR BEST TIMING TOOLS FOR INTEREST SENSITIVE AREAS IS THE DOW JONES 20 BOND AVERAGE, A COMPOSITE OF 10 HIGH GRADE INDUSTRIAL AND 10 PUBLIC UTILITY BONDS. LIKE MUTUAL FUNDS, WE USE P&F "BUY" & "SELL" SIGNALS AND ALSO "HIGH POLES" & "LOW POLES".

SHOWN ABOVE IS THE 20-BOND ACTION SINCE JULY '85, SPLIT ON TWO FRAMES BECAUSE OF THE SHARP RISE. SIGNALS SHOWN HAVE WORKED OUT VERY WELL.

Figure 8.22 Continued

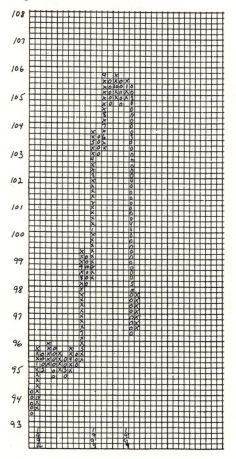

Source: Courtesy Chartcraft, Inc., New Rochelle, N.Y.

Figure 8.23
The NYSE Bullish Percentage

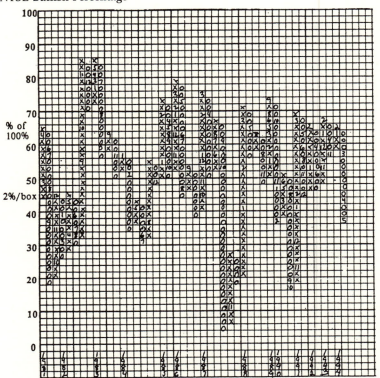

Source: Courtesy Chartcraft, Inc., New Rochelle, N.Y.

movements are of the utmost importance and its proven track record indisputable. To enhance understanding of the bullish percentage, let us analyze the Chartcraft approach to interpretation. When indicator declines dip below 30%, the aggregate stock market enters oversold territory. In effect, less than 30% of all NYSE stocks have bullish chart patterns. Fewer bullish chart patterns suggest that a weaker general market has negatively impacted a large number of stocks during recent downside moves. As the overall stock market slide steepens, more bearish chart patterns evolve, and the percentage reading falls. Consequently, the more deeply oversold the stock market becomes.

Understanding the bullish percentage involves the proper timing to allocate funds into equities. No commitments should be made in stocks during indicator declines until a three-box reversal occurs. Since each square amounts to 2%, a 6% movement constitutes a change in direction. Upside market reversals form from levels less than 30%. However, upturns in the indicator from below 20% and 10% indicate greater bullish potential as the rallies originate from more deeply oversold markets.

When a three-box reversal upturn occurs from below 10%, 20%, or 30%, we have a *bull alert market.* Both traders and investors should purchase stocks because of the oversold market condition. Stock trades and call options should be concentrated in the strongest groups, although long-term investors can afford to be less discriminating if they remain patient. Maximum profit potential rests with transactions in the early stages of a bull alert market. Whenever a buy signal takes place from a column of X's in the NYSE bullish percentage, we have a *bull confirmed market.* Both traders and investors can engage in transactions with higher levels of confidence as the uptrend should be sustainable for the foreseeable future with broad-based advances until the late phases of the bull market.

After upside reversals occur from below 10%, 20%, or 30%, what happens if the NYSE bullish percentage experiences another decline below 30%? Chartcraft refers to such dips as *bear market bottoms,* which serve as interruptions in the newly formed advance. One or more drops below 30% may develop, but such declines suggest the market is probing for a bottom. Hence, the term bear market bottoms aptly describes this phase of the advance. Do not allow dips below 30% to alter your interpretation of the market's strength.

When the indicator readings reverse downward from above 30% but below 70%, we refer to such declines as *bull correction markets.* Corrections in the bullish percentage trend are usually of short duration because of the absence of a sell signal. Falling indicator readings from less than 70% are caused from a retracement in the aggregate market. Corrections ensure the long-term health of a bull market and should not force a change in investment posture yet.

As indicator readings reach 70% and higher, we are entering into an overbought market and downside vulnerability increases dramatically. Once more than 70% of all stocks show bullish chart patterns, we must conclude that almost everyone agrees that a bull market is underway. Downmoves from above 70%, 80%, or 90% to below 70% signal a *bear alert market.* Traders and option players should liquidate long positions until the market outlook becomes more definitive. Once a sell signal materializes, a *bear confirmed market* occurs. All long positions should be liquidated and consideration should be given to puts and short sales. The downtrend in stock prices takes on an aura of certainty and all doubts should be erased.

Upmoves from above 30% but below 70% during a bear confirmed market should be termed *bear correction markets.* Increases in the percentage reading result from rally attempts in the general stock market, but they usually prove to be disruptions within the overall downtrend. Do not seek long positions, and such disruptions in the downmove may be used to build additional short positions and puts. Once the first downmove below 70% occurs, you may expect one or more rally attempts back above 70% readings. These attempts are termed *bull market tops* and should not alter your original perceptions of a major downtrend.

Greed and fear can be depicted in the NYSE bullish percentage. Once readings move below 30%, most investors have reached panicky stages. Indicator levels below 10% and 20% suggest even higher levels of anxiety among investors. Bull markets have their inception in an environment of pessimism and fear. Conversely, percentage readings above 70% suggest public awareness of rising prices and a willingness to participate by most investors. Levels exceeding 80% and 90% indicate extreme optimism and warn of the vulnerability that may arise early in the bear market.

INTERPRETING THE NYSE BULLISH PERCENTAGE

Michael Burke and John Gray of Chartcraft offer several rules for accurate evaluation of the NYSE bullish percentage.[10] The number one rule stresses that most members of the investing public are aware of a bull market when 70% or more of all chart patterns are bullish. For in-and-out traders and relatively nimble investors, begin some profit taking at the 70% level. Although the indicator may move above 80% or 90% and also may remain there for a while, never count on being quick enough to identify a reversal and exit positions "just in time." Remember, the easy money has been made before readings hit 70%. The major change from above the 70% level is that the market will become more discriminating.

Second, understand the significance of the 70% level. Movements from above 70% to below 70% place the indicator in a *bear alert status,* which means that downside risk increases. Although the bull market may continue, 70% represents a line of demarcation. A decline below 70% suggests that more chart patterns have reached near-term targets. Changing from bull confirmed to bear alert status indicates profit taking and warns that the advance may encounter some resistance. Unless your investment horizon spans unusually long time periods, take advantage of gains, liquidate, and reenter the market once the technical position improves.

Rule 3 deals with a declining bullish percentage reading, which ultimately moves from above 72% to 68% or below. Once the reading dips to less than 70%, the downmove becomes more protracted. Expect the bullish percentage to drop to 50% or between 40% and 50% within a period of two to six months. Understand that when the readings hits 68%, we are uncertain whether the market decline represents a correction or a full-fledged bear market. Corrections usually conclude between 40% and 50%, with 50% serving as a good approximation. However, major bear market movements will decline to less than 30% with a good possibility of reaching below 10% or 20%.

The fourth rule warns speculators to protect paper profits on puts and short positions once the NYSE bullish percentage reading hits the general area of 50%. Using protective stop orders is advisable. If the bullish percentage has been in a *bull correction market,* long positions may be resumed once a three-box reversal to the upside occurs. If the chart indicates *a bear confirmed market,* do not make purchases until a reversal develops from below 30%. Most mistakes result from making commitments too early.

A fifth rule yields a conservative approach for speculators who own puts or sold short when the reading drops to 68%. Since an average decline level from the 68% reading is about 44%, close out puts and shorts when the indicator approaches the mid–40s. Although positions may sometimes be closed out too soon, it is better to be "safe than sorry." A better rule may be to maintain puts and shorts until a three-box reversal surfaces in the bullish percentage. Subjectivity enters the picture on rule 5 because unusually weak stocks will move lower and reverse last. However, volatile issues and stocks in strong groups need to be closed out when a column of X's appears in the bullish percentage. If a three-box reversal in the X column quickly concludes and another column of O's forms, short positions and puts may be renewed.

Rule 6 helps clarify the aggregate market picture for short sellers and put buyers when the reading moves below 68%. On the first upturn from below 50%, look at the previous columns of X's to see if it exceeded the top of the preceding X column. A buy signal placed the indicator (and market) in a bullish posture, so the decline more than likely indicates a correction that will conclude with a reading between 40% and 50%. We have a *bull correction market* and long positions are acceptable once the bullish percentage shows a three-box reversal in a column of X's. If the preceding column of X's failed to yield a buy signal, the bullish percentage (and market) is bearish, and you should continue to avoid long positions until the indicator reaches oversold territory.

Rule 7 applies to a *bull correction market* where the previous column of X's gave a buy signal and the current column of O's has failed to yield a sell signal. Confine long positions to stocks that display positive relative strength. More market risks are present under these circumstances because a three-box column of X's could always be quickly changed if another column of O's appears. Other indicators treated in this chapter should also be evaluated before decisions are finalized. Key measures include the percentage of stocks above ten-week and thirty-week moving averages, high-low indexes, and other bullish percentages (to be discussed shortly).

An eighth rule can be summarized briefly.[11] Most profits are made when various bullish percentages turn up from low levels and move to 70%. Once the 70% level comes into play, the subtlety of the advance disappears amidst media attention and frantic sales spiels from brokers. Profits generally become smaller as the market reaches more selective stages. Similarly, profits from short sales are realized more easily when bullish percentages decline below 70% but remain above 30%. Once the 30% level enters the picture, the market becomes more discriminating and profits from shorts and puts either disappear or shrink. The prevailing downtrend becomes apparent to the public and media, both of whom thrive on negative thoughts. In effect, the easy money is made on both sides of the market prior to public awareness and market extremes.

The final rule advises portfolio managers that asset allocations should change to common stocks once the readings indicate oversold extremes. Bullish percentage levels below 10%, 20%, and 30% warn of inordinate amounts of pessimism. The lower the reading, the more oversold the market, so portfolio managers need to time their movements accordingly. Long positions should be established at the first sign of a three-box reversal in a column of X's from below 30%. Stronger, more enduring rallies will emerge if upside movements originate from below 10% or 20%. Similarly, short positions or an exodus from the stock market should occur on either the first sell signal, first three-box reversal from above 70%, 80%, or 90%, or on the initial drop below 70%.

THE DJIA, ASE, AND OTC BULLISH PERCENTAGES

Chartcraft also follows bullish percentages for the DJIA, the American Stock Exchange, and the over-the-counter markets. The same rules and interpretation apply to each. The underlying significance lies in the speculative nature of the OTC and ASE markets. Since OTC stocks fail to meet any listing criteria, they trade on the NASDAQ rather than a particular exchange. OTC stocks are considered the most speculative, whereas ASE issues follow closely behind. Meanwhile, the DJIA stocks represent blue chip activity.

The bullish percentages for the OTC and ASE markets generally signal problems early by changing directions first. Speculative markets often make their moves early in either direction and precede activity in higher-quality markets. Asset managers should place heavy emphasis on trends and levels of the OTC and ASE bullish percentages because their interpretation serves as a preview of later action on the NYSE. Although the bullish percentage indicator for the DJIA serves as a useful tool in following blue chip issues, remember its use is in analyzing price trends of stocks which lag the market.

Although much involvement in certain asset management and allocation deals with higher quality issues because of the fiduciary responsibility attached, strategies may be formulated by closely scrutinizing the more speculative trends. The DJIA bottoms last and "tops out" last. OTC and ASE bullish percentages stand the best chance of serving as leading indicators. Figure 8.24 provides a look at the ASE bullish percentage, and Figure 8.25 shows the underlying stocks bullish percentage. Underlying stocks can be defined as all stocks that have listed options traded. This bullish percentage is the same in format and interpretation and merely helps gauge trading activity in the options markets.

APPLYING THE MOVING AVERAGE CONCEPT

The concept of moving averages assumes a key role in technical analysis. When a stock price exceeds its moving average, a bullish trend exists; prices below moving averages are in bearish trends. Extending such logic allows us to conclude that if a large percentage of stocks exceed their moving averages, the overall market must be bullish. Similarly, when large percentages of stocks fall below their moving averages, the general trend of the market has to be bearish.

Much of our market analysis focuses on greed, fear, investor sentiment, and identifying these well-defined extremes in thought and behavior. Logically, if we

Figure 8.24
The ASE Bullish Percentage

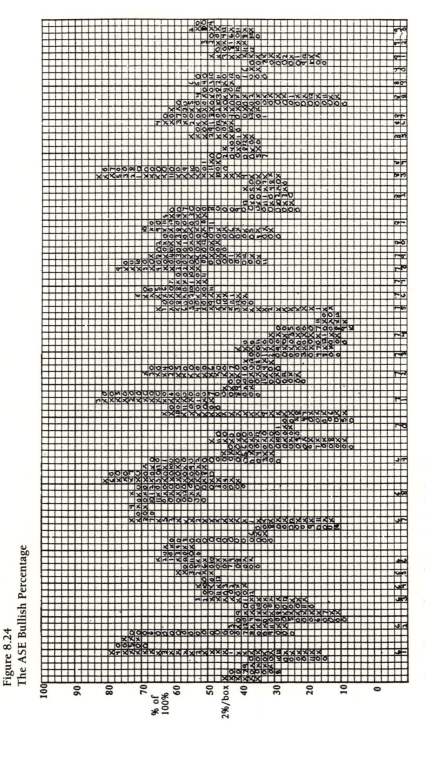

Source: Courtesy Chartcraft, Inc., New Rochelle, N.Y.

Figure 8.25
Underlying Stocks Bullish Percentage

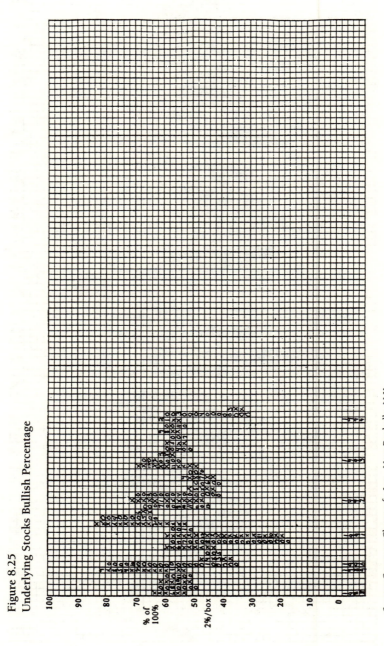

Source: Courtesy Chartcraft, Inc., New Rochelle, N.Y.

are able to identify extremes, we can forecast directional changes in the general market. Let us approach moving averages from a composite point of view. As more stocks rise above their moving averages, the greater the public optimism as investors realize that something is taking place in the market. When 70%, 80%, or 90% of all stocks on a given exchange are above their moving averages, bullish extremes appear. Similarly, when large numbers of stocks begin to fall below their moving averages, investors are obviously liquidating positions in pessimism and fear. When less than 10%, 20%, or 30% of all stock prices drop below moving averages, bearish extremes surface.

For interpretation ease, the Chartcraft approach (see Figures 8.26 and 8.27) categorizes extremes for indicators in the same fashion. Below 30%, we have a bullish market environment when the indicator gives a three-box reversal to the upside. The most extreme oversold levels originate from below 20% and 10%. Similarly, above 70% provides a potentially bearish situation as the market reaches overbought territory. However, readings above 80% and 90% offer potentially the steepest declines because of the excessive optimism.

Chartcraft offers proprietary data for ten-week and thirty-week moving averages on both the NYSE and ASE. Interpretations remain the same for each, although traders observe the ten-week moving averages more closely because of its greater sensitivity to shorter-term trends. Longer-term investors express more interest in the thirty-week moving averages because they are less sensitive to day-to-day fluctuations and exclude less meaningful prices moves. However, penetrations of the thirty-week moving average in either direction have more significance due to their relative permanence. Moving averages for the ASE should be examined closely because speculative extremes can be followed and identified quickly. Remember, what shows up in OTC and ASE markets presages a preview of what is to come on the NYSE markets.

HIGH-LOW INDEXES

The Chartcraft version of the high-low index can be constructed by dividing the number of stocks making daily new highs on an exchange by the total number of stocks on the same exchange which make new highs and new lows. A ten-day moving average is then calculated to reduce aberrations and provide a smoothing effect. High-low indexes are illustrated for the NYSE, OTC, and ASE markets, respectively, in Figures 8.28, 8.29, and 8.30.

Let us analyze the high-low index from a commonsense perspective. As increasing numbers of stocks make new highs, more investors show tendencies to "chase stocks" during their advance. Although new highs remain technically positive in keeping with the importance of Dow's works, an excessive number suggests extremes and an awareness of a strong bull market. When the high-low indexes reach 70%, 80%, or 90% and above, well-defined extremes of optimism exist. In effect, more than 70% of all stocks on a given exchange are making new highs. The obvious strength in the market induces uninformed investors to enter

Figure 8.26
Percentage of NYSE Stocks above Ten-Week Moving Averages

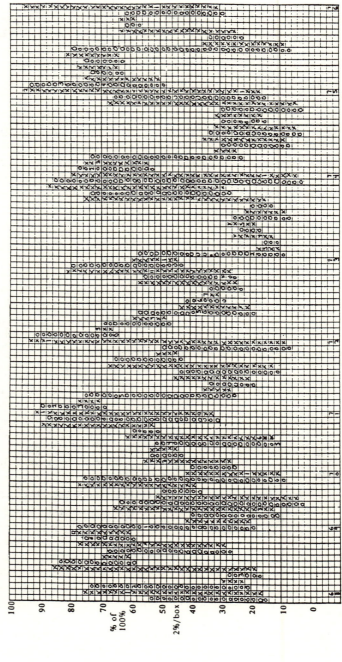

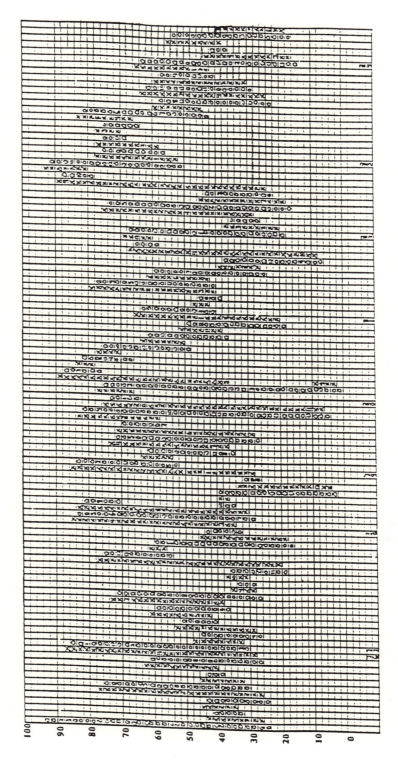

100 90 80 70 60 50 40 30 20 10 0

Figure 8.26 Continued

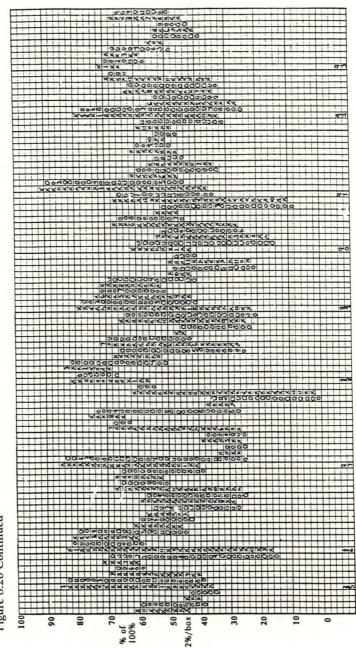

% of
100%

2%/box

Figure 8.27
Percentage of NYSE Stocks above Thirty-Week Moving Averages

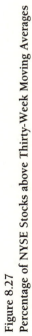

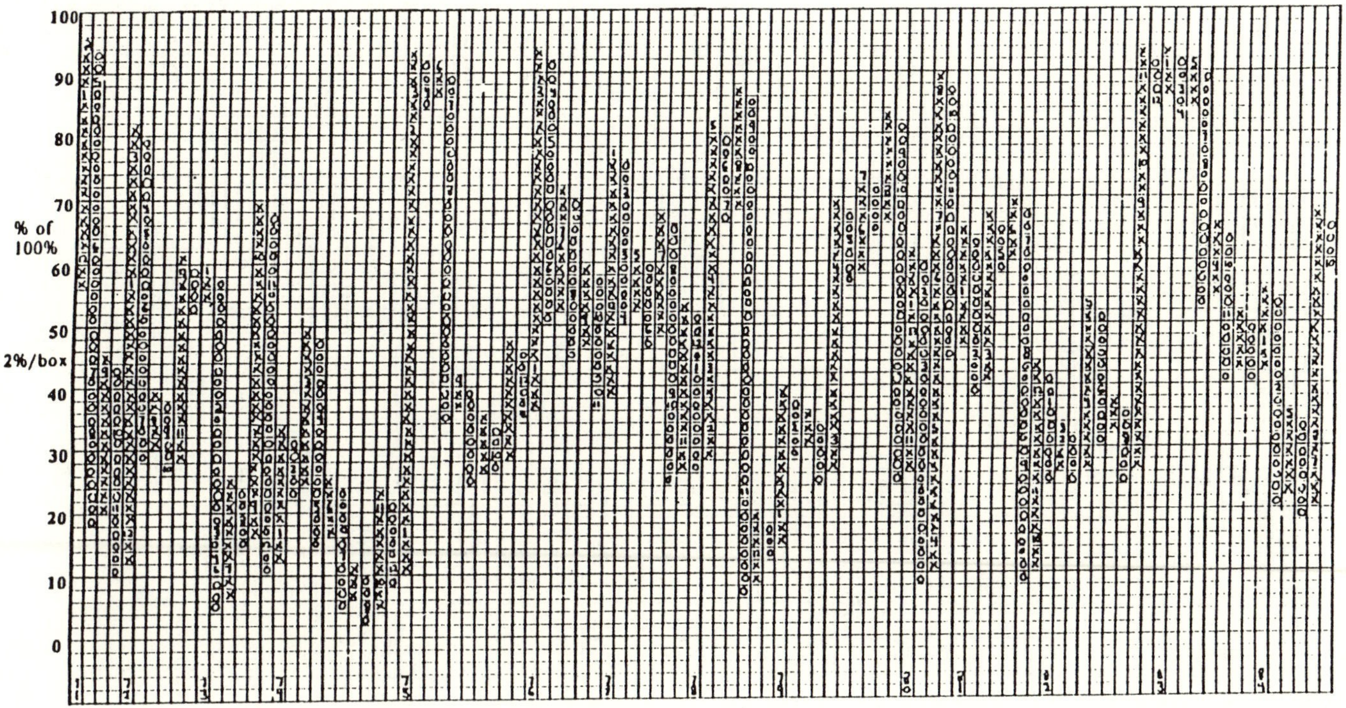

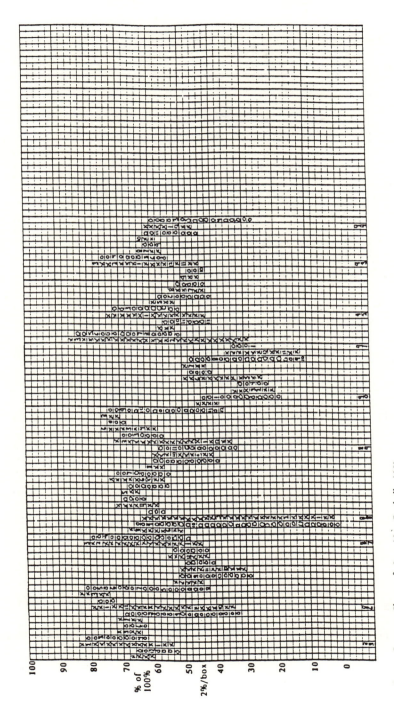

Source: Courtesy Chartcraft, Inc., New Rochelle, N.Y.

100
90
80
70
% of
100%
2%/box
50
40
30
20
10
0

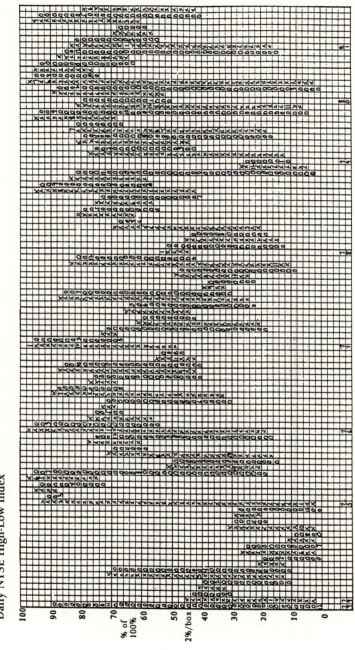

Figure 8.28
Daily NYSE High-Low Index

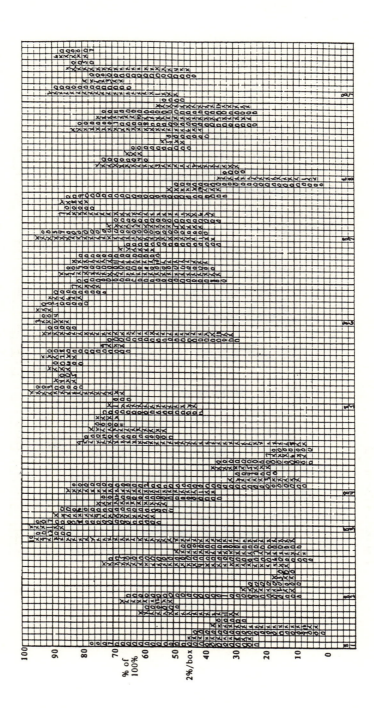

Figure 8.28 Continued

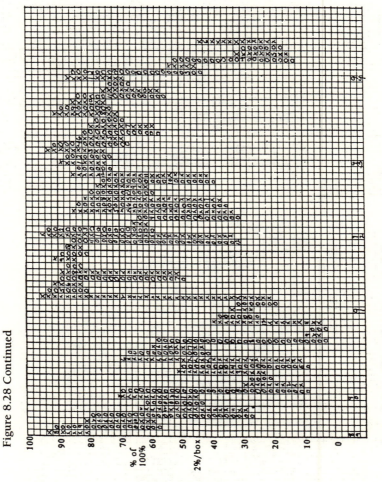

Source: Courtesy Chartcraft, Inc., New Rochelle, N.Y.

Figure 8.29
Daily Over-the-Counter High-Low Index

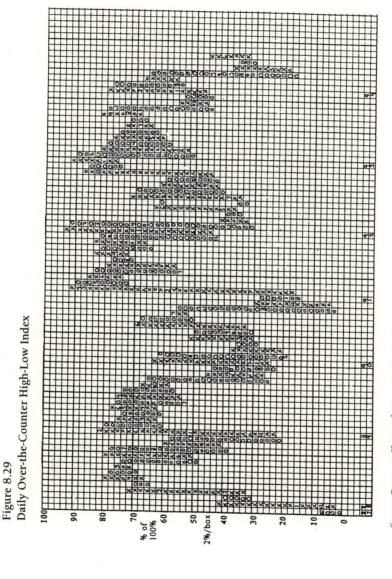

Source: Courtesy Chartcraft, Inc., New Rochelle, N.Y.

245

Figure 8.30
ASE Daily High-Low Index

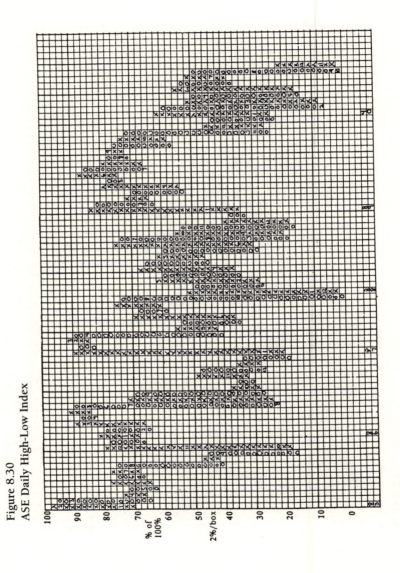

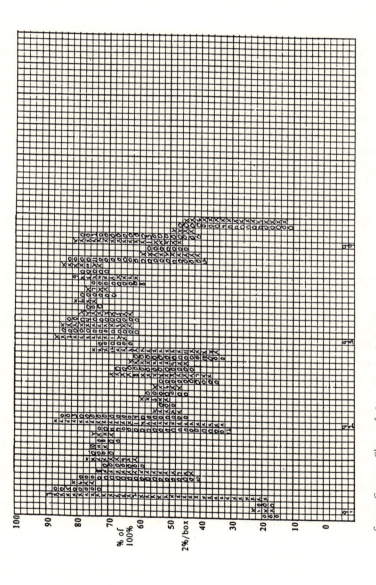

247

the market on a broad scale. Such speculative excesses can be eliminated by corrections in the general market. Downturns in the high-low index from above 70% warn of impending declines.

In the same vein, high-low index readings of less than 10%, 20%, or 30% signify a deeply oversold market where few individual stocks make new highs and large numbers of issues reach new lows. Public pessimism is widespread as fundamentals worsen. Asset managers must reach decisions to accumulate equities at the first sign of a three-box reversal to the upside while negative outlooks broaden. Follow all three high-low indexes (NYSE, ASE, and OTC) to understand activity in each market segment. As with the bullish percentage, a final observation should be interjected in connection with established parameters. Enter the market with no doubts when indexes give buy signals and exit on sell signals. Further, go long on the first three-box reversal from below 10% (and usually 20%) with no reservations and liquidate on the first three-box downmove from above 90% (and normally 80%).

THE ADVANCE-DECLINE LINE

The advance-decline (A-D) line measures underlying technical strength and remains the best measure of breadth available in market analysis. When more stocks advance in price compared to declining issues, the market is technically stronger and has positive plurality. If more stocks decline in price relative to advancing issues, the market is technically weaker and shows negative plurality. Declining and advancing totals are accumulated daily in order that a "running total" may be retained for plotting purposes. Figure 8.31 graphically portrays the A-D line.

Two key ideas remain central to the interpretation of the A-D line. First, it normally parallels the stock market in trend. If the A-D line suddenly turns down while the market continues to advance, we call this *divergence*. The market weakens technically and will soon follow the A-D line as breadth deteriorates. During a downtrend, the A-D line may turn upward while the market continues lower. The rising A-D line in the face of a declining market is termed *convergence* and signals a turnaround in the stock market over the near term. The A-D line generally tops out before the market and serves as a leading indicator. However, A-D lines may coincide with market movements near bottoms.

Second, there are three important A-D lines. Breadth for the NYSE, ASE, and OTC markets provides an idea of underlying technical strength or weakness for different market segments. Chartcraft views A-D lines as positive when all three exceed their levels of ten days ago. Levels less than their readings ten days ago cause suspicion because breadth has deteriorated. If the OTC and ASE A-D lines fail to reach levels of ten days ago while the NYSE surges well above comparable tops, avoid speculative markets and stay with higher quality issues.

Figure 8.31
The NYSE Daily Cumulative A-D Line

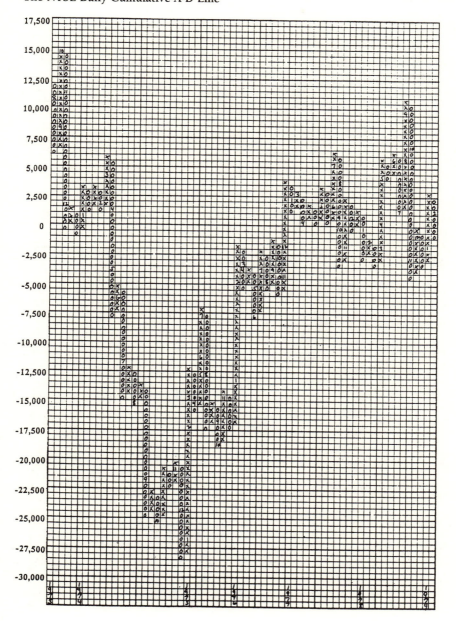

Figure 8.31 Continued

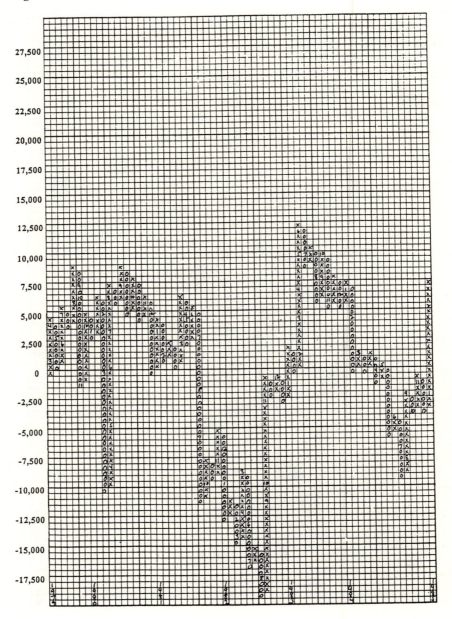

Figure 8.31 Continued

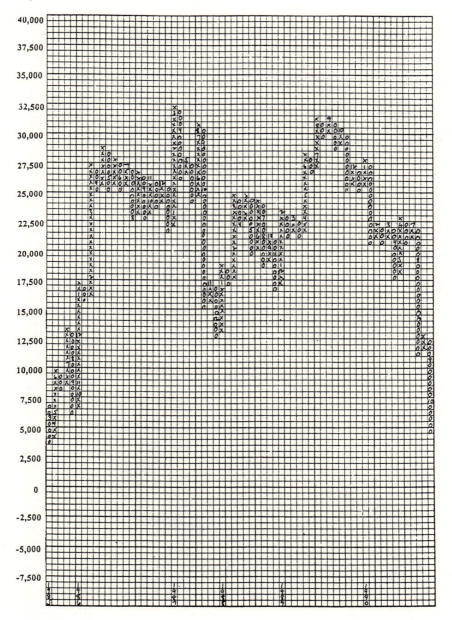

Figure 8.31 Continued

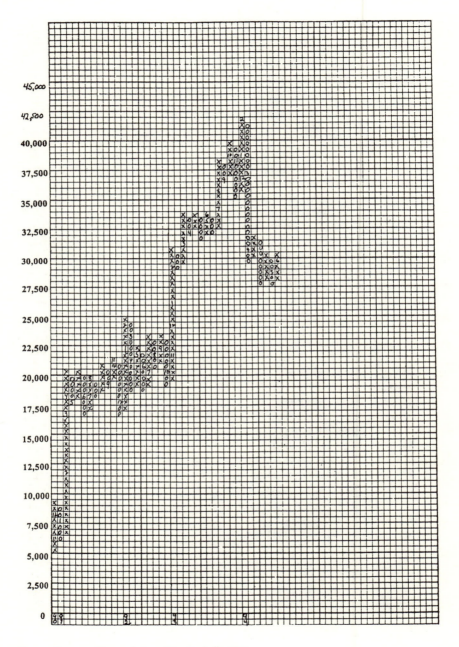

Source: Courtesy Chartcraft, Inc., New Rochelle, N.Y.

PUTTING A STRATEGY TOGETHER

Although heavy emphasis is placed on group analysis in Chapter 12 with our treatment of mutual funds, let us introduce the importance of different sectors of the market. When allocation decisions focus on individual issues, we should buy strong stocks in an advancing industry group during a rising market. By definition, strong stocks should have positive relative strength. Short sales (or liquidations) should center on weak stocks with negative relative strength in declining industry groups (sectors) in a falling market. The industry grouping is of paramount importance.

Let us assume in the spring of 1991 we are looking at the investment brokerage firms with the idea of accumulating some stocks. In Figure 8.32 we look at Merrill Lynch and its chart pattern in early 1991 shows signs of building a major bottom. Morgan Keegan also shows a bottoming pattern, although not quite as impressive as Merrill Lynch. Next, we examine the relative strength (inserted for illustration purposes) of each issue in the upper right-hand corner of the chart (using Chartcraft charts works easier than doing your own calculations). Merrill Lynch's RS shows a buy signal in 4/91, whereas Morgan Keegan's RS turns positive in 5/91. Both the bullish chart patterns and their positive RS charts meet our criteria.

Next, we look at the "Finance-Investment Brokers" group chart, which bottomed and now shows a strong 1991 upmove that proves to be a low pole. The "Wall Street" group bullish percentage shows a strong rally from below 10% in early 1991. Since all bullish percentage charts require the same interpretation, we recognize that the investment group is in the formative stages of what should be a major upmove. Finally, we look at the aggregate market as evidenced by the S & P 500. The market also appears to have completed the bottom to a very nasty downmove.

Figure 8.32 shows how we put the pieces together for our total strategy. We buy bullish stocks with positive RS charts in strong groups and a rising market. Although the market will experience setbacks during the advance, our stocks should do well and outperform the market.

SUMMARY

This chapter concludes our treatment of P & F charting as an integral aspect of technical analysis. By virtue of its timing advantages, technical analysis emerges as a vital part of portfolio management and asset allocation strategies. Not only do P & F charts assist in decisions relating to individual issues, they play a role in analyzing groups and the aggregate market.

We have learned that some of the older, more traditional chart patterns may need some updating. Thus we included high poles, low poles, triple bottom failures, triple top failures, key reversals, shakeouts, and spikes, among others. Each new pattern helps combat criticisms of P & F charting techniques. Finally, we put together a total strategy that asset managers can use in the selection or liqui-

Figure 8.32
The Whole Picture

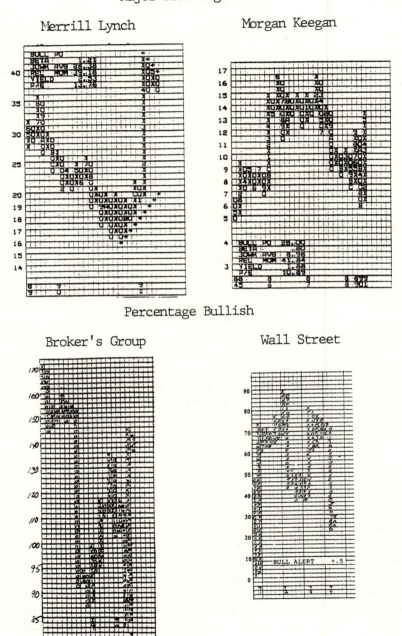

Major Brokerage Firms

Merrill Lynch   Morgan Keegan

Percentage Bullish

Broker's Group   Wall Street

Figure 8.32 Continued

S & P 500

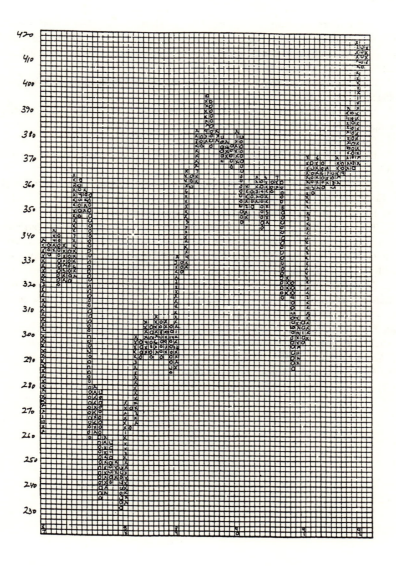

Source: Courtesy Chartcraft, Inc., New Rochelle, N.Y.

dation of individual stocks. Later, many of these same techniques will serve as viable strategies in selecting other assets.

NOTES

1. The authors gratefully acknowledge the contributions of Mike Burke, John Gray, and all of the Chartcraft staff in the completion of this manuscript. In addition to furnishing all of the point and figure charts, their spirit of cooperation and valuable insights made the completion of the book possible.

2. Earl Blumenthal, *Chart for Profit Point and Figure Trading* (Larchmont, N.Y.: Investors Intelligence, 1975), 42–45.

3. Michael L. Burke, *Three-Point Reversal Method of Point & Figure Construction and Formations* (New Rochelle, N.Y.: Chartcraft, Inc., 1990), 70–71.

4. Blumenthal, *Chart for Profit Point and Figure Trading*, 37.

5. Burke, *Three-Point Reversal Method of Point & Figure Construction and Formations*, 54–55.

6. Carroll D. Aby, Jr., *The Complete Guide to Point and Figure Charting* (Birmingham, Ala.: Colonial Press, 1992), 131–33.

7. Blumenthal, *Chart for Profit Point and Figure Trading*, 45.

8. The original work on the NYSE bullish percentage was performed by Earl Blumenthal and called "the bullish-bearish index." Later work was initiated by A. W. Cohen, *How to Use the Three-Point Reversal Method of Point and Figure Stock Market Trading*, 9th ed. (New Rochelle, N.Y.: Chartcraft, Inc., 1987).

9. All of the current refinements concerning the NYSE bullish percentage should be attributed to Michael L. Burke, Editor, Chartcraft, Inc. Mike has been a close friend for many years and he and John Gray have been of immeasurable help.

10. For more treatment of these and other ideas relating to the NYSE bullish percentage, see Michael L. Burke and John E. Gray, eds., *Chartcraft's Options Service* (New Rochelle, N.Y.: Chartcraft, Inc., 1989–1993), select issues.

11. Aby, *The Complete Guide to Point & Figure Charting*.

Chapter 9

SELECTING TIMELY INDUSTRIES

Many investment advisors suggest that selecting industries whose companies are being accumulated by large institutional investors and other buyers is of greater significance to earning above average stock market profits than seeking out individual firms with growth appeal. Several approaches can be followed in these endeavors, including time series analysis approaches, fundamental approaches, technical approaches, and the Value Line approach. Many of these are illustrated in this chapter, and certain market anomalies are tested in Chapter 10.

The groups of stocks to be studied can be broken down in a number of different ways, and investment services vary widely as to the different groups of stocks. For example, Moody's Investors Service provides historical and current information in four basic breakdowns—financial, utilities, transports, and industrials. Any firm that does not fit into one of the first three groups, generally, is classified as an industrial. The several federal agencies use about ten sectors for classifying private companies. This grouping can further be broken down into three or four digit industry classifications.

Value Line, Inc., generally follows this classification in its EDP Data Base plus. These major sectors are agriculture, extracting, construction, manufacturing, utility, transport, wholesaling, retailing, financial, and services. Standard & Poor's breaks the stocks into about sixty to sixty-five major industry groups, whereas Value Line, Inc., uses about ninety-five groups, including some geographic breakdown for banks and electric utilities. Dow Jones (in *Barron's*) uses about thirty-seven groups, including the DJIA, DJTA, and DJUA. Studies from most of these services are included in this chapter to show how they might be utilized in selecting groups of timely stocks selected to meet certain investment objectives.

Before selecting a method, the rational investor should determine her or his investment objective. A short-term trader, for example, might become a technician or buy groups of stocks that usually move in a predictable annual manner. A technician seeking a one- or two-year investment might concentrate on cyclical swingers, whereas someone wanting long-term growth appeal should seek out strong firms in industries with long-term potential for growth in sales and profits.

Recall from Chapter 2 that the major components of the business swings include seasonal, cyclical, and long-term secular trends. Each of these are reviewed in this order in this section.

SEASONAL TRADING IN STOCKS

Overall, January appears to be the month with the strongest upside bias in stock prices. The first quarter generally performs better than others, followed by the second, and fourth. The third quarter often sees substantial market declines, at least during bear market years. Having some general impression about the overall stock market action, however, is inadequate for selecting stocks from industries with strong appeal. Let us consider the average quarterly moves as shown from *Value Line Data Base* from the six years of data ending with October 1991. This is reflected in the two pages of information, Table 9.1. The reader is encouraged to study the table carefully.

Most investors are interested in earning stock market profits by being long in the market. Thus the ten (of ninety-five) stock groups showing the greatest returns during quarters one through four of the preceding study are listed here.

Rank	Industry	% Return	Rank	Industry	% Return
		Quarter One			
1	Home appliance	24.60	2	Auto./trucks	23.87
3	Homebuilding	23.28	4	Recreation	21.12
5	Semiconductor	20.27	6	Toys/sch. supp.	20.27
7	Shoes	20.05	8	Steel: integra.	19.77
9	Retail: bldg. supp.	19.27	10	Apparel	19.08
		Quarter Two			
1*	Retail: bldg. supp.	12.13	2	Broadcast/cable	11.48
3	Hotel/gaming	10.22	4	For. elect./entr.	9.12
5	Drugstores	9.00	6	Grocery stores	8.73
7	Retail stores	8.04	8*	Shoes	7.41
9	Medical supplies	7.36	10	Telecomm. equip.	6.88
		Quarter Three			
1	Gold/silver	14.35	2	Copper	9.08
3	Tobacco	4.83	4	Aluminum	4.73
5	Petrol producing	4.08	6*	For. elect./entr.	3.98
7	Toiletry/cosmetics	3.38	8*	Shoes	3.03
9	Railroads	2.60	10	Tire/rubber	2.42

Quarter Four

1*	For. elect./enter.	5.86	2	European divers	5.75
3	Household prod.	4.64	4	Telecomm. svc.	3.98
5	Comp. software/svc.	3.67	6	Elect. util.: East.	3.69
7	Elec. util.: Cent.	3.47	\8	Drug	2.67
9*	Toiletry/cosmetics	2.66	10	Food processing	2.55

*Denotes repeats from the previous quarter.

Information gleaned from Table 9.1 for the above quarterly list of ten best performing groups (based on six years of data) should suggest a quarterly trading strategy into issues representative of good movers. Alternately, pools of assets with monthly cash inflows might seek to invest in those groups of stocks showing near-term price appeal. For example, new funds in January might be substantially allocated to shoe issues, since they usually perform well in quarters 1, 2, and 3. New monies in March might flow toward foreign electronic entertainment, as the issues do well the following three quarters, and so forth.

The individual who wishes to short issues might do so on the basis of usual price decline for the group of stock during certain quarters of the year. Quarter one would be a poor period for shorts, on average, but with petroleum producing and utilities (on a relative basis) being the poorest performers. Quarter two offers several groups of usually downside movers, including manufactured housing/RV, steel, integrated, gold/silver, advertising, real estate and thrift. Downside movers in quarter three are more numerous and include declines exceeding 5% for the following industries: homebuilding, textiles, apparel, home furnishings, publishing, semiconductors, toy-school supplies, maritime, telecommunications equipment, retail, building supply, restaurant, drugstore, thrift, real estate, hotel/gaming, advertising, and recreation. Substantial losers in quarter four included the following: gold/silver, petroleum producing, apparel, cement/aggregate, steel, integrated, aluminum, machinery for construction and mining, auto./truck, aerospace/defense, maritime, thrift, real estate, and hotel/gaming.

CYCLICAL TRADING IN STOCKS

Although efficient market proponents suggest that some switching into high-beta stocks during periods of expected market upside moves is appropriate, and switching back to low-beta groups when stock downturns appear likely is an appropriate market strategy, this approach will miss many of the early and later movers. At the end of each month, *Value Line Data Base Plus* provides about fifty variables on each of about 1,600 large firms in EDP personal computer format. A complete run of the data (about thirty-five pages when grouped by SIC industry designations) provides average group betas as of February 1, 1992, and May 1, 1994. There appears to be only moderate consistency between betas for groups of stocks determined at diverse time periods. For example, some forty of the ninety-one industry groups witnessed shifts in beta values of at least ten points

Table 9.1
Value Line Group Quarterly Returns

(Average of 6 years)

INDUSTRY GROUP	QU 1	QU 2	QU3	QU4
Metals/mng (div)	14.5%	1.18%	2.20	-3.78
Copper	17.22	-1.54	9.08	-4.86
Metals/mng (ind)	13.03	2.62	-0.15	-1.82
Gold/silver	7.47	-3.71	14.35	-7.68
Coal/alt energy	7.85	0.53	1.75	-2.50
Canadian energy	7.37	0.79	1.33	-2.81
Petr producing	4.40	0.72	4.08	-8.95
Homebuilding	23.28	0.58	-9.88	-0.37
Food Processing	11.37	6.85	-1.57	2.55
Beverages/alcohol	13.08	6.07	0.63	1.67
Tobacco	10.27	6.56	4.83	1.46
Beverages/soft	Combined	with	beverages/alcohol	
Textiles	14.88	6.39	-6.67	-4.47
Apparel	19.08	4.20	-6.08	-6.49
Home furnishings	15.75	4.55	-6.17	-4.76
Paper/forest products	13.50	3.86	-0.87	-2.38
Packaging/containers	13.73	5.72	-2.85	-4.05
Publishing	16.67	4.57	-0.43	-7.01
Newspaper	11.33	6.96	-5.95	-3.97
Chemicals: Basic	12.27	5.70	-2.98	-1.77
Chemical: Diversif	14.87	3.08	-1.73	-1.48
Chemical: Specialty	12.95	5.37	-1.67	-1.48
Drug	18.47	4.98	1.80	2.67
Household Prods	12.35	6.52	-1.83	4.64
Toiletries/cosmetics	14.85	5.35	3.38	2.66
Petro: Integrated	9.87	1.35	1.67	-1.54
Tire/rubber	18.25	4.78	2.42	-0.20
Shoe	20.05	7.41	3.03	-4.38
Building materials				
Cement/aggregate	17.68	1.14	-4.15	-7.71
Steel: general	15.00	6.65	-1.90	-0.57
Steel: integrated	19.77	-2.82	-4.50	-8.29
Steel: specialty	10.78	4.49	-0.03	-4.38
Aluminum	12.05	6.23	4.73	-5.12
Metal fabricating	16.28	2.75	-3.48	-3.76
Machinery	14.92	3.48	-4.33	-2.35
Mche/constr & mining	17.25	5.83	-7.22	-7.74
Oilfield svc/equip	15.50	1.87	-0.65	1.58
Machine tool	16.02	2.08	-7.15	-4.53
Office equip/supply	12.57	1.43	-3.57	-0.36
Computer/periph	18.98	3.47	-7.20	1.05
Comp software/svc	16.88	5.34	-2.70	3.67
Electrical equip	12.33	6.16	-4.52	0.57
Home appliances	24.60	4.22	-7.93	-0.31
Electronics	14.42	1.37	-4.48	-2.89
Semiconductor	20.27	3.24	-10.68	-4.54
Auto/truck	23.87	-1.44	-2.00	-5.73
Auto parts: repl	11.87	2.46	-3.75	-3.38
Auto parts: OEM	16.62	4.82	-5.10	-3.97
Aerosp/defense	11.58	1.28	-2.40	-6.80
Manuf housing/RV	18.20	-5.56	-6.58	0.04

Table 9.1 Continued

Precision instr	16.08	1.87	−4.85	−2.80
Toy/school supp	20.27	3.24	−10.68	−4.54
Railroad	12.10	1.37	2.60	−1.27
Truck/trans lsg	10.10	1.64	−1.75	−0.25
Maritime	18.33	4.69	−6.70	−6.36
Air transport	18.08	3.08	−2.37	−3.31
Telecomm svc	6.37	5.12	2.00	3.98
Telecomm equip	6.52	6.88	−6.87	−3.11
Foreign telecomm				
Broadcastg/cable	14.73	11.48	−1.68	−0.59
Elec util: east	2.67	1.87	1.03	3.69
Elec util: cent	4.27	1.50	0.70	3.47
Elec util: west	5.20	3.09	−1.32	1.60
Nat Gas: distr	4.15	2.90	1.12	0.91
Nat gas: divers	6.30	2.83	0.35	−3.35
Environmental				
Food wholesale	8.48	5.92	−4.23	0.34
Retail: bldg supp	19.27	12.13	−10.42	−1.09
Retail stores	18.23	8.04	0.23	−2.11
Grocery	11.12	8.73	−0.67	−0.50
Retail specialty	17.53	5.89	−4.42	−4.56
Restaurant	14.65	6.77	−5.52	−3.88
Drugstore	15.10	9.00	−5.20	−3.89
Bank	11.88	4.87	−3.87	−3.02
Bank: midwest	11.38	5.32	−1.47	−1.09
Bank: Canadian				
Financial svcs	16.45	−2.33	−1.22	−1.85
Thrift	13.37	2.55	−10.83	−5.41
Secur brokerage	17.67	0.73	0.18	−3.35
Insurance: life	12.57	2.19	−2.00	−1.74
Insurance: divers	11.78	0.01	−1.90	−0.22
Insurance: P/C	12.32	1.12	−3.78	0.14
Real estate	13.80	−4.45	−10.95	−8.72
Hotel/gaming	18.38	10.22	−7.97	−5.83
Industrial svcs	12.27	4.89	−3.25	−0.24
Advertising	14.48	−2.17	−8.05	−4.30
Recreation	21.12	3.25	−5.30	−1.44
Medical services	14.82	5.02	−3.95	−3.49
Medical supp	17.42	7.36	1.22	1.64
Diversif cos	13.80	2.53	−0.07	−1.13
European divers	11.73	4.27	−0.22	5.75
For elec/entrtn	6.63	9.12	3.98	5.86
Unclassified	18.02	2.27	−4.68	−2.21

Source: Developed from *Value Screen* +, Value Line, Inc., 10–1 and 4–1 PC disks, 1986–1992.

Table 9.2
Value Line Group Betas for Two Different Dates

Industry Group	Avg Beta Feb. 1992	Avg Beta May 1994
EXTRACTING		
Metals/mng	1.14	.92
Copper	1.08	0.98
Gold/silver	0.61	0.28
Coal/alt energy	0.94	0.77
Canadian energy	0.73	0.58
Petr producing	0.91	0.74
CONSTRUCTION		
Homebuilding	1.33	1.37
MANUFACTURING		
Food Processing	0.96	0.95
Beverages/alcohol	0.94	0.88
Tobacco	0.92	1.02
Beverages/soft	1.09	1.14
Apparel	1.20	1.09
Home furnishings	0.91	0.89
Paper/forest products	1.21	1.07
Packaging/containers	0.96	0.95
Publishing	1.03	0.99
Newspaper	1.04	1.00
Chemical: Diversif	1.07	0.92
Chemical: Specialty	1.08	1.00
Drug	1.18	1.37
Household Prods	1.01	1.11
Toiletries/cosmetics	1.12	1.11
Petro: Integrated	0.90	0.78
Tire/rubber	1.04	1.09
Shoe	1.22	1.23
Building materials	1.06	0.95
Cement/aggregate	1.05	0.92
Steel: general	1.04	0.93
Steel: integrated	1.12	1.02
Steel: specialty	1.02	n.a.
Aluminum	1.30	1.18
Metal fabricating	1.09	0.92
Machinery	1.10	1.01
Mche/constr & mining	1.13	1.13
Oilfield svc/equip	1.11	0.98
Machine tool	1.11	1.10
Office equip/supply	1.02	1.00
Computer/periph	1.40	1.40
Comp software/svc	1.33	1.33
Electrical equip	1.08	0.98
Home appliances	1.14	1.27
Electronics	1.24	1.09
Semiconductor	1.57	1.51
Auto/truck	1.17	1.18
Auto parts: repl	1.12	0.99
Auto parts: OEM	1.05	0.93
Aerosp/defense	1.03	0.98
Manuf housing/RV	1.09	1.16
Precision instr	1.12	0.94
Toy/school supp	1.18	1.56
TRANSPORT		
Railroad	1.07	1.17
Truck/trans lsg	1.18	1.14
Maritime	1.26	1.10
Air transport	1.19	1.29
UTILITIES		
Telecom svc	0.99	1.09
Telecom equip	1.08	1.02
Foreign telecom	0.93	0.93
Broadcastg/cable	1.23	1.18
Elec util: east	0.65	0.66
Elec util: cent	0.67	0.63
Elec util: west	0.65	0.68
Nat Gas: distr	0.66	0.61
Nat gas: divers	0.96	0.84
Environmental	1.21	1.21
WHOLESALING		
Food wholesale	0.90	0.78
Retail bldg supplies	1.17	1.16
RETAILING		
Retail stores	1.23	1.23
Grocery	1.03	1.04
Retail specialty	1.28	1.33
Restaurant	1.05	1.13
Drugstore	0.99	0.91
FINANCIAL		
Bank	1.10	1.29
Bank: midwest	0.95	1.06
Bank: Canadian	0.78	0.92
Financial svcs	1.24	1.28
Thrift	1.22	1.43
Secur brokerage	1.38	1.60
Insurance: life	1.05	1.12
Insurance: divers	1.08	1.16
Insurance: P/C	0.98	1.00
Real estate	1.16	n.a.
Hotel/gaming	1.13	1.33
SERVICES		
Industrial svcs	1.06	0.99
Advertising	1.13	1.06
Recreation	1.24	1.23
Medical services	1.15	1.45
Medical supp	1.20	1.21
Diversif cos	1.10	0.97
European divers	0.82	0.84
For elec/entrtn	0.84	0.81
Unclassified	1.09	1.18
Avg for list	1.06	1.05

Source: Compiled from *Value Line +,* Value Line, Inc., PC disks dated 2–1–92 and 5–1–94.

over the twenty-seven-month period. Please study Table 9.2 for these Value Line provided beta values.

Nevertheless, those investors who wish to concentrate on low-beta stocks will find that the following groups have below average relative stock price volatility: gold/silver, Canada energy, elect. util., natural gas, Canadian banks, foreign firms, and petroleum: integrated. Their counterpart, or high-beta groups, include the following: semiconductor, computer/peripheries, brokerage, computer software, aluminum, maritime, financial services, recreation, electronics, and thrift.

The reviewer of Table 9.2 determines that many of the stocks predicted to do well by Value Line over the next three-five years are cyclical issues with above average betas, and a few growth industries with slightly above average betas. This list of stocks with Value Line's expected average annual returns exceeding 25% is as follows: copper, coal, petroleum producing, steel: integrated, oilfield service/ equipment, telecommunications equipment, and environmental.

Value Line, Inc., in its hard copy service and PC data base predicts near-term market performance and expected performance for three to five years into the future. Its selection of stocks for one year performance, given the highest value line performance rating (1 on the hard copy and 5 on the PC data base) provides very good market returns when followed. The three- to five-year forecast is thought to be much less accurate (by these writers). The reader might be shocked to discover that the three- five-year return prediction by Value Line, Inc., in early 1992 for such growth groups as drugs, medical services, and medical supplies fall into the average category of 16 to 18% returns. The relative accuracy of these forecasts will not be known for a few more years. This forecasted lackluster performance was due to the fact that most of these issues had already gained 200% or more in price from their bear market lows of late 1990, and possibly from early indication of a national health care bill. Some consolidation in these prices toward a more normal price-earnings or cash flow per share multiple is/was expected (by Value Line analysts).

One probable reason for expected poor performances of utilities is that they are highly correlated to moves in interest rates. When rates are falling, generally, utility shares move higher. When interest rates are rising, conversely, they are stagnant in price (as a group), and investors look mainly to dividend yields as their returns. Other groups of interest-sensitive stocks include homebuilding, building materials, home furnishings, manufactured housing/RV, autos and trucks, heavy equipment, hotel/gaming, recreation, and heavily leveraged individual firms.

PRICE CHANGE LEADERS AFTER BEAR MARKET BOTTOMS

In the Appendix, Table 9.8 provides insight into stocks that in the three market upturns of 1986–1987, 1988–1990 and 1991 did the best, relatively, during the first two quarters after the bear market bottom and those that did best during the third and fourth quarters (later movers) after the bear market bottoms. Unfortunately, the list offered only a few consistently early leaders, but the list of early gainers did contain several repeats in at least two of the three bull market rallies. Early substantial movers during the three bull markets are reported below for the three bull market recoveries. Selected data from Table 9.8 are shown in Table 9.3. The industry groups are arranged in SIC order, and for the three periods, are as shown in Table 9.3.

The list in Table 9.3 suggests that some of the more cyclical swingers (big ticket items such as homes, autos, home furnishings, and their suppliers) are the earliest significant price gainers, especially during periods of low interest rates. During the third and fourth quarters following a bear market bottom, more growth-oriented industries appear to fare best. Since greater profits are usually available during the first two quarters after a bear market bottoms out, it behooves return-oriented portfolio managers to stay attuned to the market and take bold positions before the upturns in the business cycle become apparent from a study of the widely followed business indicators (reviewed in Chapter 2).

Similarly, the financial analyst (reader) might review Table 9.8 in the Appendix and determine which industry groups faired most poorly (small gains or losses) during the first two quarters and during the second, six-month period after these three bear market bottoms. Consistency in poor performances would suggest that these groups should (1) be avoided for significant long purchases or (2) be the groups where short-sale candidates are sought (see Table 9.4).

LONG-TERM PRICE MOVERS

A review of the industry groups carried regularly in *Barron's* for the twenty-three-year period 1964 through 1987 provides some insights into the industry groups that provided the greatest historical returns. The data are divided into two time periods. The first of these time periods shows group price changes from their average in 1964 through 1979. The stock market was generally moving sideways during this period. The second time period was the eight years of 1979 through 1987. The year 1987 was used as a cutoff since the market took a major dip in late 1987 and was thought to be more reflective than going to 1988 or 1989. Table 9.5 provides the index numbers for the industry groups and the annual compounded price gains over this fifteen and eight year period, respectively.

An analysis of Table 9.5 reveals that the best fifteen-year gainers (from 1964 to 1979) were the following: gold mining, meat packing, motion pictures, aircraft manufacturers, television, machinery, railroad equipment, and drugs. The best eight-year gainers (1979–1987) included motion pictures, drugs, food and beverages, liquor, meat packing, retailing, air transport, tobacco, and tire and rubber. Statistics for other industry group gains are shown in Table 9.5. Although past price action does not necessarily ensure future performances, long-term growth in sales, earnings, and prices do tend to move in the same direction for extended time periods.

Groups of stocks that showed little price change, on balance, over the earlier

Table 9.3
Best Early (Six-Month) and Intermediate (Six-Month) Gainers after Selected Bear Markets

First and second six-months after 1986 bear market

INDUSTRY	% RETURNS	INDUSTRY	% RETURNS
Metals/mng: divers	45%	Copper	34%
Copper	47	Metals/mng: industrial	30
Gold/silver mining	54	Gold/silver mining	49
Canadian energy	47	Publishing	36
Paper/forest products	49	Toiletries/cosmetics	30
Chemical: diversified	42	Steel: general	34
Drug	42	Steel: integrated	31
Shoe	41	Aluminum	44
Oilfield svc/equip	46	Oilfield svc/equip	39
Computer/peripherie	47	Auto/truck: foreign	30
Computer software/svc	43	Railroad	30
Home appliance	41	Foreign elect/entert	62
Semiconductor	54		
European: diversified	46		
Unclassified	43		

First and second six-months after 1987 bear market

INDUSTRY	% RETURNS	INDUSTRY	% RETURNS
Textiles	35%	Tobacco	26%
Tire/rubber	40	Maritime	21
Cement/aggregate	43	Telecomm equipment	14
Steel: general	36	Grocery	16
Home appliances	70	Foreign elect/entertn	15
Maritime	34		
Food wholesale	33		
Retail bldg supp	34		
Banks: midwest	34		
Hotel/gaming	39		
Medical supplies	35		

First and second six-months after 1990 bear market

INDUSTRY	% RETURNS	INDUSTRY	% RETURNS
Homebuilding	66%	Homebuilding	36%
Apparel	43	Tobacco	36
Tire/rubber	40	Drug	34
Semiconductor	44	Toiletries/cosmetics	40
Toy/school supply	51	Tire/rubber	42
Maritime	48	Computer software/svc	37
Retail bldg supply	46	Toy/school supply	33
Retail specialty	54	Foreign telecomm	28
Drugstore	45	Bank: midwest	28
Thrift	48	Security brokerage	42
Security brokerage	58		
Real estate	40		
Hotel/gaming	57		
Manufactured housing/RV	42		

Source: Compiled from *Value Line Data Base,* selected dates.

Table 9.4
Poorest Early (Six-Month) and Intermediate (Six-Month) Movers after Three Bear Markets

INDUSTRY	RETURNS	INDUSTR	RETURNS
After Bear Market Lows of 1986			
Maritime	0%	Apparel	10%
Electric util: east	1	Computer software/svc	-5
Electric util: central	6	Elect util: cent	-9
Electric util: west	3	Natural gas distr	-6
Drugstores	10	Thrift	-16
Thrift	10	Medical service	-6
Insurance: life	7	Manuf. housing/RV	-9
Real estate	5		
Medical service	6		
Foreign elect/entertn	-2		
After Bear Market Lows of 1987			
Copper	6%	Gold/silver mining	-18%
Gold/silver mining	-5%	Petroleum producing	-10
Tobacco	6	Cement & aggregate	-20
Newspaper	5	Machinery: constr/mng	-10
Drugs	7	Oilfield svc/equip	-12
Computer software/svc	8	Machine tool	-10
Electric util: West	7	Computer/peripherie	-10
Thrift	7	Semiconductor	-30
Advertising	6	Auto/truck	-12
European diversified	5	Precision instruments	-10
Foreign elect/entertn	8	Thrift	-13
After Bear Market Lows of 1990			
Canadian energy	-1%	Copper	-8%
Petroleum producing	-7	Metals/mng: indust	-7
Oilfield svc/equip	-3	Gold/silver mining	-14
Electric util: East	2	Cement and aggregate	-9
Electric util: Central	6	Aluminum	-7
Electric util: West	0	Auto/truck	-20
Natural gas: distr	1	Telecomm equipment	-24
Natural gas: diversified	-1	Food wholesaling	-10
European diversified	-1	Advertising	-7

Source: Compiled from *Value Line Data Base,* selected dates.

fifteen-year period, included air transport, automobiles, building materials, closed-end investment firms, chemical firms, installment finance, retailers, tire and rubber, steel and iron, textiles, and utilities. Stocks with the smallest relative gains (or actual price declines) from 1979 to 1987, on balance, included the following: farm equipment, steel and iron, television, closed-end investment companies, and railroad equipment firms. These are based on *Barron's* price averages and do not reflect dividend yields over the periods studied.

Table 9.5

Compounded Growth Rate in *Barron's* Group Stock Averages, 1964–1979 and 1979–1987

INDUSTRY	1964 AVG.	1979 AVG.	ANNUAL G	MID-1987	ANNUAL G
Aircraft mfg	143.54	438.52	7.7%	1,139	4.2%
Air transp	173.67	85.16	-3.5	384	20.2
Autos	179.72	78.31	-5.8	206	12.9
Auto equip	111.36	166.73	2.7	514	15.0
Banks	193.81	288.57	2.7	470	6.2
Bldg mat/eq	204.07	222.82	0.5	533	8.3
Chemicals	374.36	280.77	-2.0	822	14.4
Cl end inv cos	41.65	32.05	-1.9	45	4.3
Drugs	427.09	1020.97	6.0	6042	25.0
Elect equip	338.30	438.54	1.7	1635	17.9
Farm equip	290.04	609.92	5.0	384	-5.9
Food/beverage	203.35	292.96	2.5	1540	23.0
Gold mining	62.26	438.71	13.9	790	6.8
Grocery chains	300.27	322.73	0.4	1090	16.5
Install finan	198.45	193.52	-0.2	672	16.9
Insurance	790.57	982.96	1.5	1872	8.6
Liquor	300.98	490.42	3.3	2820	24.2
Machine tool	64.98	128.49	4.9	296	11.0
Machinery, hvy	53.07	146.99	7.0	318	10.1
Motion picture	91.13	377.92	10.0	2879	29.0
Nonferr mtls	100.95	152.80	2.9	325	10.1
Office equip	1083.70	2573.21	6.0	6025	11.1
Oils	336.72	491.85	2.6	1198	13.9
Meat packing	44.31	196.01	10.4	1090	24.0
Paper	147.31	254.62	3.7	805	15.5
Railroad eq	76.16	193.18	6.2	288	5.1
Retailing	422.35	407.30	-0.2	2125	22.9
Tire/rubber	388.78	221.72	-3.8	929	19.8
Steel/iron	285.21	174.53	-3.4	136	-3.2
Television	178.20	504.15	7.2	380	-3.7
Textiles	226.74	177.02	-1.6	722	19.1
Tobacco	118.39	132.87	0.7	755	20.9
DJIA	874.39	882.98	0.0	2445	13.5
DJT	207.46	243.86	1.1	1035	20.1
DJU	146.12	106.22	-2.1	208	8.8

1964/79 data: Avg of quarterly ending figures

1987 average: Avg of June 16th and July 2nd ending figures.

Source: *Barron's,* issue dates April 6, 1964; July 6, 1964; October 5, 1964; January 4, 1965; April 2, 1979; December 31, 1979; June 26, 1987; and July 2, 1987 averages. Series discontinued for later years.

FUNDAMENTAL SELECTION APPROACHES

Stocks bought for long-term holding periods are usually selected on the basis of above average return on stock equity, much below average price-earnings levels (or cash flow multiple levels), or based on a more complicated intrinsic value calculation with an array of the issues into those most underpriced in the market.

Value Line Investment Survey estimates the average returns for three to five years into the future, and some subscribers use this technique for identifying stocks to include in their portfolio. Rather than to do this for individual stocks, the average of twelve industry groups (from the Value Line ninety-five) are shown with highest/lowest return on book equity and returns for the following five, semiannual periods, with a striking date of April 1, 1988 in Table 9.6 Table 9.7 shows the twelve groups of stocks with the highest/lowest price-earnings multiples on that date and with the semiannual performances for the following five periods. The investment literature generally leads an investor to believe that firms with superior returns on book equity, but those trading at below average price-earnings multipliers, will perform superiorly in the marketplace. Tables 9.6 and 9.7 should shed some light on these generally held beliefs.

Table 9.6 covers the price moves, broken into six-month periods from April 1988 through September 1990, for a dozen industry groups with the highest and lowest return on equity to attempt to detect any shift in market values during rising and falling markets generally. The stocks with above average return on book equity for their companies ran from a high (in 1988) of 23.8% for toys and school supplies to a low of 14.9% on home furnishings and chemical: specialty firms. The low return on equity groups ran return on investment (ROI) figures from a high of 8.6% on petroleum: integrated to a low of 3.4% on steel: integrated firms.

Several conclusions may be drawn from a review of the data in Table 9.6. During the first of five, semiannual periods covered, the entire group of Value Line stocks rose by 3.7% (price alone, not inclusive of dividend yields). The high-ROI stocks rose an average of 0.6%, whereas the low-ROI stocks gained an average of 3.5%. In the second period, the high-ROI stocks rose 6.8% compared to a market gain of 6.9%. The low-ROI groups rose an average of 10.7%. The six-month period ending with September 1989 witnessed a run-up in all Value Line stocks of 14.3%; the highest-ROI groups had an average gain of 19.3%; and the lowest-ROI stocks had gains of 11.2%. The lowest-ROI stocks hardly declined from then to April 1, 1990, compared to a Value Line average drop in price of 6.5% and a retrenchment in price of 9.4% for the highest-ROI groups. Both groups performed about the same from then to October 1, 1990, with each doing poorer than the universe from which they were drawn. Thus we can conclude that the low-ROI stocks trade at low price-earnings multiples, generally, and are somewhat less volatile than those with much above average ROI figures.

Some fundamental security analysts, when selecting stocks, take the approach of buying those trading at unusually low price-earnings multiples, while selling or avoiding those with higher than average multiples of earnings. To test the desirability of this approach for a group of stocks, the twelve groups of Value Line industries trading at the lowest price-earnings were compared to the twelve trading at the highest average P-E multiples. The returns for each of five six-month assumed holding periods were contrasted to these low versus high P-E stocks, and the results are reported in Table 9.7.

Table 9.6
Group Stock Price Moves for High and Low Return on Equity, April 1988 through September 1990

		SIX-MONTH PRICE MOVEMENT IN STOCKS TO:				
INDUSTRY	ROI	OCT 88	APR 89	OCT 89	APR 90	OCT 90
HIGH RETURNS ON NET WORTH GROUPS						
Food proc	15.9%	6.8%	9.4%	21.3%	-0.5%	-6.4%
Home furn	14.9	-4.4	7.6	13.1	-19.1	-22.8
Newspaper	18.1	-4.5	3.4	19.9	-15.5	-26.1
Chem: spec	14.9	1.2	7.3	16.6	-2.3	-13.4
Drug	21.6	-0.2	12.5	16.6	8.6	1.6
Toiletry/ cosmet	20.9	1.6	8.6	24.5	-7.0	-16.9
Toys/sch supply	23.8	4.3	17.4	42.1	-12.5	-35.8
Fin svc	16.8	-1.0	-3.6	14.9	-4.7	-21.3
Thrift	20.1	-9.0	-10.0	9.6	-35.8	-38.9
Sec brok	18.7	15.4	-3.6	20.7	-18.1	-22.8
Europ div	18.2	-3.7	22.9	14.9	2.2	-4.5
Unclass	15.4	1.1	9.9	17.0	-7.6	-18.5
Avg of 12		0.6	6.8	19.3	-9.4	-18.8
LOW RETURNS ON NET WORTH GROUPS						
Copper	4.8%	3.6%	15.7%	18.6%	-7.2%	-9.1%
Canada ene	7.6	-4.1	7.7	2.3	-2.8	4.7
Petr: integ	8.6	0.5	17.4	8.6	3.9	-0.9
Cement/aggr	8.0	-6.7	-4.4	14.2	-10.1	-26.7
Steel: intg	3.4	9.3	0.2	-0.6	-10.1	-34.7
Steel: spec	7.1	29.8	13.6	-0.6	-4.4	-0.2
Mche: const	6.5	0.8	7.2	7.9	10.8	-28.3
Oilfield sv & equip	5.4	-17.6	24.2	18.8	28.5	3.6
Railroad	7.6	2.3	7.6	13.5	-2.3	-20.6
Maritime	5.9	18.1	25.0	9.9	3.2	-40.8
Nat gas diversif	6.4	9.0	15.2	24.7	-0.8	1.2
For elect/ entertn	6.2	-3.2	-0.8	17.3	-4.5	-17.9
Avg of 12		3.5	10.7	11.2	0.4	-14.1
Avg of VLDB		3.7	6.9	14.3	-6.5	-18.5

Source: Compiled from *Value Line +,* Value Line, Inc., PC data disks, for April 1 and October 1 (1988–1990).

Table 9.7

Groups of the Twelve Lowest P-E and Highest P-E Stocks with Six-Month Price Moves from April 1, 1988 to October 1, 1990

INDUSTRY	P-E	10-1-88	SIX MONTH PRICE MOVES TO 4-1-89	10-1-89	4-1-90	10-1-90
			FAR ABOVE AVERAGE P-E STOCK GROUPS			
Gold/silver	27.6x	-7.5%	-2.9%	8.6%	7.4%	-3.9%
Canada ener	24.0	-4.1	7.7	2.3	-2.8	4.7
Petr: integ	19.7	0.5	17.4	8.6	3.9	-0.9
Mche/constr	20.0	0.8	7.2	7.9	10.8	-28.3
Oilfield eq	26.9	-17.6	24.2	18.8	28.5	3.6
Mche tool	19.3	-12.4	10.2	12.6	3.8	-27.7
Semiconductr	20.2	-7.9	-16.8	3.6	4.1	-31.9
Toys/sch sup	19.4	4.3	17.4	42.1	-12.5	-35.8
Broadcst/cbl	32.9	8.8	18.0	37.7	-16.3	-21.4
NG diversif	22.1	9.0	15.2	24.7	-0.8	1.2
Real estate	22.6	2.9	11.9	-5.2	-17.0	-49.2
For electrn Entertnm	32.9	-3.2	-0.8	17.3	-4.5	-17.9
Avg, 12 gps	24.0x	-2.2	10.3	14.9	0.4	-15.8
			FAR BELOW AVERAGE P-E STOCK GROUPS			
Metals/mng	11.0x	4.4%	26.9%	10.3%	-1.8%	-22.5%
Tobacco	10.6	8.5	16.0	18.0	-13.4	-8.9
Mfgd housng	10.8	7.2	1.6	-6.3	-14.6	-14.5
El Util: Est	8.8	4.8	0.1	12.8	-0.1	-10.9
El Util: Cen	9.4	3.4	-1.9	2.6	0.4	-8.9
El Util: Wst	10.6	-1.9	-4.1	9.0	-2.1	-13.3
NG distrib	10.8	3.4	1.9	18.1	-3.2	-3.3
Banks	9.6	10.1	2.4	18.2	-25.0	-35.5
Bks: Midwst	11.2	14.5	2.4	21.1	-15.4	-16.6
Thrift	6.4	-9.0	-10.0	9.6	-35.8	-38.9
Ins: diversi	9.6	9.5	3.7	21.5	-5.4	-22.2
Ins: prop/cas	8.4	2.6	11.8	17.5	-4.3	-17.1
Avg, 12 gps	9.8x	4.8%	3.4%	12.7%	-10.1%	-18.6%
Avg, VLDB	14.0x	3.7%	6.9%	14.3%	-6.5%	-18.5

Source: Compiled from *Value Line +,* Value Line, Inc., PC data disks, for April and October (1988–1990).

The industry groups with far above average P-Es (as of April 1, 1988) were as follows: gold/silver, Canadian energy, petroleum: integrated, machinery/construction and mining, oilfield equipment and service, machine tool, semiconductor, toys and school supplies, broadcasting/cable, natural gas/diversified, real estate and foreign electronic entertainment. These industries were arranged in the order of their standard industrial classification (SIC) codes, with P-Es on the assumed investment date (a market of average strength) ranging from 19.2× to 32.9. The mean average P-E for the twelve high P-E industry groups at that time was 24.0 times.

On balance, high P-E stocks tended to be laggards in the market, often performing not as well in early stages of market swings, but performing somewhat better as the bull-market forces became more pronounced. Broadcasting and cable, the highest P-E group at the outset of the period reviewed, moved up more rapidly than the market as a whole, but when declines began, price retrenchments were much more severe than for the entire market. The performance of this one group was more extreme than others in the comparison. On the lower end of P-Es (in the high P-E groups), petroleum integrated and natural gas: diversified moved up in rising markets but fell below average in declining markets.

The dozen lowest P-E groups as of April 1, 1988, included the following: metals/mining; tobacco; manufactured housing; electric utility: east, central, and west; natural gas distribution; banks; banks: midwest; thrifts; insurance diversified; and insurance: property and casualty. P-E ratios for these groups ranged from a low of 8.4 to a high of 11.2 times. On balance, these stocks tended to move up early in bull markets but to decline more than average during bear markets. The severe declines were limited to very cyclical swingers, including metals, banks, and thrifts. The utility and other groups generally moved in line with, or somewhat less than, market average swings.

In total, the limiting of a portfolio to low P-E groups of stocks does not appear to be a discriminating way for selecting stocks. Selecting individual issues from across industries that trade at low P-E ratios is tested in Chapter 10 to gauge the effectiveness of the strategy applied to individual stocks (rather than groups of stocks). Stock groups that trade at above average P-E ratios are thought to do so because of probable near-term improvements in earnings per share, and/or their superior ability to promote above average growth in earnings per share and dividends per share in the next few years. Stocks that consistently trade at far below average P-E ratios generally do so because of their lack of potential for growth in earnings per share and dividends per share during the next few years. Low P-E stocks often pay out 60–80 percent of E/S to stockholders, as few internal investment opportunities exist for the firms (i.e., utilities). Banks and thrifts were trading at much below average P-E ratios in the early 1990s because of the large number of bank/thrift failures during recent years and the above-average mortgage delinquency rate in their portfolios of mortgage loans in early 1988 and later years.

TECHNICAL SELECTION OF GROUPS OF STOCKS

Upward market momentum for a group of stocks usually lasts for a year or longer during a bull-market period. The attempt is to detect those industries that are (or will be) rising at an above average rate during the next six or twelve months. Several methods will be suggested for making such a selection.

Most issues of the *Wall Street Journal* provide a detailed breakdown of industry groups, along with a listing of price changes from the beginning of the year to the current date. By the end of January, one should contrast the moves in a group of stocks with its usual seasonal move in the first quarter. Remember that about half the first quarter's move is expected in January (for most groups of stocks). Those that appear to be gaining in prices more than normal are candidates for continued price appreciation. After about twelve to eighteen months, most industry groups begin to tire and to consolidate their prices. Early gainers (strong stocks with rapid growth in reported E/S) should probably be liquidated. Later in the year, price changes for industry groups can be computed for a period of about two months to detect strong and weak momentum groups of stocks. Some funds might be transferred into laggards in the industry. Still other funds might be transferred to other groups of stocks that appear to be under accumulation.

Current Market Perspectives (see Figure 9.1 for an example) also provides a price comparison for the past twelve months. One would probably wish to avoid those industries that have moved upward by 50% or more during the past year, or perhaps book profits on issues that have reached resistance levels from a technical sense, and instead concentrate on accumulating those issues that still have significant upside potential.

Another possible way to detect attractive industry groups using *Current Market Perspectives* is to interpret the industry line charts (about the same as suggested in Chapters 4 and 5 for vertical bar charts), and buy issues that are reasonably priced, but in industry groups that have breakout patterns. For example, Figure 9.2 provides eight graphs (eight of sixty-four in total). The reader should draw in lines and determine which of these groups appear to be headed toward a major breakout with a strong base pattern and which are merely in a technical recovery (partial recovery of past decline). The latter groups should be avoided, or perhaps shorted, as they are likely to decline further when the market turns weak.

SUMMARY

Stock market timing, or placing stock investments in the right industry group at the right time, is critical to earning an above average stock return. One approach to this endeavor is to estimate likely upswings in the economy and to concentrate in issues with high betas (relative price volatility), or to concentrate in low-beta stocks during market selloffs. Some stock traders concentrate only on certain months or days of the week. Still others buy and hold for the long term.

In this chapter, we attempted to identify groups of stocks that are usually early, mid-market, and late cycle movers so as to sequence the group selection process. Fundamental approaches for selecting groups of timely stocks are then tested.

Some technicians use industry bar charts, attempting to identify strong and

Figure 9.1
Trendline's Twelve-Month Industry Performance

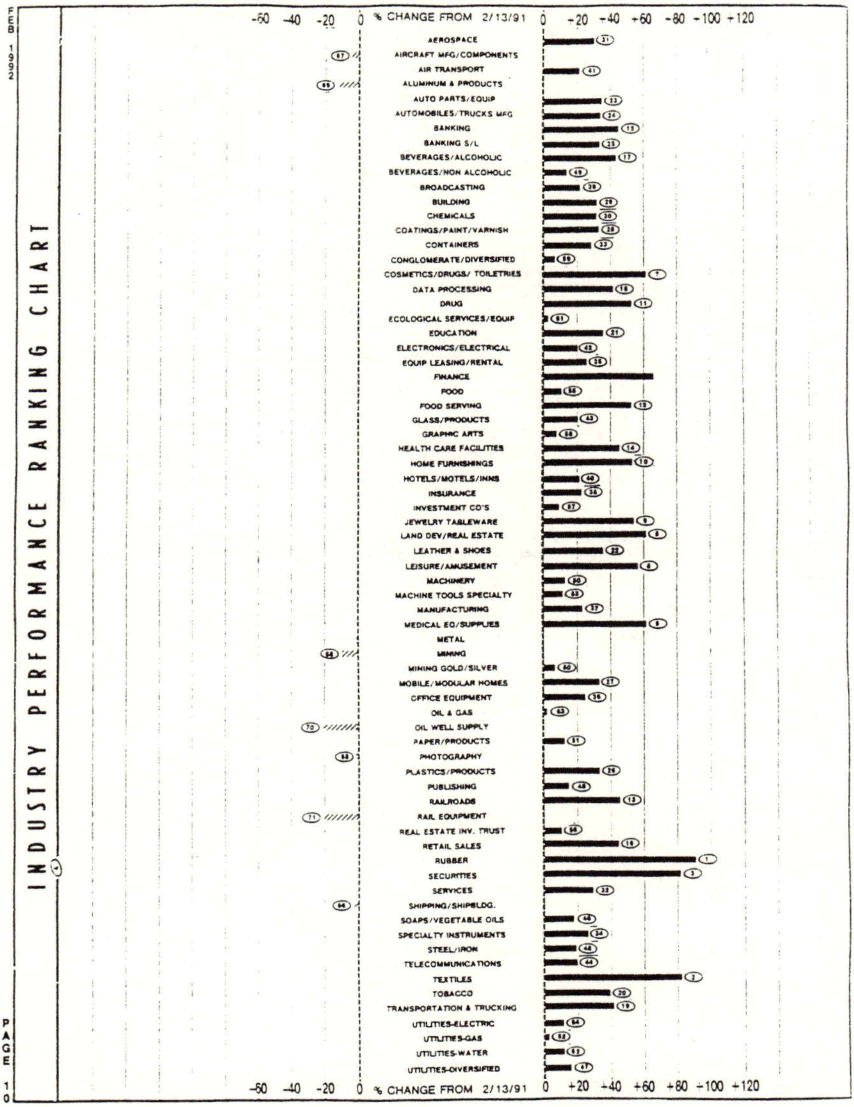

FEB 1992

INDUSTRY PERFORMANCE RANKING CHART

% CHANGE FROM 2/13/91

-60 -40 -20 0 +20 +40 +60 +80 +100 +120

AEROSPACE
AIRCRAFT MFG/COMPONENTS
AIR TRANSPORT
ALUMINUM & PRODUCTS
AUTO PARTS/EQUIP
AUTOMOBILES/TRUCKS MFG
BANKING
BANKING S/L
BEVERAGES/ALCOHOLIC
BEVERAGES/NON ALCOHOLIC
BROADCASTING
BUILDING
CHEMICALS
COATINGS/PAINT/VARNISH
CONTAINERS
CONGLOMERATE/DIVERSIFIED
COSMETICS/DRUGS/TOILETRIES
DATA PROCESSING
DRUG
ECOLOGICAL SERVICES/EQUIP
EDUCATION
ELECTRONICS/ELECTRICAL
EQUIP LEASING/RENTAL
FINANCE
FOOD
FOOD SERVING
GLASS/PRODUCTS
GRAPHIC ARTS
HEALTH CARE FACILITIES
HOME FURNISHINGS
HOTELS/MOTELS/INNS
INSURANCE
INVESTMENT CO'S
JEWELRY TABLEWARE
LAND DEV/REAL ESTATE
LEATHER & SHOES
LEISURE/AMUSEMENT
MACHINERY
MACHINE TOOLS SPECIALTY
MANUFACTURING
MEDICAL EQ/SUPPLIES
METAL
MINING
MINING GOLD/SILVER
MOBILE/MODULAR HOMES
OFFICE EQUIPMENT
OIL & GAS
OIL WELL SUPPLY
PAPER/PRODUCTS
PHOTOGRAPHY
PLASTICS/PRODUCTS
PUBLISHING
RAILROADS
RAIL EQUIPMENT
REAL ESTATE INV. TRUST
RETAIL SALES
RUBBER
SECURITIES
SERVICES
SHIPPING/SHIPBLDG.
SOAPS/VEGETABLE OILS
SPECIALTY INSTRUMENTS
STEEL/IRON
TELECOMMUNICATIONS
TEXTILES
TOBACCO
TRANSPORTATION & TRUCKING
UTILITIES-ELECTRIC
UTILITIES-GAS
UTILITIES-WATER
UTILITIES-DIVERSIFIED

PAGE 10

-60 -40 -20 0 % CHANGE FROM 2/13/91 0 +20 +40 +60 +80 +100 +120

Source: Courtesy Standard & Poor's/Trendline.

Figure 9.2
Trendline's Group Stock Averages (Eight of Seventy-Two)

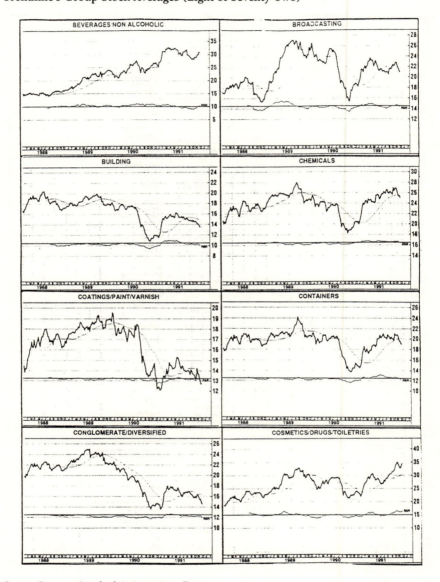

Source: Courtesy Standard & Poor's/Trendline.

weak patterns for industry groups. The patterns are interpreted in the same way on industry graphs as for those on individual issues. These and other topics are discussed and illustrated in this chapter.

APPENDIX: VALUE LINE INDUSTRY RANKINGS

Some investors that subscribe to either *Value Line Investment Survey* (weekly) or *Value Line Data Base Plus* select their stocks on the basis of the industry rankings (see, for example, Table 9.8). To test the relative performance of these rankings, the average stock appreciation for the top decile and a bottom decline (nine of ten issues) were compared for one, two, three, and four years with rankings as of April 1, 1986, 1987, and 1988. The results are provided in Table 9.9. In the table, the SIC Code, the industry, and the estimated three-to five-year appreciation (mean average for groups) are provided. Other columns show price changes for six months after striking date, the second six months, and for years zero to two, zero to three, and zero to four.

Results from using either high- or low-ranked industries (for the year ahead) or for high versus low estimates of three- to five-year price appreciation were mixed. The bottom ranked industries often did better in year one from the top ranked industry. On a longer-term basis, the groups with much above average estimated price appreciation usually outperformed those estimated to do below average. In general, however, actual four-year price appreciation was only about one-third to one-half the estimate for three- to five-year average group appreciation. The market performance for the Highest Value Line rated industries for the same period are presented in Table 9.10.

The conclusion from this study suggests that the group ranking selection method is not effective for a year or longer time periods. Use of Value Line estimate of price appreciation (for three–five years) appears to offer some merit, although actual price increases averages only one third to one half of those forecasted by Value Line for the periods tested.

Table 9.8
Moves during Quarters 1 and 2 and 3 and 4 after Bull Markets Began, 1985–1991

SIC	1986-87 Bull Mkt. Q4,86 & Q1, 87	Q2 & Q3 1987	1988-89 Q1 & Q2 1988	Bull Mkt Q 3 & Q4 1988	1991 Bull Mkt Q1&Q2 1991	Q3&Q4 1991
1000	45	2	19	-33	12	-7
1021	47	34	6	5	12	-8
1031	25	30	26	7	20	-7
1041	54	49	-5	-18	11	-14
1210	13	2	27	-3	15	7
1299	47	12	26	5	-1	-3
1300	28	-0-	17	-10	-7	1
1521-40	27	-0-	31	-6	66	36
2000	25	8	18	12	18	6
2082	31	26	11	5	17	7
2085	19	11	5	26	38	36
2087	---	---	---	---	---	---
2200	19	7	35	-2	39	16
2300	24	-10	26	-2	43	12
2500	32	8	27	-5	32	-3
2600	49	5	20	-6	30	-2
2640	29	9	21	-1	26	7
2700	34	36	32	-5	14	12
2710	37	18	5	1	16	3
2810	34	6	16	+4	21	-2
2813	42	22	20	-7	19	11
2820	33	14	22	-6	22	19
2834	42	5	7	3	27	34
2840	30	10	10	4	23	24
2844	38	30	28	-4	18	40
2900	31	4	19	4	8	-3
3000	37	15	40	1	40	42
3140	41	7	31	9	34	18
3200	---	---	---	---	---	---
3240	29	9	43	-20	31	-9
3311	16	34	36	4	21	3
3312	25	31	28	-9	23	-3
3313	15	25	21	10	22	3
3350	30	44	23	5	8	-7
3400	30	18	32	-8	23	-5
3530	21	28	27	-10	15	0
3533	46	34	16	-12	-3	-20
3540	21	14	22	-10	21	5
3570	25	23	18	6	30	15
3573	47	13	16	-10	28	9
3579	43	-5	8	-5	28	37
3600	23	20	20	-3	30	2
3670	26	11	24	-7	34	8
3674	54	23	21	-30	44	6

Table 9.8 Continued

SIC	1986-87 Bull Mkt.		1988-89 Bull Mkt		1991 Bull Mkt	
	Q4,86 & Q1, 87	Q2 & Q3 1987	Q1 & Q2 1988	Q3 & Q4 1988	Q1&Q2 1991	Q3&Q4 1991
3710	31	39	21	-12	36	-20
3712	---	---	---	---	---	---
3714	26	3	26	5	19	7
3716	27	7	28	2	29	19
3720	13	5	22	-7	29	0
3792	32	-9	22	07	42	23
3800	31	6	27	-10	32	7
3940	13	17	9	-3	51	33
4002	27	30	18	2	16	22
4200	16	1	17	7	33	13
4400	0	5	34	21	48	4
4510	27	10	24	9	30	17
4810	13	13	20	14	3	8
4811	N/A	10	28	-2	24	-24
4812	---	---	---	---	---	---
4830	33	27	26	3	12	13
4911	1	-3	11	2	2	18
4912	6	-9	9	2	6	16
4913	3	-4	7	-3	N.C.	15
4920	16	-6	13	-2	1	11
4929	29	0	16	7	-1	-3
4953	---	---	---	---	---	---
5140	24	-2	33	7	8	-10
5211	35	-2	34	-8	46	0
5300	28	28	30	4	38	10
5400	15	23	21	16	26	-3
5600	22	-4	30	2	54	7
5812	20	-4	21	7	33	3
5910	10	4	26	-7	45	1
6000	14	0	22	-4	36	19
6001	14	6	34	-1	24	28
6002	N/A					
6081	---	---	---	---	---	---
6100	28	-2	17	-9	29	21
6120	10	-16	7	-13	48	3
6210	20	12	22	0	58	42
6310	7	8	17	3	33	23
6320	12	-2	15	2	20	9
6330	15	-2	10	-5	24	4
6500	5	2	24	-1	40	8
7000	30	9	39	0	57	10
7300	27	15	17	-4	27	-1
7310	34	2	6	-3	25	-7
7900	26	4	31	4	31	13
8000	6	-6	30	-8	30	17
8060	29	8	35	-4	31	25
9913	25	25	27	0	19	9
9970	46	11	5	10	-1	22
9975	02	62	8	15	8	-5
9991	43	-3	25	-7	13	15

Source: Based on SIC group averages from *Value Screen +*, Value Line, Inc., PC data runs, end-of-quarter disks, 1987–1991.

Table 9.9
Market Performance for Value Line Rated Industries for Years Ended April 1, 1992

				Value Retaining Relative			
		Est	1+6mos	6mos			
		3-5yr	to10-1-86	to 4-1-87		Price change for	
SIC	Industry	Appr	(1+1% chg)	(1+1% chg)	0-2 yrs	0-3 yrs	0 - 4 yrs
				Bottom 10 Groups as of 4-1-86			
2200	Textiles	37%	.901	1.197	9.5%	27.7%	7.5
3570	Off/Eq/Sup	43%	.837	1.263	-5.1	-7.2	-9.5.
3579	Software	106%	.934	1.470	29.6	22.9	47.3
5140	Food:WS	40%	.902	1.245	-8.5	11.3	11.7
6100	Fin Svc	65%	.933	1.286	-6.5	10.7	-2.3
6120	Thrift	68%	.884	1.099	-39.1	-50.4	-65.3
6320	Ins. Divers	31%	.932	1.113	-16.9	-5.4	8.5
7300	Ind. Svcs.	55%	.927	1.290	15.0	19.8	27.0
8060	Med. Supp.	64%	.986	1.299	23.4	36.5	69.6
Avg of 10 (or all)		59%	.908	1.247	-2.7	4.8	7.6
				Bottom 10 Groups as of 4-1-87			
1000	Metals/Mining	-1	101.5	70.6	-12.5	-5.3	-26.1
1041	Gold/Silver	-12	153.9	65.9	-8.9	6.2	-24.2
2600	Paper	9	104.3	82.6	-5.9	-2.3	-6.8
2710	Newspaper	44	118.7	80.4	0.5	1.0	-9.8
2813	Chem Divers	27	122.9	88.9	17.4	16.1	24.6
3000	Tire/Rubber	13	114.9	99.4	21.9	32.0	35.8
3573	Peripherals	63	113.1	75.4	-19.8	-16.1	5.5
3579*	Software	83	118.9	79.4	-8.7	9.4	19.4
9970	European	10	110.9	83.8	10.0	29.2	46.2
Avg. of 10 (or all)		38	116.4	80.2	-1.7	8.9	14.7
				Bottom 9 Groups as of 4-1-88			
1021	Copper	91	103.6	115.7	31.9	11.3	17.3
1031	Metals/Mang	60	105.2	125.1	51.0	-12.3	-11.7
2813*	Chem:Divers	63	100.5	106.9	6.2	13.7	34.4
2820	Chem:Spec	57	101.2	107.3	23.7	46.6	88.4
3311	Steel:Gen	54	114.4	111.5	39.9	42.8	73.9
5910	Drugstore	99	99.5	112.3	2.4	27.8	45.5.
7300	Ind. Svc	101	104.4	99.8	10.4	10.9	22.9
8060	Med. Supp	106	106.6	103.8	37.5	104.0	135.1
9975	For Elec	20	98.6	99.2	7.6	-1.3	-23.0
Average		77	103.6	109.1	23.4	27.1	42.5

Source: Compiled from April 1 and October 1, *Value Screen +,* Value Line, Inc., PC data disks, 1986–1992.

Table 9.10
Market Performance for Highest Value Line Rated Industries for Years Ended April 1, 1992

				Value Retaining Relative			
		Est	1+6mos	1+6mos			
		3-5yr	Price	Price		Price Charge for	
SIC	Industry	Appr	Chg	Chg	0-2 yrs	0-3 yrs	04 yrs
				Top 10 Groups as of 4-1-86			
1044	Gold/Silver	107	.955	1.415	-2.3	-12.3	2.3
1300	Petro:Prod	79	.911	1.274	-4.7	-9.5	13.6
3313	Steel:Spec.	61	.969	1.139	-12.3	29.3	22.9
3520	Mche/Const	207	.997	1.207	22.9	32.8	48.1
3670	Electronics	78	.828	1.259	13.4	13.7	15.5
4929	NG:Divers	83	.944	1.292	-11.4	+11.2	-37.6
6002	Banks:Other	111	1.056	0.817	=	=	=
Avg of 10 (or all)		106	.824	1.139	1.4	6.0	22
				Top Groups as of 4-1-87			
3716	Auto Parts	43	107.5	75.9	-1.0	-15.7	-19.9
4400	Maritime	104	105.8	80.8	26.2	43.1	26.6
4913	ElecUtil: Wst	17	95.8	94.7	-14.7	-86.9	-11.8
5812	Restaurant	44	95.9	83.3	-9.1	5.6	12.0
5910	Drugstore	78	104.3	92.9	8.0	0.5	24.3
6002*	Banks	73	68.1	31.3	—	—	—
6500	Real Estate	65	97.5	78.7	-11.6	-30.5	-63.3
7000	Hotel/Gaming	60	103.8	80.9	3.5	0.9	-13.3
7310	Advertising	63	102.7	80.9	-18.6	-20.1	-42.5
8000	Med. Svcs	107	97.0	74.5	-17.4	-21.7	57.4
Average		59	98.3	77.4	-3.8	-5.2	-3.3
				Top Groups as of 4-1-88			
2300	Apparel	117	97.2	118.5	8.2	7.3	49.7
3716*	Auto Pts	90	110.8	109.5	3.4	-1.3	66.9
2792	Mfg. Housing	139	107.2	101.6	-12.8	19.4	92.9
3940	Toy/Sch Sup	103	104.3	117.4	52.2	42.5	108.1
4929	N.G. Divers	92	109.0	115.2	55.3	50.6	26.1
5300	Retail Store	112	105.8	112.2	20.1	26.4	83.1
6120	Thrift	172	91.0	90.0	-42.4	-53.7	-40.5
6210	Sec. Brok.	117	115.4	100.5	14.6	42.9	133.5
Average		121	104.6	109.9	15.4	18.9	66.8

*Report from year earlier

Source: Compiled from April 1 and October 1, *Value Screen +,* Value Line, Inc., PC data disks, 1986–1992.

Chapter 10

STOCK MARKET ANOMALIES

BEATING THE MARKET

The argument has been long and furious as to whether or not an investor (individual or institution) can beat the return on the market consistently over a long period of time without assuming above average risk. Efficient market advocates would argue that this is not likely to happen. Fundamentalists and technicians would apply their formulas or use their graphs and attempt to beat the market.

Efficient market advocates have suggested three theories as to market efficiency. The first of these is that it is weakly efficient, or that past stock prices are reflected in current values. The semistrongly efficient market advocates would argue that all past stock action and known public information is already embodied in the current price of stock. The advocates of a strongly efficient stock market would suggest that all known public information, past stock prices, and important known and nonpublic information would all be embodied in current stock price levels.

Other investors would argue that too many market anomalies exist to assume that the stock market is truly efficient in the short run. They mention the calendar year-end effect, especially for small firms; the day of the week effect; the turn of the month effect; market reaction to strong earnings reports or changing cash dividend payouts; and the like. Some financial analysts argue that the emergence of more powerful computers, larger data bases, and the proliferation of market analysts all make the market more vulnerable to swift upsurges and downsurges than in past decades.

In this chapter, we examine several anomalies that occur with a high degree of consistency and some that infrequently occur but generally produce a predictable result; we then draw conclusions from portfolio simulation into Value Line Data Base firms as to the usefulness of these so-called anomalies. We use prior market studies and those conducted especially for this endeavor in support of a strongly inefficient, or somewhat predictable price behavior, for certain known events.

CONSISTENTLY REPEATING ANOMALIES

The January Effect

The year-end stock market rally that reoccurs with a high degree of repetitiveness has become known as the January effect. From about December 20 of one year to roughly February 7 of the following year, stock prices are usually in a strong uptrend. This has sometimes been attributed to year-end tax selling of stocks that have been in a downtrend for most of the year and carry trading losses to recent purchasers who wish to recognize them or to rapid gainers on which holders might wish to book realized gains. Selling prices in both situations would depress such stock prices for a time.

S. L. Jones, W. Lee, and R. Apenbrink, in a study of the comparison of the turn-of-the-year effect and the June–July turn-of-the-month effect for two major time periods: yearly, 1900–1917 and 1918–1929. They concluded that a major portion of the gains achievable by holding stocks during January was attributed to tax-loss selling and such selling pressure occurring in previous months.[1] However, a study by P. Arowin from more recent data concluded that of the 13.7% cumulative annual returns on stock portfolios, some 8.2% was attributed to the earnings in January alone. Returns in July of 1.6%, on average, was not statistically different from the average earned by months.[2]

C. G. Lamoureux and G. C. Sanger applied the turn-of-the-year effect to small firms, especially those traded in the OTC markets, and reached somewhat different conclusions. Their findings were that the spread between bid and ask quotations were as broad as 33.1% for small firms but as narrow as 3.2% for the largest firms. They also witnessed very large spreads around the turn of the year but narrowing spreads through August of each year. They concluded that, due to the very broad spreads between bid and ask around the turn of the year, it would not be possible for traders to consistently earn above average risk-adjusted returns from this anomaly.[3]

G. N. Pettengill and B. D. Jordan published a study of the overreaction hypothesis and reached some useful conclusions about the turn-of-the-year effect. They followed the contrarian strategy of buying stocks of firms with the largest net negative loss returns over three years and holding them for three years. Their conclusions were that 21.5% excess returns, with 67% of this occurring in January, was possible with this portfolio strategy. Their conclusions were that the greatest losses in one period were those with the greatest gains in the following period. Monday returns were found to be uniformly negative, whereas Friday's returns were the highest for each of the twenty groups of stocks studied.[4]

Trading by the calendar suggests that certain times of the year often witness strengths in the market, whereas others witness weaknesses. The year-end effect and the end-of-the-month effect (strong last three and first three trading days), especially around the turn of the quarter, appear to exist. The first month of each quarter is usually strong and the last month of each quarter is weak. Stock prices are usually weak on Mondays, strong on Fridays, and about average during the other trading days of the week. Certain of these patterns might be repeated due to (1) year-end tax selling and overreaction price hypothesis, (2) window dressing by institutional holders of stocks at the end of months or quarters, (3) early reporting of good earnings reports and late reporting of poor results, and (4) heavy reinvesting on Fridays so as to take advantage of possible positive weekend news with some selling pressure on Mondays.

Size-Related Anomalies

Several financial researchers and publishers have suggested that much of the year-end effect occurs for small rather than for large firms, suggesting that the market is more efficient where more trading takes place, and in auction rather than dealer dominated markets (OTC).

B. McDonald and R. E. Miller, in a study of abnormal returns from small, medium, or large firms (broken down into seventy-five different size categories), found that the abnormal return series exhibits a very consistent inverse relationship with market value. That is, firms with smaller total market values produced more abnormal returns than did their larger counterparts.[5] This is generally consistent with published data by Ibbotson. Much of the gains, or abnormal returns, occurred in January.

K. C. J. Wei and S. R. Stansell revisited the small-firm effect and found similar results. They determined that the smaller the firm size, the larger are the alphas and betas. Alphas ranged from a +.78 per month on the smallest firms to a −.12 for the largest category. Betas ranged from 1.36 to 0.98 for the portfolios that were structured into five percentile groups, with the highest beta values for the smaller firms. The January effect was very significant, especially for the smaller firms.[6] This is consistent with the capital asset pricing model that suggests that high betas (relative price volatility) are expected to lead to above average returns.

I. Friend and H. P. Lang generally found that quality rankings for common stocks are superior over beta and variance measures of risk in explaining returns. They found that the size effect phenomenon largely occurs in January, but that the size effect reflects a risk effect not wholly caught by beta or variance measures.[7]

D. B. Keim, in a study of NYSE and AMEX stocks from 1951 to 1986 found that the earnings-price ratio and the size effect are significant in January. The findings suggest that the size effect is largely associated with that month, but that the earnings/price (E/P) ratio is significant during the rest of the year as well.[8]

Most of the preceding studies are gross return comparisons and do not assess the portfolio a transaction cost. This was done in a study by G. W. Kester, who when imposing a transaction cost of 2% to buy and 2% to sell, found that switching from large firms to small firms and back again was probably not profitable during most years. If transaction costs are 1% or less, such switches might be profitable, as might be switches out of fixed-income portfolios and into small stocks for the turn of the year returns and then back again.[9]

A very good review of previously published studies on certain market anomolies was published by B. I. Jacobs and K. N. Levy in 1989.[10] Their general concusions were about as follows:

1. Gordon suggested in 1962 that common stock returns are inversely related to a firm's size.

2. Bantz shows that risk-adjusted returns are higher for small firms than for large firms on the NYSE.

3. Reinganum showed that the small firm effect applied to both NYSE and AMEX stocks, 1963–1977, but not in all four- to five-year time periods.

4. Size effect is largely evidenced in January, but there are wider bid-ask spreads for small than for large firms.

5. Larger spreads could be due to lower liquidity for the stocks in small firms or more trading by insiders, thus requiring higher returns to attract public traders.

6. Risk, and hence expected returns, vary over time.

7. Higher returns are generally associated with stock not held or little held, by institutional accounts, suggesting a neglected effect.

8. Low P-E stocks, risk adjusted, produce higher returns than do high P-E stocks.

9. Studies have shown that P-E and size are independent.

10. Returns are highest on Friday and lowest on Monday. One half of the size effect occurs in January with a quarter in the first five trading days of January.

11. Stocks tend to oscillate from low returns one year to high returns the next year.

12. Investors tend to ride with losers too long, thus magnifying year-end selling and excess downward pressure on the stocks. Some rebounding the following year then occurs.

Stock Impact of Earnings Announcements

Several studies have recently been published concerning the short-term impact on stock prices from unexpected earnings or dividend declaration announcements. Some of these are reviewed in the following paragraphs.

J. B. Wiggins concluded that market-adjusted stock returns, controlling for firm size, are directly related to earnings price ratios and standard unexpected earnings ratios.[11] S. J. Chang and S. N. Chen noted that there is no interaction between the unexpected announcement of earnings per share and dividend declarations released concurrently rather than individually.[12]

M. Ettredge and R. J. Fuller concluded that, on average, stocks of companies with negative earnings in one year generated positive, abnormal risk and market-adjusted returns in the subsequent year. This suggests a market overreaction to bad earnings reports. Buying stocks of such firms and holding them for twelve months would have generated positive abnormal returns of about 11.6% before transaction costs. The largest abnormal returns were experienced by repeat offenders.[13]

R. J. Fuller, L. C. Hubers, and M. J. Levinson found in an eighteen-year study from April 1973 through March 1991 that low P-E stocks did generate positive alphas and high P-E stocks generated low alphas. These differences were not accounted for by changes in earnings per share growth rates, analysts' forecasting errors, or omission of risk differences.[14]

Value Line Ranking Studies

The *Value Line Investment Survey* (VLIS) ranks stocks into one of five categories for expected stock performance over the next twelve months. Of the 1,700 firms reviewed by the survey, about 100 are ranked I for performance (tops); about 300 are ranked II; roughly 900 are ranked average, or III; about 300 are ranked IV; and the lowest category, V, occurs for about 100 firms.

G. Huberman and S. Kandel state that several stock price studies have concluded that such ranking and superior results from holding such stocks points to an inefficient stock market. They make this claim to support the semistrong hypothesis. Studies show that excess returns in buying Value Line ranked I and II stocks and shorting those in the IV and V groups produced positive annual returns of 19%. Huberman and Kandel go on to say that investing in the smallest 20% of NYSE and AMEX stocks, compared to the largest 20% of the firms, provided similar results. About 60% of the returns on small firms occurred in January. The writers point out that although VLIS top two ranked stocks do produce high returns for twelve months following ranking, negative risk-adjusted returns followed the next year.[15]

David Peterson studied the security price reaction to initial review of common stocks by Value Line. He argued that significant price moves occurred one day before and after the announcement date of a Value Line ranking change.[16] The ranking of stocks by Value Line is largely based on a fifty-day market momentum index and on recent unexpected earnings-per-share reports.

Other Considerations on Market Efficiency

Two writers suggest that the purchase of recent winners and that of selling losers is the way to go to earn excess profits on stock trading. In a 1993 study, N. Jegadeesh and S. Titman found that selecting stocks on the basis of a high, six-month return and holding them an added six months would realize a compounded excess return above market of 12.01%, on average. Such excess returns were not due to systematic risk due to risk differences but were attributed to delayed price reactions to firm-specific information.[17]

Richard C. Grinold researched the question "Are benchmark portfolios efficient?" He applied tests for the market benchmarks in Australia, Germany, the United Kingdom, the United States, and Japan. He generally concluded that they were not very efficient.[18]

Ippolito, in an article published in 1993, reviewed after-expense returns of mutual funds from twenty-one previously cited studies and concluded that there was no significant difference in their returns and those for index funds. The findings generally concluded that mutual funds are sufficiently successful in finding and implementing new information to offset their expenses.[19]

INFREQUENTLY OCCURRING ANOMALIES

Mergers and Acquisitions

Several articles have recently been published concerning the relative performance of shares of target versus acquiring firms. Results found in a few of the studies will be surveyed in the paragraphs which follow.

Jay F. Shepherd discovered the following about mergers: they usually come in waves corresponding to market highs; the selling firms gain from the mergers; and the acquiring firms may or may not gain from the mergers, buy any gain is usually delayed to the acquiring firm. Shepherd suggests several reasons why selling stockholders may not win in such a transaction. Owners might not be fully aware of the worth of their firm, few selling firms use specialists as intermediaries, the sellers might have a compulsion to sell, and the prices received by the sellers are discounted due to their poor marketability.[20]

Over time, the mergers and acquisition markets appear to have grown more efficient. To make profitable acquisition, Shepherd suggests the following strategies: locate companies with limited buyer interest; acquire them when the economy is not booming; and if the acquiring firm has surplus management talent, acquire sick firms and replace their top level management. Historically, premium prices of 25 to 50% were paid in bear markets, but premiums have shrunk in recent years. The buyer, or acquirer, is advised to shun acquisitions when the IPO market is booming, as owners want too high a price.

K. P. Scanlon, J. W. Trifts, and R. H. Pettway, in a 1989 article, reviewed NYSE and AMEX mergers from 1968 to 1985 where no other mergers took place a year before or a year after the subject acquisitions.[21] Some 135 mergers were identified. Generally, the shareholders of the acquiring firms lost wealth, especially when the two firms were operating in different industries. The larger the acquisition, generally, the greater the relative loss to the shareholders in the acquiring firms.

A. Agrawal, J. Jaffe, and G. Mandelker, in a 1992 article, reviewed 937 mergers of firms that disappeared from the CRSP (Center for Research on Stock Prices) tapes from 1955 to 1987. They found that premium prices were paid by the acquiring firms and that the performance of the shares of acquiring firms were inferior for two or more years. Average loss in wealth was 10% over the five years following a merger completion. Loss of wealth did not appear to be present with cash tender offers.[22]

Leveraged Buyouts

K. M. Torabzadeh and W. J. Bertin compared returns to shareholders in forty-three business combinations and for forty-three leveraged buyouts (LBOs) over the 1982 to mid-1987 period. After controlling for transaction costs and firm-specific financial characteristics, target firms in business combinations were found to capture significantly greater abnormal returns than counterparts that were engaged in leveraged buyouts resulting in restructuring a public firm into a private concern.[23]

W. F. Long and D. J. Ravenscraft investigated the impact of a leveraged buyout on the spending for research and development (R & D). They compared seventy-two R & D performing LBOs with 3,329 non-LBO control observations and 126 LBOs with little or no R & D expenditures. They made four statistically significant findings, as follows: Pre-LBO R & D intensity is roughly one half of the overall manufacturing mean and two thirds of the firm's industry industry average; LBOs cause R & D intensity to drop by 40%; large firms tend to have smaller LBO-related declines in R & D intensity; and R & D intensive LBOs outperform both their non-LBO industry peers and other LBOs without R & D expenditures.[24]

Initial Public Offerings

C. B. Barry and R. H. Jennings published a paper in 1993 reviewing 152 operating firms that first went public and fifty closed-end investment firms. They generally found that the initial pricing incorrection for the IPOs was small and that any incorrection was generally corrected within a few minutes of initial trade for the stocks. The two groups of shares were offered at median prices of $10 and $12 per share, respectively. Mean secondary volume of trading compared to shares offered was 30% for operating firms and 2% for closed-end investment company shares. The study generally supported the efficient market hypothesis.[25]

Jon A. Garfinkel, in a 1993 article, studied 494 firms with IPOs that took place during 1981–1983. The firms were followed for seven years after first being IPOs to determine whether or not seasoned secondary offerings were made. In about 20% of the instances, such occurred at an average interval of 24 months following the initial public offering. Stocks at the point of IPO were deemed to be about 11% underpriced. Such underpricing appeared to have little incremental signaling as to the likelihood for incremental reissuance of more shares or for abnormal returns during subsequent years. Little impact was noted on insider trading from the apparent underpricing.[26]

J. Affleck-Graves, S. P. Hegde, R. E. Miller, and F. K. Reilly studied IPOs that

first traded on the NYSE, the AMEX, the NASDAQ/NMS, and the NASDAQ/
nonNMS from 1983 to 1987. Some 55, 41, 158, and 824 IPOs, respectively, came
to these markets. Owners retained from 53 to 66% of total voting shares, with
the smaller ratio for the AMEX listed stocks. Underpricing was slightly below 5%,
on average, for NYSE IPOs; about 3% for AMEX IPOs; about 5.6% for NASDAQ/
NMS; and over 10% for NASDAQ/nonNMS listings. Greater likelihood of trading,
then, tended to reflect less underpricing of the IPOs.[27]

PORTFOLIO SIMULATIONS

In the next several pages, extracted portfolios from Value Line Data Base that
use one of seven investment selection criterion are reviewed. In the first set of
twelve portfolios selected at six-month intervals from Value Line disks of information, we select those twenty-five to thirty stocks with strong negative performances in one period and determine their performances in the following six
months. We then follow this with stocks showing high earnings-per-share growth,
high book value to market value, small company stocks, low price-earnings ratio
stocks, strong positive momentum stocks, and those judged by Value Line to be
timely (i.e., highest company rating and in the top eight or ten industries for
ranking). In Tables 10.1 through 10.7 six-month data base performances are
compared to those for these seven different selection criterion. The averages for
the twelve periods are reflected on the bottom line of each table.

In simulating an investment into twenty to thirty Value Line Data Base stocks
with the largest negative momentum for six months ended with the first or third
quarter and assuming an investment for six more months, results are poorer than
those achievable on the entire data base, as shown in Table 10.1. Some half of
the periods witnessed continued heavy downside moves in the negative movers
of a six-month period. This strategy is not to be recommended by a long purchaser
of stocks but could be a good method for locating appropriate issues to short sell.

Making an investment into stocks with the highest earnings per share growth
rate were simulated in similar fashion with the results reported in Table 10.2.

Those twenty to thirty stocks on the Value Line Data Base with the highest
book-to-market values were selected for six-month simulations. The results are
shown in Table 10.3.

On balance, the prices of high book-to-market value stocks tend to move in
the same direction as the stock data base, but the method did not provide results
as good as the average for all stocks in the portfolio during six-month holding
periods, 1986–1992.

Small firms are expected to perform better in terms of capital gains than the
average for the base from which the stocks are drawn. The selection of twenty to
thirty such stocks with portfolio restructuring after six months are shown in Table
10.4.

The strategy of selecting small stocks in a portfolio of twenty to thirty Value
Line Data Base (VLDB) issues, holding them for six months, and then replacing

Table 10.1

Six-Month Performance of Stocks with Strong Negative Performances over Six Months, 1986–1992

Period	No.	6-mo perf.	VL base perf.	Nonlisted EOP
4/86 - 9/86	21	-18.9%	-5.3%	0
10/86 - 3/87	26	43.5	26.1	6
4/87 - 9/87	21	8.6	7.1	0
10/87 - 3/88	25	-25.3	-16.4	3
4/88 - 9/88	27	6.7	3.7	5
10/88 - 3/89	20	-8.2	6.9	4
4/89 - 9/89	25	10.1	14.3	5
10/89 - 3/90	22	-23.7	-6.5	5
4/90 - 9/90	30	-42.4	-18.5	13
10/90 - 3/91	29	29.0	28.6	9
4/91 - 9/91	21	-4.1	5.4	1
10/91 - 3/92	29	28.2	12.2	9
Average of 12 Periods		0.3%	4.8%	

Source: Portfolios of twenty–thirty stocks selected as of April 1 and October 1 of each year from Value Screen +, Value Line, Inc., PC data base and evaluated six months later.

them with a similar number of small firms' shares did not do appreciably better than the average on the data base over the six-year period.

The next strategy for simulating twelve, half-year investment into twenty to thirty stocks from the VLDB was to use stocks with low price-earnings ratios, hold them for six months, and then repeat the procedure for a total of twelve simulations. The results are shown in Table 10.5.

The strategy of buying low price-earnings ratio stocks and selling them after a six-month holding period and then seeking other, low P-E stocks did not perform as well as the average for the total of the data base over the years 1986–1992.

The sixth simulation strategy was to buy strong upside momentum stocks, hold them for six months, and then repeat the process with about twenty to thirty stocks selected from the Value Line Data Base. The results are shown in Table 10.6.

The strategy of buying fast upside momentum stock provided slightly above average returns during the six-year period under review. For the most part, the strong upside momentum stocks tended to move in the same direction as the overall market but to move upside or downside at a more rapid rate, generally.

Table 10.2
Six-Month Performance of Stocks with Rapid Growth in Earnings per Share,
1986–1992

Period	No.	6-mo perf.	VL base perf.	Nonlisted EOP
4/86 - 9/86	27	-3.3%	-5.3%	5
10/86 - 3/87	26	51.0	26.1	0
4/87 - 9/87	28	0.4	7.1	0
10/87 - 3/88	27	-16.3	-16.4	2
4/88 - 9/88	26	-1.9	3.7	0
10/88 - 3/89	30	2.8	6.9	0
4/89 - 9/89	28	26.7	14.3	0
10/89 - 3/90	27	-1.7	-6.5	0
4/90 - 9/90	26	-11.0	-18.5	0
10/90 - 3/91	25	42.8	28.6	0
4/91 - 9/91	26	29.0	5.4	0
10/91 - 3/92	21	22.9	12.2	0
Average of 12 Periods		11.8%	4.8%	

Source: Portfolios of twenty–thirty stocks selected as of April 1 and October 1 of each year from
Value Screen +, Value Line, Inc., PC data base and evaluated six months later.

Table 10.3
Six-Month Performance of Stocks with High Book-to-Market Values, 1986–1992

Period	No.	6-mo perf.	VL base perf.	Nonlisted EOP
4/86 - 9/86	18	-18.2%	-5.3%	5
10/86 - 3/87	20	25.3	26.1	4
4/87 - 9/87	27	18.2	7.1	0
10/87 - 3/88	25	-26.3	-16.4	5
4/88 - 9/88	27	3.9	3.7	0
10/88 - 3/89	25	-7.9	6.9	1
4/89 - 9/89	23	-.5	14.3	2
10/89 - 3/90	21	-21.0	-6.5	2
4/90 - 9/90	25	-23.4	-18.5	0
10/90 - 3/91	26	9.3	28.6	2
4/91 - 9/91	27	-5.5	5.4	0
10/91 - 3/92	30	40.8	12.2	0
Average of 12 Periods		-0.4%	4.8%	

Source: Portfolios of twenty–thirty stocks selected as of April 1 and October 1 of each year from
Value Screen +, Value Line, Inc., PC data base and evaluated six months later.

Table 10.4

Six-Month Performance of Stocks of the Smallest Firms on the Value Line Data Base, 1986–1992

Period	No.	6-mo perf.	VL base perf.	Nonlisted EOP
4/86 – 9/86	27	8.5	-5.3%	1
10/86 – 3/87	26	27.1	26.1	5
4/87 – 9/87	30	6.6	7.1	0
10/87 – 3/88	20	-21.4	-16.4	4
4/88 – 9/88	21	-1.7	3.7	0
10/88 – 3/89	22	6.1	6.9	0
4/89 – 9/89	25	15.1	14.3	0
10/89 – 3/90	24	-2.1	-6.5	0
4/90 – 9/90	22	-12.5	-18.5	0
10/90 – 3/91	24	34.3	28.6	0
4/91 – 9/91	25	1.6	5.4	0
10/91 – 3/92	21	7.2	12.2	0
Average of 12 Periods		5.7	4.8%	

Source: Portfolios of twenty–thirty stocks selected as of April 1 and October 1 of each year from *Value Screen +*, Value Line, Inc., PC data base and evaluated six months later.

Table 10.5

Six-Month Performance of Stocks with Low Price-Earnings Ratios, 1986–1992

Period	No.	6-mo perf.	VL base perf.	Nonlisted EOP
4/86 – 9/86	25	-9.7%	-5.3%	1
10/86 – 3/87	29	16.2	26.1	0
4/87 – 9/87	27	1.7	7.1	0
10/87 – 3/88	25	-14.5	-16.4	0
4/88 – 9/88	25	10.2	3.7	0
10/88 – 3/89	25	4.2	6.9	1
4/89 – 9/89	29	8.1	14.3	2
10/89 – 3/90	30	-21.4	-6.5	1
4/90 – 9/90	31	-38.8	-18.5	0
10/90 – 3/91	26	35.9	28.6	1
4/91 – 9/91	23	15.5	5.4	1
10/91 – 3/92	20	14.7	12.2	0
Average of 12 Periods		1.8%	4.8%	

Source: Portfolios of twenty–thirty stocks selected as of April 1 and October 1 of each year from *Value Screen +*, Value Line, Inc., PC data base and evaluated six months later.

Table 10.6
Six-Month Performance of Stocks with Strong Upside Market Price Momentum, 1986–1992

Period	No.	6-mo perf.	VL base perf.	Nonlisted EOP
4/86 – 9/86	19	-8.1%	-5.3%	5
10/86 – 3/87	18	54.9	26.1	7
4/87 – 9/87	22	10.7	7.1	0
10/87 – 3/88	22	-21.1	-16.4	4
4/88 – 9/88	21	2.3	3.7	0
10/88 – 3/89	25	2.6	6.9	2
4/89 – 9/89	26	13.1	14.3	0
10/89 – 3/90	21	-7.4	-6.5	0
4/90 – 9/90	22	-11.1	-18.5	0
10/90 – 3/91	20	5.8	28.6	0
4/91 – 9/92	30	10.9	5.4	0
10/92 – 3/93	26	12.7	12.2	0
Average of 12 Periods		5.4	4.8%	

Source: Portfolio of twenty–thirty stocks selected as of April 1 and October 1 of each year from *Value Screen* +, Value Line, Inc., PC data base and evaluated six months later.

Table 10.7
Six-Month Performance of Stocks with the Highest Individual and Industry Ranking, 1986–1992

Period	No.	6-mo perf.	VL base perf.	Nonlisted EOP
4/86 – 9/86	27	-.6%	-5.3%	0
10/86 – 3/87	25	34.5	26.1	2
4/87 – 9/87	30	14.1	7.1	0
10/87 – 3/88	22	-16.9	-16.4	0
4/88 – 9/88	23	2.1	3.7	0
10/88 – 3/89	21	8.4	6.9	1
4/89 – 9/89	22	24.0	14.3	0
10/89 – 3/90	25	-4.0	-6.5	0
4/90 – 9/90	30	-5.1	-18.5	0
10/90 – 3/91	29	49.9	28.6	0
4/91 – 9/91	27	11.0	5.4	0
10/91 – 3/92	25	16.5	12.2	0
Average of Periods		11.2%	4.8%	

Source: Portfolio of twenty–thirty stocks selected as of April 1 and October 1 of each year from *Value Screen* +, Value Line, Inc., PC data base and evaluated six months later.

The last simulated method was to select about thirty stocks that were ranked the highest by Value Line and those that were in the top eight or ten (of about ninety-five) industry top-ranked groups of stocks. The results are shown in Table 10.7.

The Value Line highly recommended stocks (highest rank for twelve-month expected price performance) selected from the top eight or ten top-ranked industry groups performed about 150% better than did the entire portfolio from which the stocks were drawn.

Value Line predominantly uses market momentum and better than expected quarterly earnings reports to select its expected near-term, much above average stock performers. Over this six-year period, the Value Line selection method appeared to be superior to the other methods simulated.

SUMMARY

Several stock market anomalies are reviewed in this chapter. These include the January effect, other trading-by-the-calendar patterns, size-related anomalies, Value Line ranking (on the basis of market momentum and E/S surprise factor), and special situations such as merger candidates or initial public offerings.

Certain portfolio selection strategies are then tested using *Value Line Data Base Plus* for twelve recent semiannual time periods. The buying of strong momentum stocks, those with rapid gains in E/S and those with high Value Line stock ranking, generally did outperform the base returns. Small firms' stocks tended to do only slightly better than large firms during a six-month period.

Other methods of selection attempted showed little improvement over average base returns. Negative E/S and negative price momentum selection approaches produced portfolios with poorer than average returns.

NOTES

1. S. L. Jones, W. Lee and R. Apenbrink, "New Evidence on the January Effect before Personal Income Taxes," *The Journal of Finance* 46, no. 5 (December 1991): 1909–24.

2. P. Arowin, "Size, Seasonality, and Stock Market Overreaction," *Journal of Financial and Quantitative Analysis,* 25, no. 1 (March 1993): 113–125.

3. C. G. Lamoureux and G. C. Sanger, "Firm Size and Turn-of-the-Year Effect in the OTC/NASDAQ Market," *The Journal of Finance,* 44, no. 5 (December 1989): 1219–46.

4. G. N. Pettengill and B. D. Jordan, "The Overreaction Hypothesis, Firm Size, and Stock Market Seasonality," *The Journal of Portfolio Management* 16, (Spring 1990): 60–63.

5. B. McDonald and R. E. Miller, "Additional Evidence on the Nature of Size-Related Anomalies," *Journal of Economics and Business* 40, no. 1, (1988): 61–68.

6. K. C. J. Wei and S. R. Stansell, "Benchmark Error and the Small Firm Effects: A Revisit," *The Journal of Financial Research* 14, no. 4 (Winter 1991): 359–369.

7. I. Friend and H. P. Lang, "The Size Effect on Stock Returns," *Journal of Banking and Finance* 12 no. 1, (1988): 13–30.

8. D. B. Keim, "A New Look at the Effects of Firm Size and E/P Ratio on Stock Returns," *Financial Analysts Journal* 46, (March-April 1990): 56–66.

9. G. W. Kester, "Market Timing with Small versus Large-Firm Stocks: Potential Gains and Required Predictive Ability," *Financial Analysts Journal* 46, (September-October 1990): 63–69.

10. B. I. Jacobs and K. N. Levy, "Forecasting the Size Effect," *Financial Analysts Journal* 45, (May-June 1989): 38–54.

11. J. B. Wiggins, "The Earnings-Price and Standardized Unexpected Earnings Effects: One Anomaly or Two?" *The Journal of Financial Research* 14, no. 4 (Winter 1991): 163–175.

12. S. J. Chang and S. N. Chen, "Information Effects of Earnings and Dividend Announcements on Common Stock Returns: Are They Interactive?" *Journal of Economics and Business* 43 no. 2, (1991): 179–192.

13. M. Ettredge and R. J. Fuller, "The Negative Earnings Effect," *The Journal of Portfolio Management* 17, (Spring 1991): 27–33.

14. R. J. Fuller, L. C. Hubers, and M. J. Levinson, "Returns to E/P Strategies, Higgledy-Piggledy Growth, Analysts' Forecast Errors, and Omitted Risk Factors," *The Journal of Portfolio Management* 19, (Winter 1993): 13–24.

15. G. Huberman and S. Kandel, "Market Efficiency and Value Line's Record," *Journal of Business* 63, no. 2 (1990): 187–215.

16. David R. Peterson, "Security Price Reactions to Initial Review of Common Stock by the *Value Line Investment Survey,*" *Journal of Financial and Quantitative Analysis,* 22, no. 4 (December 1987): 483–493.

17. N. Jegadeesh and S. Titman, "Return to Buying Winners and Selling Losers: Implications for Stock Market Efficiency," *The Journal of Finance* 48 (March 1993): 65–91.

18. R. C. Grinold, "Are Benchmark Portfolios Efficient?" *The Journal of Portfolio Management* 18 (Fall 1992): 34–41.

19. R. A. Ippolito, "On Studies of Mutual Fund Performance, 1962–1991," *Financial Analysts Journal* 49 (January-February 1993): 42–50.

20. J. F. Shepherd, "How Mergers and Acquisition Market Inefficiencies Work for Bargain Hunters," *Mergers & Acquisitions* 27, (November-December 1992): 5–8.

21. K. P. Scanlon, J. W. Trifts, and R. H. Pettway, "Impact of Relative Size and Industrial Relatedness on Returns to Shareholders of Acquiring Firms," *The Journal of Financial Research* 12, no. 2 (Summer 1989): 103–112.

22. A. Agrawal, J. Jaffe, and G. Mandelker, "The Post-Merger Performance of Acquiring Firms: A Re-examination of an Anomaly," *The Journal of Finance* 47, no. 4 (September 1992): 1605–1621.

23. K. M. Torabzadeh and W. J. Bertin, "Abnormal Returns to Stockholders of Firms Acquired in Business Combinations and Leveraged Buyouts," *Journal of Accounting, Auditing and Finance* 7, (Spring 1992): 231–239.

24. W. F. Long and D. J. Ravenscraft, "LBOs, Debt and R&D Intensity," *Strategic Management Journal* 14 (Summer 1993): 119–135.

25. C. B. Barry and R. H. Jennings, "The Opening Price Performance of Initial Public Offerings of Common Stock," *Financial Management* 22 (Spring 1993): 54–63.

26. J. A. Garfinkel, "IPO Underpricing, Insider Selling and Subsequent Equity Offer-

ings: Is Underpricing a Signal of Quality?" *Financial Management* 22, (Spring 1993): 74–83.

27. J. Affleck-Graves, S. P. Hegde, R. E. Miller, and F. K. Reilly, "The Effect of the Trading System on the Underwriting of Initial Public Offerings," *Financial Management* 22, (Spring 1993): 99–108.

Chapter 11

INTERMARKET ANALYSIS AND FIXED-INCOME ALLOCATION STRATEGIES

When we think of asset allocation in terms of bonds and other fixed-income investments, the standard approach involves interest rate risk, inflation, and trends in the economy. In other words, traditional treatments concerning fixed-income portfolio management seem to focus heavily on the bond market.

We are unable to accept the view that the bond market stands almost in isolation with little or no relationship to other financial markets. Granted, bond prices depend on rising and falling trends in interest rates. The key for management, however, is anticipating these interest rate trends and determining what causes them. It seems logical to assume financial markets are related. Bonds should respond to developments in gold, foreign currencies, the dollar, and other factors.

The thrust of this chapter suggests that market interrelationships do exist.[1] In his book entitled *Intermarket Technical Analysis,* John Murphy espouses the virtues of financial market interrelationships in forecasting different price movements. This chapter uses Murphy's analysis as an approximate guideline to look at cash prices on a number of indexes, including the dollar, the German Mark, gold, the CRB Index, bonds, utilities, energy prices, and stocks. As opposed to Murphy's contention that futures charts should be used, we apply our analysis to cash prices.

AN OVERVIEW OF MURPHY'S VIEWPOINTS

According to John Murphy, a sustained decline in the dollar is inflationary. However, it requires a while for a dollar with reduced value to circulate and exert an inflationary impact. To extend the inflation scenario, the one commodity most sensitive to price movements in the dollar is gold. Gold moves diametrically opposite or contrary to the dollar. As the dollar falls, gold rises and forms an uptrend.

Rising gold prices warn of the potential for inflation. A partial explanation can be traced to the thought that movements in gold often precede other commodity price movements. In addition, silver prices typically parallel gold trends and confirm its price action. Energy prices also provide an interesting insight. Oil prices often move with gold and support the inflation or disinflation picture unfolding at the current time. Rising oil, gold, and silver prices fuel the inflation outlook. Meanwhile, a declining dollar signals stronger foreign currencies because U.S. financial reporting measures foreign currency values relative to the dollar.

Commodity prices gauge inflation and can be followed by the Commodities Research Bureau (CRB) Index, a widely followed tool for measuring price level changes. As commodity prices increase and the CRB Index rises, inflation makes its presence felt. Once inflation rears its ugly head, interest rates climb as bond and stock prices retreat.

When interest rates increase and bond prices decline, the stock market must be scrutinized closely. Investors are risk averse and gravitate toward conservative investments with guaranteed high yields rather than assume larger risks from the vagaries of the stock market. Money flows toward safer fixed-income alternatives rather than the less secure equities market. As a result, stocks move lower.

Conversely, a low interest rate environment makes certificates of deposit (CDs) and other fixed-income options less attractive. To secure a higher return, investors look to common stocks as an investment choice. Funds are redirected from fixed-income instruments toward the stock market.

In contrast, let us develop a noninflationary scenario. First, a rising dollar is disinflationary. Gold and energy prices decline along with lower CRB Index readings and weaker foreign currency values. The ultimate result is strong performances in bond and stock prices.

Now that we have established a background of market interrelationships, let us apply this logic to actual market situations. We will look at the 1987 and 1990 markets, which resulted in a top and bottom, respectively, for common stocks. By taking an anecdotal approach, we can track the trends and performances of different markets and determine whether such interrelationships actually prove helpful in forecasting for asset allocation decisions.

THE MARKET TOP OF 1987

Figure 11.1 reveals a sharply lower 1987 dollar stemming from a sustained downtrend. Actually, the dollar appeared to reach peak levels during the 1985 calendar year based on an evaluation of longer-term P & F charts. The principal point of interpretation with the dollar centers on its primary trend. Throughout 1987, the dollar fell precipitously with its inflationary connotations warning of potential weakness in both bonds and stocks. Figure 11.2 represents a graphic

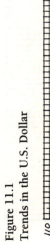

Figure 11.1
Trends in the U.S. Dollar

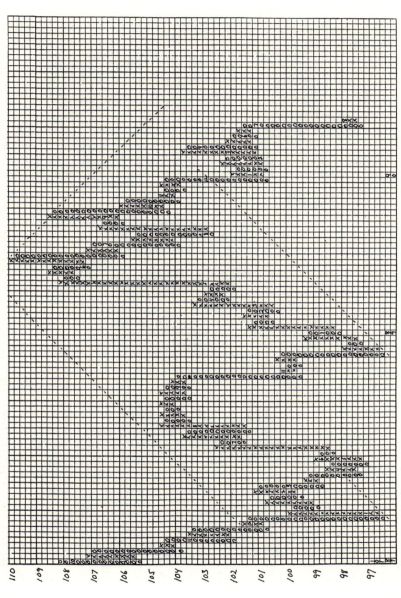

Figure 11.1 Continued

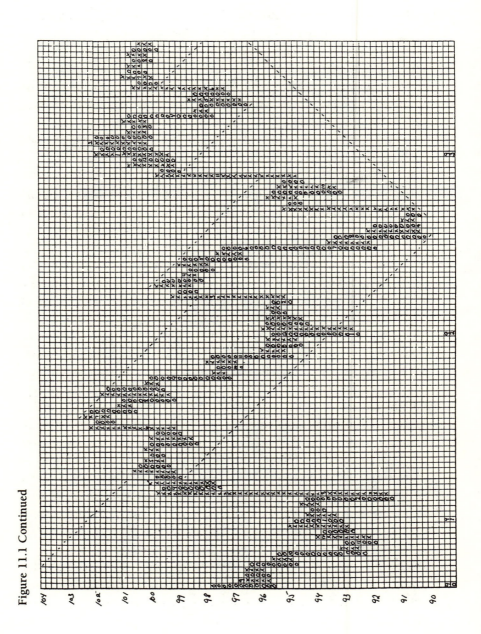

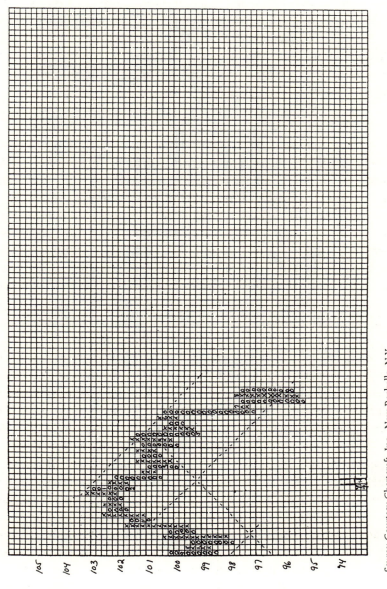

Source: Courtesy Chartcraft, Inc., New Rochelle, N.Y.

Figure 11.2
Foreign Currencies—A Look at the German Mark

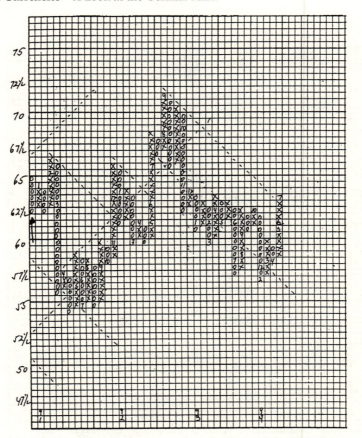

Figure 11.2 Continued

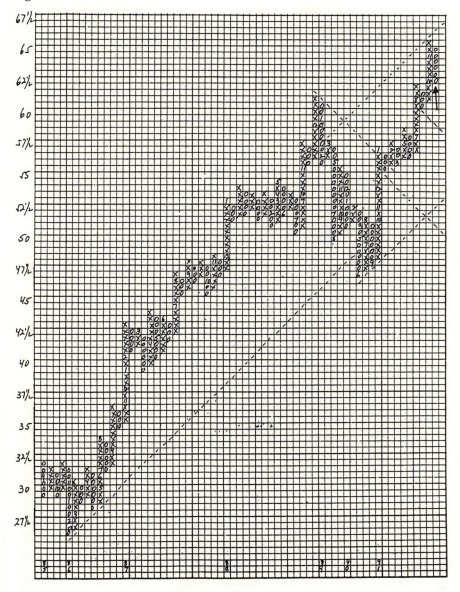

Source: Courtesy Chartcraft, Inc., New Rochelle, N.Y.

Figure 11.3
Trends in Gold Prices

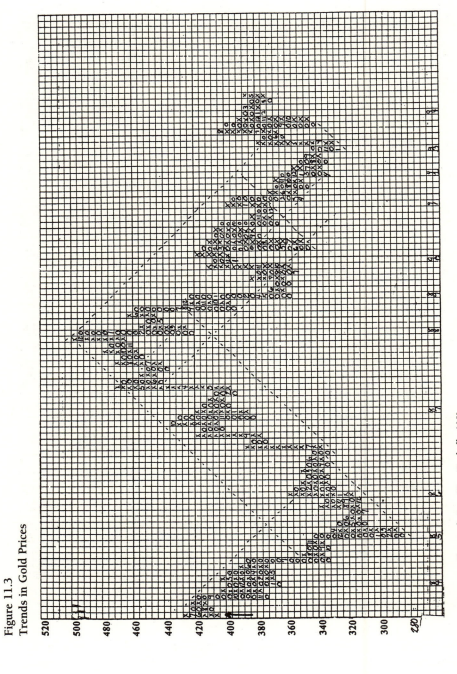

Source: Courtesy Chartcraft, Inc., New Rochelle, N.Y.

Figure 11.4
The CRB Index

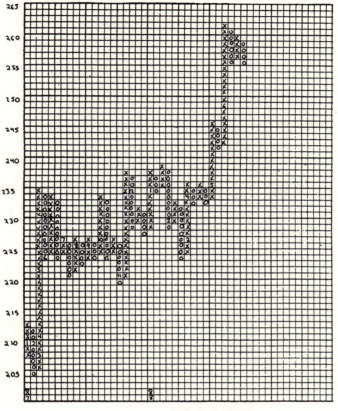

C.R.B. INDEX

Source: Courtesy Chartcraft, Inc., New Rochelle, N.Y.

view of foreign currencies by providing a look at the German Mark. The Mark gave a buy signal in July, 1987, and a strong uptrend continued until late 1988. Firm price action in foreign currencies confirmed the weakness in the U.S. dollar.

The progress of gold can be tracked in Figure 11.3. A low pole buy signal occurred in the first quarter of 1985, with a more definitive upside breakout in early 1986. Gold's solid advance gave ample forewarning of possible inflation and the risks associated with fixed-income investments. The CRB Index in Figure 11.4 helps make judgments about price changes. In early 1987, a buy signal and strong upmove took place. As was the case with the dollar, foreign currencies, and gold, we received early notice of possible problems in the bond sector. As we see shortly, what affects bonds also serves as a laggard problem for common stocks.

Let us turn our attention to Figure 11.5 and the Dow Jones Bond Average. A

Figure 11.5
Reviewing Bond Prices

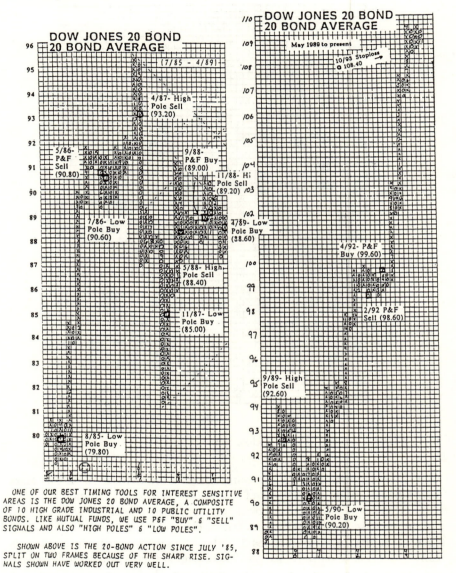

ONE OF OUR BEST TIMING TOOLS FOR INTEREST SENSITIVE
AREAS IS THE DOW JONES 20 BOND AVERAGE, A COMPOSITE
OF 10 HIGH GRADE INDUSTRIAL AND 10 PUBLIC UTILITY
BONDS. LIKE MUTUAL FUNDS, WE USE P&F "BUY" & "SELL"
SIGNALS AND ALSO "HIGH POLES" & "LOW POLES".

SHOWN ABOVE IS THE 20-BOND ACTION SINCE JULY '85,
SPLIT ON TWO FRAMES BECAUSE OF THE SHARP RISE. SIG-
NALS SHOWN HAVE WORKED OUT VERY WELL.

Source: Courtesy Chartcraft, Inc., New Rochelle, N.Y.

Figure 11.6
The Dow Jones Utility Average (A)

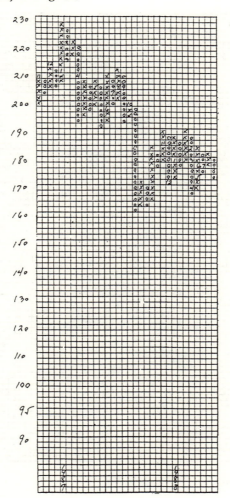

Source: Courtesy Chartcraft, Inc., New Rochelle, N.Y.

high pole sell signal occurs in April 1987, with a downside breakout following shortly thereafter. Portfolio managers must constantly review these events as they unfold. Any sell signal or downside break in bond prices should never go unnoticed. Let us see why.

A quick referral to Figures 11.6 and 11.7 provides a look at the Dow Jones Utility Average (DJUA). Notice that a sell signal develops in March, 1987. The breakdown in utility prices preceded the sell signal in bonds by one month. Obviously, a correlation exists between bonds and utility stocks. Keep in mind

Figure 11.7
The Dow Jones Utility Average (B)

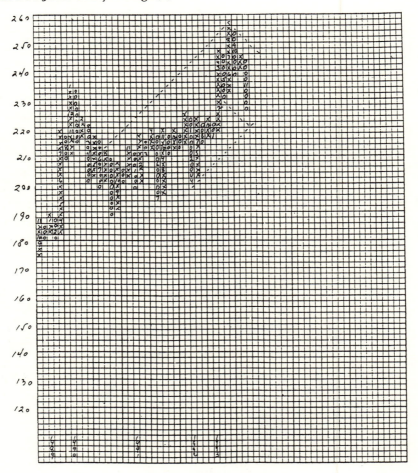

Source: Courtesy Chartcraft, Inc., New Rochelle, N.Y.

that utility stocks serve as investment competition to bonds because of their high dividend yields. Logically, long-term interest rates must impact both sets of securities. Interestingly, utilities serve as a leading indicator for stock and bond prices.[2]

Figure 11.8 provides an overview of energy trends with the chart on West Texas Crude Oil spot prices. Rising prices appeared throughout most of 1986 and 1987. Oil reached price levels of almost $22.50 per barrel. The energy sector previewed inflationary expectations as oil prices more than doubled in the 1986–1987 period. Although oil declined late in 1987, energy had already corroborated

Figure 11.8
Energy Prices

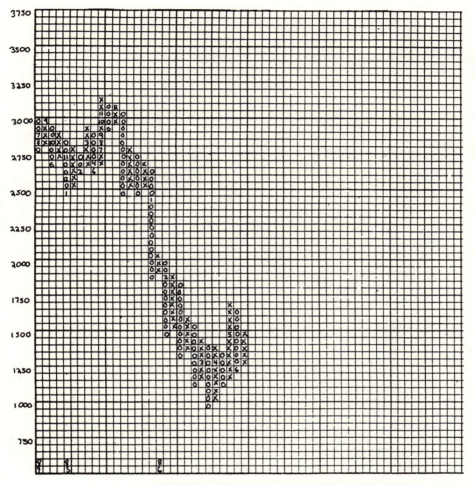

CRUDE OIL – WEST TEXAS INTERM

Figure 11.8 Continued

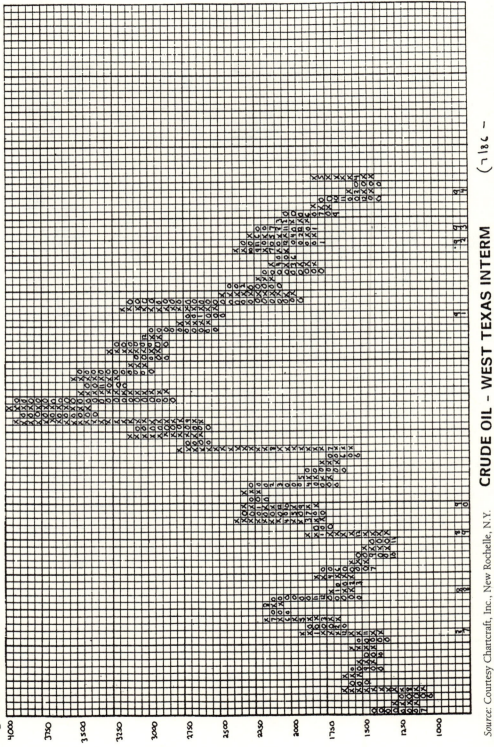

CRUDE OIL – WEST TEXAS INTERM

trends in gold, the CRB Index, and other indicators, thereby warning of potential problems in the financial markets.

To conclude our synthesis, let's examine common stocks, our final step in extending these interrelationships. A chart of the Dow Jones Industrial Average (DJIA) appears in Figure 11.9. A sell signal in October 1987 carried the DJIA downward from the 2,600–2,700 level to near the 1,700 level. We experienced a short-term bear market, which not only exceeded everyone's worst expectations but was worse than the crash of 1929. Leading indicators such as the dollar, foreign currencies, gold, the CRB Index, oil prices, and utilities gave ample warning to shift the allocation of funds away from bonds (and stocks). In turn, bond price slides served as a precursor of the most infamous reversal in common stock history.

THE MARKET BOTTOM OF 1990

Now that we have completed our integrative treatment of financial markets at a top in the stock market, let us develop a similar analysis for the subtle bottom of 1990. The dollar seems to reach bottom in late 1990 and then begin an abridged rally phase. However, it seems appropriate to interject some added thoughts on the area of intermarket analysis at this point. Overall, the dollar seems to be the most difficult aspect to interpret. Perhaps the safest rules to use are the simplest.

First, the primary trend of the dollar should be weighted heavily since persistently rising or falling trends are either noninflationary or inflationary, respectively. Second, a buy signal that follows a lengthy downtrend is bullish for the dollar and a healthy sign for investors. Conversely, a sell signal that occurs after an extended uptrend is bearish for the dollar and a warning signal for investors. Otherwise, dealing with the dollar and its multifaceted relationships is exceedingly complex and makes attempts to factor in many other rules too difficult.

From Figure 11.2 we observe the Mark declining throughout most of 1989 and 1990 followed by a buy signal and uptrend in November 1990. The bullish period in the Mark continues into early 1991 when the U.S. stock market begins to strengthen. Gold turns bearish with a sell signal in January 1988 and declines until the first quarter of 1993.

We note in Figure 11.4 that the CRB Index turns bearish in May 1990 from a sell signal. For the most part, the downtrend also continues into early 1993. Gold and the CRB Index confirm each other and indicate a disinflationary period with lower prices and lower interest rates. Despite the interpretational difficulties associated with the dollar, both gold and the CRB Index warn of low inflation and portend of a highly positive investment climate.

As we move to Figure 11.5, the Dow Jones bond chart furnished by Chartcraft shows a low pole buy signal in May 1990. As further evidence of the value of low poles (and high poles), the upside breakout did not occur until January 1991. Rising bond prices (and lower interest rates) reinforce the favorable outlook for

Figure 11.9
The Dow Jones Industrial Average

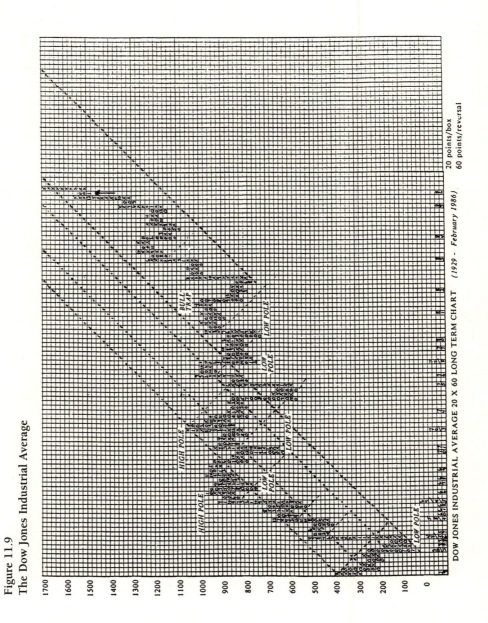

DOW JONES INDUSTRIAL AVERAGE 20 X 60 LONG TERM CHART   (1929 - February 1986)

20 points/box
60 points/reversal

312

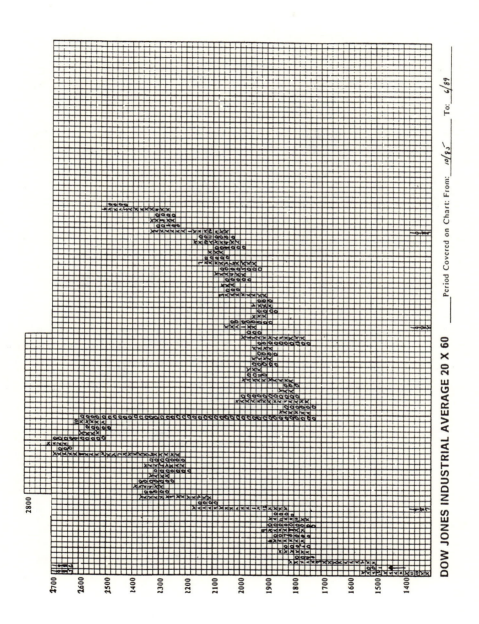

DOW JONES INDUSTRIAL AVERAGE 20 X 60

Period Covered on Chart: From: _10/85_ To: _6/89_

2800

2700
2600
2500
2400
2300
2200
2100
2000
1900
1800
1700
1600
1500
1400

313

Figure 11.9 Continued

DOW JONES INDUSTRIAL AVERAGE 20 X 60

Period Covered on Chart: From: 7/89 To: 4/93

314

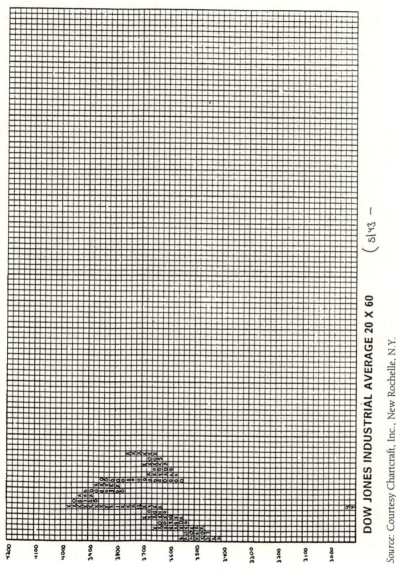

DOW JONES INDUSTRIAL AVERAGE 20 X 60

(5143 –

Source: Courtesy Chartcraft, Inc., New Rochelle, N.Y.

financial markets and remind portfolio managers of the close correlation between bond and stock markets.

The Dow Jones Utility Average again provided advance warning with a low pole buy signal followed by an upside breakout on the chart in November, 1990. A sell signal on the West Texas Crude chart (Figure 11.8) in September 1990 confirmed the noninflationary expectations and provided an impetus for the stock market. The DJIA in Figure 11.9 bottomed in late 1990 and gave a buy signal from a breakout above a large base pattern in January 1991. A well-defined, explosive bull market followed.

INTERMARKET ANALYSIS AND ASSET ALLOCATION

The evidence from this chapter appears significant in the analysis of turning points in both stocks and bonds. Traditional asset allocation postures in the fixed-income sector often develop from theoretical, quantitative forecasting. Such approaches to shifts in interest rate expectations appear to be staid and ineffective, suggesting that there may be room for improvement.

The underlying viewpoint among some involved with asset allocation seems to be predicated on the belief that fixed-income management must focus on the bond market as an autonomous entity. The bond market can no longer be evaluated with the approach that fixed-income securities are detached from the financial arena. Bonds, as well as stocks, seem highly dependent on other market places.

The dollar must be evaluated from sustained primary moves in either direction. Reversals (i.e., buy or sell signals) conclude these trends and seem to be effective in forming ideas for general expectations. Foreign currencies ordinarily perform counter to the dollar and help allocation decisions.

A review of long-term P & F charts reinforces our findings. The 1970s were characterized by an unprecedented bull market in gold, an advance in the CRB Index, rising oil prices, and a decline in the dollar. The result was unparalleled inflation, a gold price near $900 an ounce, and turbulent financial markets. The 1970s extended into 1980 and 1981 and contained the worst period on record for bond prices.

The 1980s were greeted by a reversal in the dollar. Remember, buy and sell signals in the dollar following long-term trends in either direction are highly significant and represent a key to accurately interpreting its movements. The CRB Index and gold began twelve-year bear markets that reversed in 1993. Declining interest rates, a disinflationary economy, and rising utility prices were the impetus for record performances in both bonds and stocks. The principles underlying financial market interrelationships performed in harmonious fashion. A longer-term perspective confirms our evaluation of the junctures in 1987 and 1990.

Asset allocation in both debt and equity securities appears to be heavily linked to financial market interrelationships. Asset allocation principles should embrace this connectiveness in analyzing and managing diversified portfolios.

SUMMARY

Asset allocation techniques for the fixed-income sector often seem too preoccupied with interest rate changes and economic forecasting. Although such items remain important to switching in and out of bonds, frequently they do not help portfolio managers with market timing.

The anecdotal research approach in this chapter seems to argue that decisions relating to bond management depend on interrelationships in the financial markets. Such indicators as gold, the CRB Index, energy prices, and utility stock trends emerge as leading indicators of bond prices and interest rates. The U.S. dollar and foreign currencies are also helpful. By carefully evaluating these markets, we receive advance warning of problems which may surface in the future for fixed-income securities.

In conclusion, bonds are a viable aspect of asset allocation. Further, their price movements precede those of common stocks, another vital link in asset allocation. Pursuing this connectiveness or linkage between financial markets brings the discipline of asset allocation into sharper focus. As a final thought, one might wonder why gold, the CRB Index, oil, and related measures used throughout this chapter might not play an important role in portfolio diversification. If we argue that future contracts should be employed because of their presumed ability to predict future prices, they too could play significant roles in diversification and allocation.

NOTES

1. John J. Murphy, *Intermarket Technical Analysis* (New York: John Wiley & Sons, Inc., 1991).

2. John Murphy often writes interesting articles for a journal called *Technical Analysis of Stocks and Commodities.* For example, see John J. Murphy, "Utilities and Bonds," *Technical Analysis of Stocks and Commodities* 10 (August 1992): 34–36.

Chapter 12

ASSET ALLOCATION MANAGEMENT AND RISK REDUCTION USING MUTUAL FUNDS

One of the purest forms of asset allocation lies in the flow of money in and out of mutual funds. Investment decisions often involve the shifting of money to different mutual funds within the same family, with each fund having different investment objectives. The family of funds concept adapts well to qualified retirement plans because money can be continually transferred without incurring a tax liability from liquidating one fund's shares to purchase those of another.

Mutual funds occupy a prominent role in asset allocation because there are funds to meet almost every conceivable investment objective. Fixed-income, aggressive growth, growth, total return (growth and income), tax-exempt, and balanced funds, to name a few, now pervade the spectrum of mutual fund investment. As if these were not enough, fund offerings specializing in different sectors such as global markets, precious metals, software, computers, utilities, convertibles, investment firms, and banking are now available.

Mutual funds offer professional management and risk reduction through diversification as principal advantages. Given the levels of specialization in financial markets, many portfolio managers now achieve their results through mutual funds. Timing of decisions to move money back and forth is of paramount importance. Our approach to asset allocation through the medium of mutual funds depends on the previously utilized Chartcraft approach to point and figure charts.[1]

TRADING BUY AND SELL SIGNALS

Rules for asset allocation among different mutual funds are straightforward and relatively simple.[2] Always acknowledge the first buy signal, particularly when a downtrend has been underway for an extended period of time. By acting on the initial buy signal in a prolonged downtrend, we are usually able to catch the advance early.

Conversely, a second rule suggests that we act on the first sell signal received. Acting on the initial sell signal assumes added importance when the downside breakout occurs after a long upmove. Two of the reasons for taking buy and sell signals early lie in their durability and accuracy. Signals tend to remain intact on mutual fund charts, fewer signals develop compared to individual stocks.

Figure 12.1 illustrates how reacting to buy and sell signals on mutual fund P & F charts can result in successful trading strategies. An investor could take a long position in Centurion Growth Fund on the upside breakout in December 1987 and hold until a sell signal reverses that strategy in August 1988. A January 1989 buy signal generates another long position, which is held until sell signals appear in February and April 1990. Long positions may be resumed from a low pole in January 1991, until a trend reversal develops in July of the same year. Each breakout (or buy and sell signal) creates a strategy change that enables asset managers to be on the right side of the trend for most of the move in either direction.

ACTING ON THE FIRST BUY SIGNAL

Figure 12.2 shows the importance of taking action on the first buy signal. The first buy signal assumes added significance when it occurs at depressed price levels or in a ZOF (zone of fear) where previous bottoms formed. Such levels suggest that selling is probably overdone and that the slide has reached climactic proportions. Initial buy signals at depressed price levels must receive top priority because they not only indicate a major price reversal in most cases, but they also provide an early point of entry into an emerging new move.

EVALUATING THE FIRST SELL SIGNAL

As in the case with initial buy signals, first-time sell signals generally serve as a time for action. P & F charts on mutual funds rarely allow investors to be "whipsawed" by misleading signals. Although not yet an infallible system, breakouts for the most part are reliable and long-lasting. Therefore, we usually recommend that first-time sell signals represent a time to liquidate long positions.

Figure 12.3 illustrates the importance of acting on the first sell signal, particularly one following on the heels of an extended price advance. View sell signals occurring at extended price levels as distributional in nature. Sell signals in ZOGs

Figure 12.1
Trading Mutual Funds with Buy and Sell Signals

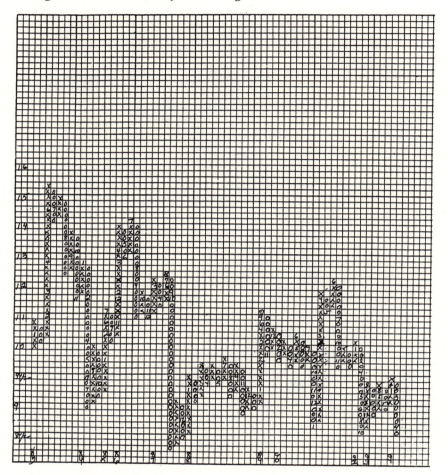

Source: Courtesy Chartcraft, Inc., New Rochelle, N.Y.

(zones of greed) typically develop where previous tops have formed and suggest vulnerability on the downside.

In the Dreyfus Strategic Growth chart, a sell signal materializes in February 1992, and the fund suffers a significant downside price reversal. Asset managers could have reallocated on the sell signal and reestablished long positions during the first quarter of 1993 from a low pole formation. In the Oppenheimer Global Bio Tech chart, a sell signal surfaced in February 1992. Asset reallocation should have been implemented on the sell signal as the fund experienced significant damage from the resulting downside price swing. A May, 1993, buy signal would

Figure 12.2
Acknowledge the First Buy Signal

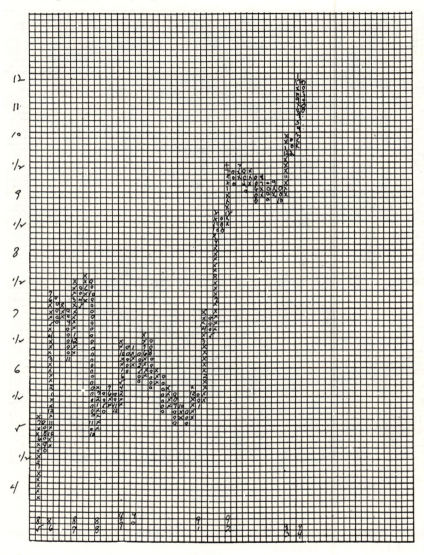

Source: Courtesy Chartcraft, Inc., New Rochelle, N.Y.

have permitted a point of re-entry and made the asset allocation process function smoothly.

THE IMPORTANCE OF ZOFs AND ZOGs

To illustrate the importance of ZOFs and ZOGs, let us review Figure 12.4. In late 1992, the Fidelity Biotech chart reveals another rally attempt to $29, an area

Figure 12.3
Acting on the First Sell Signal

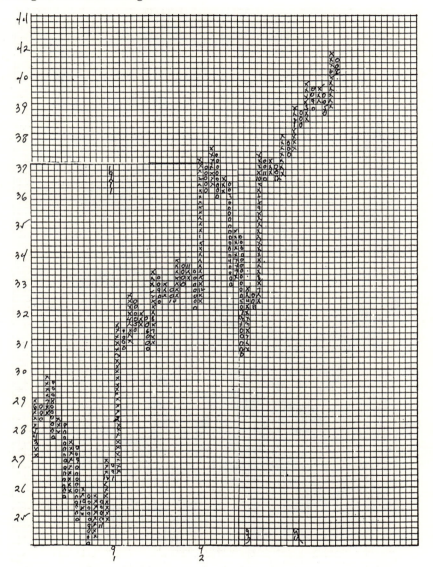

Figure 12.3 Continued

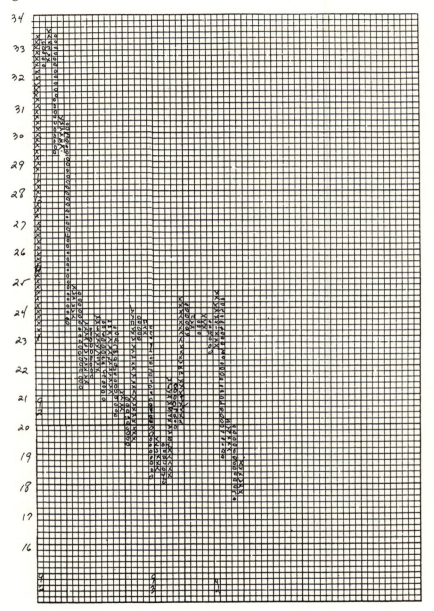

Source: Courtesy Chartcraft, Inc., New Rochelle, N.Y.

Figure 12.4
Buying and Selling in Zones of Fear and Greed

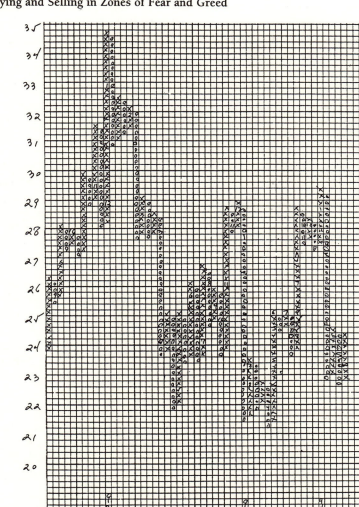

Source: Courtesy Chartcraft, Inc., New Rochelle, N.Y.

where at least one other top has previously formed. A January 1993 sell signal in this ZOG should alert chartists to allocate investment funds to other alternatives. The fund bottomed in a ZOF near the $22 area, where another major bottom previously formed. A buy signal at $23 established the basis for asset reallocation. Buy and sell signals in ZOFs and ZOGs, respectively, prove to be highly accurate and reliable. Do not underestimate their importance.

It seems appropriate to interject another strategy at this point. Once a particular market (whether it be stocks, bonds, precious metals, global, etc.) appears to have reached bottom based on the technical evidence, fund buy signals should be given even more credence. If a particular equity fund price has entered a ZOF and corresponds to an aggregate market low, accept buy signals without hesitation. The likelihood is that your point of entry will be timely and at depressed price levels.

One should reallocate funds in a similar fashion near market tops. If asset managers receive a sell signal in a ZOG in combination with a topping process in the general market, react quickly in accepting sell signals. Liquidate the fund and seek other alternatives.

Always remember that every decision should be viewed in terms of potential risk versus potential reward. A buy signal in a ZOF usually suggests minimal downside risk with the potential for advancement relatively large. A sell signal in a ZOG demonstrates large risks on the downside with reduced upside potential. Always weigh risks and rewards prior to making decisions.

SPIKES AS A PART OF THE ALLOCATION STRATEGY

From past chapters, we know that spikes are long, uninterrupted price moves in either direction. Spikes represent speculative excesses that culminate with price reversals to correct the extremes. For mutual fund investors, we regard upmoves of twenty to twenty-five squares as excessive. The charts help us recognize that the further these sustained advances carry, the greater the downside risks. Michael Burke and John Gray[3] advocate that spikes of the twenty-five-square magnitude dictate caution. Burke and Gray recommend liquidation of fund shares at the first sign of a three box reversal in a column of O's. They further maintain that long positions can be reestablished later in a column of X's.

The Merrill Lynch Phoenix Fund in Figure 12.5 includes a downside spike in August, 1990, and an upside spike in January, 1991. Had asset managers reallocated at the first sign of a three-box reversal in a column of X's or O's, respectively, their timing for allocation would have been outstanding. Re-establishing their commitment of funds with the appearance of a three-box reversal would have enhanced profitability.[4]

We may learn more on the downside spike by referring to the Fidelity Healthcare sector fund in Figure 12.5. When the downside spike from late 1992 and early 1993 culminates, we begin looking for some lateral or basing price action. Once the fund adjusts to the lower price level by consolidating and forming the base pattern, we should look to the possibility of an upside breakout and price reversal over the near term. The April–May buy signal indicated the appropriate time for shifting funds into the healthcare sector using the Fidelity fund.

HIGH POLES AND LOW POLES

As you recall, a high pole formation develops when an upside breakout in a column of X's exceeds one or more previous tops by at least three squares. The following column of O's then retraces more than 50% of the advance in the breakout column and implicitly warns of distribution. Conversely, the low pole formation occurs when a downside breakout in a column of O's exceeds one or more previous bottoms by at least three squares. The following column of X's retraces more than 50% of the decline in the breakout column and quietly suggests that accumulation is underway.

Low pole and high pole patterns prove to be very accurate in mutual funds. Therefore, we embrace such formations as a vital part of our asset allocation strategy. Remember, low poles hint of a potential buy signal that should be forthcoming. High poles warn of a sell signal in the near future. We should accept low poles and high poles as buy and sell signals, respectively, and act accordingly.

Let us examine the Calvert Social Fund in Figure 12.6. Two key points surface immediately. First, a low pole formation evolves in late 1987 and early 1988. And second, the low pole formation parallels a bottoming process in the overall market. Had a portfolio manager acted on the low pole pattern and anticipated a later buy signal, the point of commitment would have occurred at lower price levels and overall investment returns would have been enhanced. When low poles develop along with aggregate market bottoms, they generally mark a major bottom on the mutual fund chart. High poles often identify a major top in the fund price when they occur in combination with technical deterioration and a topping in the general market.

Exploring the Calvert chart further, a manager would have liquidated in December 1989, when a sell signal appeared on the chart. After the market went through a lengthy bottoming process throughout most of 1990, a February 1991 buy signal on the chart and a strengthening in the overall market suggests a logical point for reentry. With mutual funds, common stocks, and virtually all other asset investments, the strength of the underlying market remains important to performance. Generally speaking, a low pole forming during a bull market has significant upside potential. On the other hand, a low pole developing during a bear market usually signals nothing more than a short-lived rally attempt.

Another low pole formation appears in the Gradison Value fund in Figure 12.6. The Gradison low pole forms after a selling climax, which corresponds with the final weakness in the aggregate market. Once again, portfolio managers are afforded a point of early entry by acknowledging the low pole as a buy signal. Since the low pole corresponded with a bottom in the general stock market, we would interpret the Gradison chart as a major bottom.

The Brandywine Fund reveals a high pole formation in January 1993 as the advancing column contained thirteen X recordings. The sell signal prompts action once the following column of O's has seven recordings. A sell signal arrives during the consolidation or basing phase of the pattern. However, a low pole formation follows and reverses the downside breakout. The downside move after the high pole was abbreviated, but this was not unexpected because the aggregate market showed strength to the upside. As a general rule, high poles during bear markets

Figure 12.5
Dealing with Spikes

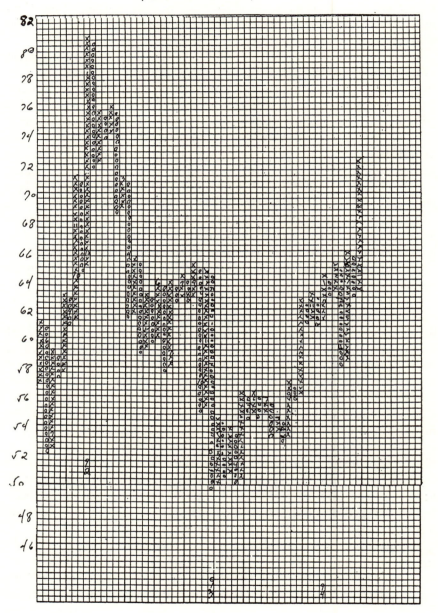

(Fedel Health Care)

Figure 12.5 Continued

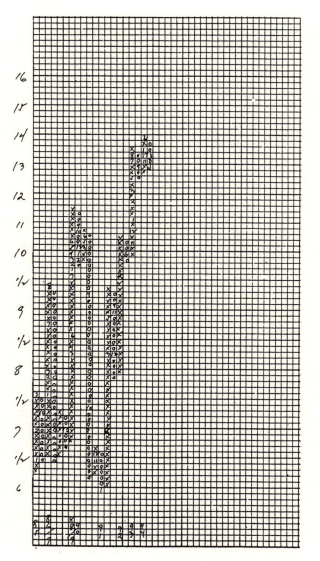

Figure 12.6
Using High Poles and Low Poles in Formulating Mutual Funds Strategies

Source: Courtesy Chartcraft, Inc., New Rochelle, N.Y.

Figure 12.6 Continued

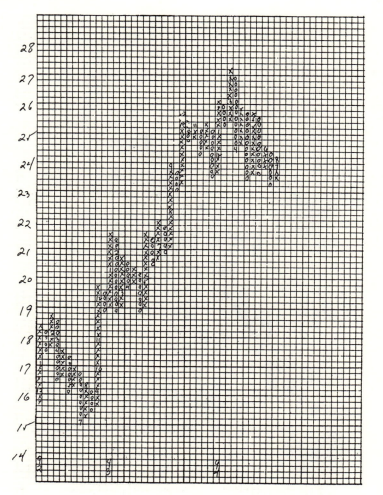

Figure 12.6 Continued

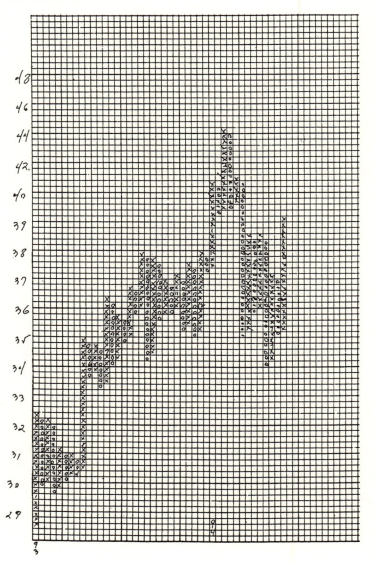

Figure 12.6 Continued

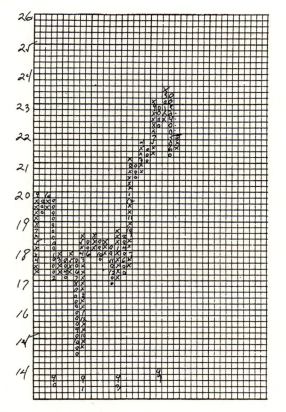

Source: Courtesy Chartcraft, Inc., New Rochelle, N.Y.

lead to major declines. High poles during bull markets result in corrections or partial retracements, which lack the severity of a major decline.

Fidelity Technology shows a high pole forming in September 1993 with a sell signal following shortly thereafter. Although the fund rallies, the chart reveals uncertainty with a pattern of lower tops beginning to appear. A high pole and a weakening aggregate market portend of uncertainty with downside risks factored into your analysis. Be careful!

LET YOUR PROFITS RUN

An old Wall Street adage suggests that investors should "cut losses and let your profits run." Mutual fund chart analysis parallels advice often given to individual stock investors—do not sell too quickly simply because you are ahead. Once trends are established, they tend to last for considerable periods of time. The very basis for trendlines is that once stocks are set in motion in a given direction, they

Figure 12.7
Let Your Profits Run

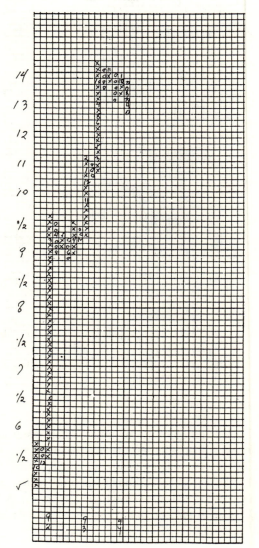

Source: Courtesy Chartcraft, Inc., New Rochelle, N.Y.

are likely to roughly approximate a straight line in their movement over the
duration of the trend. Although trendlines do not normally apply to mutual fund
charts, many of their principles underlie decision-making guidelines.

The Acorn Fund shown in Figure 12.7 reinforces the idea that prices do not
go straight up or down without some form of consolidation or interruption. Acorn

reveals volatile upside price movements once base building has been completed. Let us look at a few simple ideas that may preclude hasty decisions.

First, learn to analyze each chart individually because different funds with the same investment objectives often move in different directions. Certain funds and fund managements outperform others, so go with the leadership within the particular area of your interests. Second, we have learned normally to act on each buy and sell signal. However, remember that sell signals early in the uptrend do not normally pose the threat that they do later in the upmove. Similarly, buy signals early in a newly formed downtrend are typically short-lived.

Third, high poles often indicate corrections when they form early in the up-trend, but they warn of bear market declines if they occur late in the advance. Low poles evolving early in the downtrend usually indicate corrections in a bear market decline. However, low poles that develop late in a downtrend often reverse climactic, panicky selling and hint of the early stages of a bull market turnaround.

Fourth, aggregate market analysis can be used to supplement individual fund analysis, particularly when looking at equity and fixed-income possibilities. For example, let us assume a portfolio manager is considering a reallocation of funds into common stocks. If technical indicators such as the NYSE, ASE, and OTC bull-ish percentages and the percentage of stocks above their ten- and thirty-week moving averages are below 10% and suddenly show a three-box reversal in a col-umn of X's, chances for a positive stock market are good. Selection of the best ap-pearing charts with early buy signals in attractive groups would probably be timely.

SECTOR ANALYSIS

Perhaps the most intriguing area of asset allocation concerns is so-called sector mutual funds. Sector funds represent particular areas such as investment firms, global markets, precious metals, technology, banks, and computer software. Point and figure analysis is also important to the decision making among different industry groups.

Perhaps the premiere technical tool for industry group analysis is the bullish percentage. As you recall from earlier chapters, several categories of markets exist with the bullish percentage indicator.[5]

A REVIEW OF MARKET CLASSIFICATIONS

Bull confirmed markets result when the bullish percentage either gives a buy signal when a recording of X's moves above a previous top or when an absolute reading above 70% occurs. Such markets should be reserved for long positions. *Bull correction markets* occur when a column of O's interrupts a bull confirmed market but fails to yield a sell signal or move from above 70% to below 70%. Selective purchases can be made on pullbacks, but caution must prevail when readings have been above 70% for considerable periods of times. Bull correction markets can be tricky. For stocks, traders should only initiate short positions with scalping objectives in mind.

Bull alert markets unfold when upturns in the bullish percentage indicator develop from below 10%, 20%, or 30%. Remember, such depressed levels indicate extreme investor pessimism and usually mark points to enter the market. Long positions in stocks with positive relative strength readings and call options in similar issues are appropriate along with volatile mutual funds. Concentrate on leadership securities and funds with rising tops and/or long base patterns that appear to be breaking out to the upside. Bull alert markets evolving from low readings usually signal the end of a downtrend and provide an ideal time for purchases. Although bull alert markets are initially regarded as trading moves, they usually include a later buy signal. Moves above a previous top then converts the market status to bull confirmed.

Bear confirmed markets contain a sell signal on the bullish percentage indicator chart and warn investors to sell long positions. If you are in a family of funds, switch the allocation from equities to the money market fund. These market conditions should be reserved for short positions, hedge funds, and put options. *Bear alert markets* occur when the indicator readings drop from above 70% without a sell signal. Readings usually will drift downward to 50% or to a range between 40% and 50%. Long-term mutual fund investors usually maintain positions, whereas discriminating short positions may be assumed with a trading orientation in mind. Once a three-box reversal in a column of X's reappears, the bear alert market is negated and the bull confirmed market resumes.

Bear market bottoms originate with bull alert markets. Once the bullish percentage advances from less than 10%, 20%, or 30%, the chart often shows a decline back below the 30% level. This decline merely places doubts in the minds of those who are not convinced an upmove is underway. Bear market bottoms are not to alter your interpretation that the worst of the market slide is over. Remain focused on long positions with a bull market perspective. Learn to anticipate such interruptions. *Bull market tops* represent the bullish percentage counterpart to bear market bottoms and include rally attempts to move back above the 70% level once bear alert markets have formed. Often such rallies indicate weakened efforts and comprise of the topping process. Bull market tops and bear market bottoms generally suggest that topping and bottoming processes require longer amounts of time to complete—learn to expect them.

Bear correction markets represent a rally attempt in a bear confirmed market. A column of X's develops without penetrating a previous top, thus leaving the downtrend (and sell signal) intact. Any fund purchases or long positions in stocks are risky and should be avoided. Maintain short positions and possibly establish others on this brief show of market strength.

APPLYING THE BULLISH PERCENTAGE

Figure 12.8 reveals the bullish percentage chart for precious metals. Let us examine the unexpected move in gold (and silver) during 1993. In December

Figure 12.8
Sector Analysis: Precious Metals Bullish Percentage

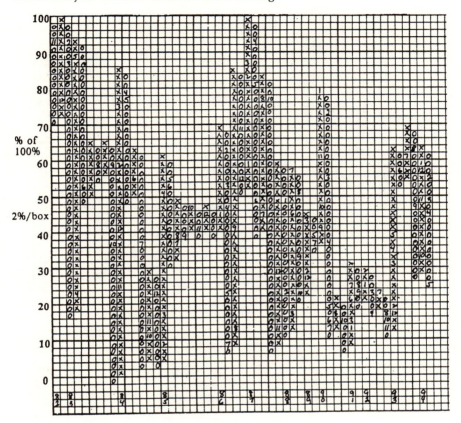

Source: Courtesy Chartcraft, Inc., New Rochelle, N.Y.

1992, the group bullish percentage turned up in a three-box reversal of X's from 12%. Initial purchase commitments could be made in the bull alert status in December, and a buy signal at 26% in February 1993 placed the group in a bull confirmed market. The three-box downturn from the 70% area in August 1993 placed the market in bear alert status. An August sell signal at 52% advised traders that the market was now bear confirmed.

By following the precious metals bullish percentage, investors would be advised of when to buy gold funds and mining stocks, when to sell or take short positions, and when to proceed with caution. Figure 12.9 includes two examples of gold funds that could have been used in the asset allocation process. The Invesco Fund gave two buy signals—one with the low pole and the other with a move above previous tops in February 1993. The Fidelity Precious Metals Fund gave a buy

Figure 12.9
Examples of Precious Metals Funds

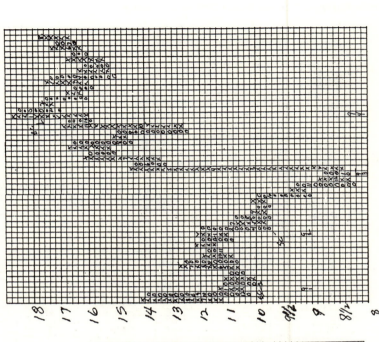

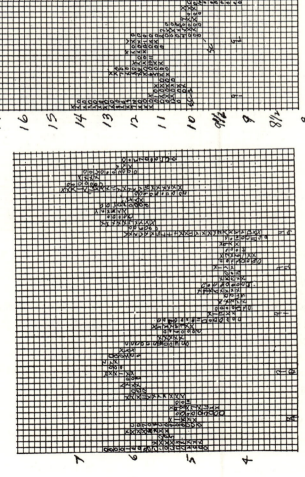

Source: Courtesy Chartcraft, Inc., New Rochelle, N.Y.

Figure 12.10
Sector Analysis: International Funds

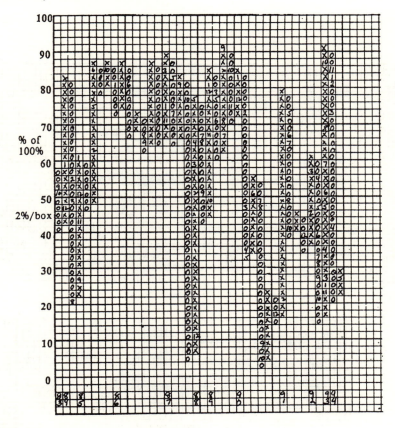

Source: Courtesy Chartcraft, Inc., New Rochelle, N.Y.

signal in February 1993 as its price rose dramatically. By using the precious metals bullish percentage with fund P & F charts, investors receive timely buy points to enter both the precious metals sector and select mutual funds within that group. Sell signals afforded timely warnings to liquidate. In each case, low pole buy signals marked points of reentry.

Let us look at the international funds sector in Figures 12.10 and 12.11. Notice that October 1992 corresponded with a three-box upturn in the international funds bullish percentage from 16%. The bullish percentage gave an early buy signal and remains in a bull confirmed market, a status that often lasts for long periods of time. We interpret the international funds bullish percentage above 70% to mean that we can make additional purchases of international funds while maintaining long positions established some time ago. Do not liquidate until either a sell signal or a move below 70% appears on the chart.

Figure 12.11
International Funds Example

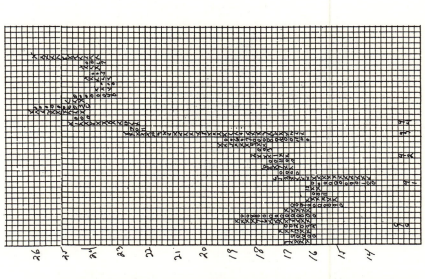

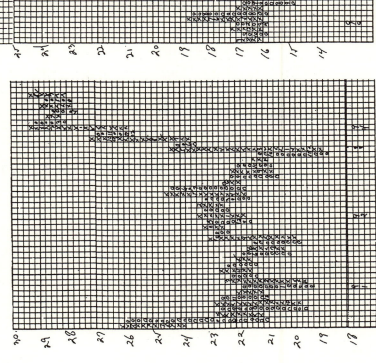

Source: Courtesy Chartcraft, Inc., New Rochelle, N.Y.

Figure 12.11 provides a look at two different international funds. The Fidelity Overseas Fund yields one buy signal in January 1993, with a low pole formation and another in March with a move above a previous top. Asset allocation was given a substantial boost, however, by early buy signals from the group bullish percentage. The ultimate result in portfolio management and asset allocation strategies is resoundingly clear—never underestimate the importance of the group bullish percentages when using mutual funds and sector analysis. The Harbor International Fund showed a low pole buy signal in February 1993. A strong upmove followed, aided in part by the underlying strength of the market. If asset managers chose to anticipate, they could have entered the Harbor Fund at the first sign of a three-box reversal simply because the international bullish percentage gave an early buy indication by turning up from 16%.

SUMMARY

One of the best vehicles to facilitate asset allocation lies in mutual funds. In turn, the point and figure chart approach to mutual fund analysis is a straightforward way to make decisions on changes in both portfolio composition and objective. Simply acknowledge buy and sell signals and use them as a means of buying and liquidating fund shares. Low poles and high poles represent accurate, reliable patterns that function efficently on mutual fund charts.

Spikes should also be used in mutual fund chart analysis to detect speculative excess in either direction. Allow your profits to run and remember that sell signals early in the advance do not pose the same threat that they do later in the upmove. Similarly, buy signals early in the decline are less meaningful than they are in the late stages of the downmove.

Finally, the industry bullish percentage represents the key analytical tool to sector analysis. Early warning signals from the group bullish percentage allow asset managers time to select individual funds and initiate the allocation process.

NOTES

1. The authors acknowledge the contributions of Michael Burke and John Gray of Chartcraft throughout this manuscript for their charts, technical assistance, and editorial approval.

2. See Michael Burke and John Gray, *The Chartcraft Mutual Funds Point & Figure Chart Book* (New Rochelle, N.Y.: Chartcraft, Inc., October, 1993), 1.

3. Many of the mutual fund rules employed herein may be applied to numerous charts in *The Chartcraft Mutual Funds Point & Figure Chart Book*. This mutual fund service is the finest of its kind and widely recognized among investors.

4. For more information on spikes, see Carroll D. Aby, Jr., *The Complete Guide to Point and Figure Charting* (Birmingham, Ala.: Colonial Press, 1992), 110–116.

5. See the *Chartcraft Long-Term Point & Figure Charts for Broad Industry Group Bullish % and the NYSE Bullish %* (New Rochelle, N.Y.: Chartcraft, Inc., 1993), 1.

BIBLIOGRAPHY

BOOKS

Aby, Carroll D., Jr. *The Complete Guide to Point and Figure Charting.* Birmingham, Ala.: Colonial Press, 1992.

Blumenthal, Earl. *Chart for Profit Point and Figure Trading.* Larchmont, N.Y.: Investors Intelligence, 1975.

Burke, Michael L. *The All New Guide to the Three-Point Reversal Method of Point and Figure Construction and Formation.* New Rochelle, N.Y.: Chartcraft, Inc., 1990.

Burke, Michael L. *Three-Point Reversal Method of Point & Figure Construction and Formations.* New Rochelle, NY: Chartcraft, Inc., 1990.

Burke, Michael L., and John E. Gray, eds. *Chartcraft's Option Service.* New Rochelle, N.Y.: Chartcraft, Inc., selected, 1989–1993.

Cohen, A. W. *How to Use the Three-Point Reversal Method of Point and Figure Stock Market Trading.* 9th ed. New Rochelle, N.Y.: Chartcraft, Inc., 1987.

Drew, Garfield A. *New Methods for Profit in the Stock Market.* Wells, Vt.: Fraser Publishing Company, 1966.

Fabozzi, F. J., ed. *Investment Management.* Cambridge, Mass.: Ballinger Publishing Company, 1989.

Ibbotson, R. G., and R. A. Singuefeld, *Stocks, Bills, and Inflation.* Chicago, Ill.: Dow Jones-Irwin, 1989.

Jones, Charles P. *Investments: Analysis and Management.* 4th ed. New York: John Wiley & Sons, Inc., 1994.

Murphy, John J. *Intermarket Technical Analysis.* New York: John Wiley & Sons, Inc., 1991.

PERIODICALS

Arowin, P. "Size, Seasonality, and Stock Market Overreaction." *Journal of Financial and Quantitative Analysis* 25, no. 1 (March 1993): 113–125.

Berman, Peter I. "An Asset Allocation Primer for Post-War Business Cycles." *American Business Review* 10 (January 1992): 88–92.

Bureau of Economic Analysis, Department of Commerce. *Survey of Current Business* (BCA Section). Washington, D.C.: U.S. Government Printing Office, June 1991.

———. *Quarterly Financial Report.* Second Quarter, 1991.

The Chartcraft Mutual Funds Point & Figure Chart Book. New Rochelle, N.Y., Chartcraft, Inc., October, 1993.

Chartcraft Long-Term Point & Figure Charts for Broad Industry Group Bullish % and the NYSE Bullish %. New Rochelle, N.Y., Chartcraft, Inc., 1993.

Chart Guide. New York, Standard & Poor's, Trendline Corporation, selected monthly issues.

Current Market Perspectives. New York, Standard & Poor's/Trendline Corporation, selected monthly issues.

Daily Basis Stock Charts. New York, Standard & Poor's/Trendline Corporation, selected weekly issues.

Ettredge, M., and R. J. Fuller. "The Negative Earnings Effect." *The Journal of Portfolio Management* 17, (Spring 1991): 27–33.

Federal Reserve Bank of New York. *Winter Review 1991.*

Federal Reserve Bank of St. Louis. *U.S. Financial Data.* October 4, 1991, and January 3, 1992.

Federal Reserve System. *Historical Chartbook.* Washington, D.C.: Federal Reserve, 1988.

Jegadeesh, N., and S. Titman. "Return to Buying Winners and Selling Losers: Implications for Stock Market Efficiency." *The Journal of Finance* 48 (March 1993): 65–91.

Jones, S. L., W. Lee, and R. Apenbrink. "New Evidence on the January Effect before Personal Income Taxes." *The Journal of Finance* 46, no. 5 (December 1991).

Keim, D. B. "A New Look at the Effects of Firm Size and E/P Ratio on Stock Returns." *Financial Analysts Journal* (September-October 1990): 63–69.

Murphy, John J. "Utilities and Bonds." *Technical Analysis of Stocks and Commodities* 10 (August 1992): 34–36.

Value Line Investment Service. New York, Value Line, Inc., selected weekly issues.

Value Screen +, New York, Value Line, Inc., selected monthly PC data base diskettes.

INDEX

About the Authors

CARROLL D. ABY, JR., is the N. B. Morrison Professor of Applied Management and Professor of Finance at Northwestern State University in Natchitoches, Louisiana. He has held investment broker positions with Merrill Lynch, A.G. Edwards & Sons, Inc., and Paine Webber, and is currently consulting in the field of investment management, financial valuation, personal financial planning, and on other related matters. He is also an investment columnist and author of numerous scholarly articles and 10 books.

DONALD E. VAUGHN is Professor of Finance at Southern Illinois University, Carbondale, Illinois. A CPA and author of eight books, including a leading textbook on investment, he gained national recognition through a series of small business profiles which he published under the auspices of the U.S. Government. He is actively engaged in research and publishes frequently in the major investment and accounting journals.